Based largely on the Thomist viewpoint, the author's discussions are provocative, easy to understand, and, above all, realistic. He helps the reader to see himself as an intelligent person, capable of working out his own destiny. In addition, Father Wuellner is convinced that a modern philosopher cannot don the toga of Cicero and remain oblivious to the lessons of history. As a result, he cannot profess ignorance of the great historical fact of Christianity. Accordingly, Father Wuellner has added an exceptionally important chapter on the contributions of Christ to a philosophy of life, in which he presents the truths which Christian theology adds to the truths that can be attained by the natural light of reason.

In brief, *A Christian Philosophy of Life* is a work that will feed the mind and fire the heart of contemporary man in his efforts to know himself and puzzle out the mysterious thing called life.

A CHRISTIAN PHILOSOPHY OF LIFE

A Christian Philosophy of Life

BERNARD WUELLNER, S.J.

JOHN CARROLL UNIVERSITY, CLEVELAND

THE BRUCE PUBLISHING COMPANY
MILWAUKEE

IMPRIMI POTEST

Leo D. Sullivan, S.J.
Praepositus Provincialis
Provinciae Detroitensis

NIHIL OBSTAT

Joannes A. Schulien, S.T.D.
Censor librorum

IMPRIMATUR

✠ Albertus G. Meyer
Archiepiscopus Milwauchiensis
July 16, 1957

Preface

LIFE WILL reveal its many splendors only to those who ponder its mysteries and prizes. Strongly convinced that mature men and women are naturally disposed to think about the main mysteries of human life and to make basic decisions about its problems, I thought that it would be good to assemble all these important issues in one volume. The opportunity to reflect on these issues is important for each cultured man and woman and for the communities in which each lives.

Being a philosopher, I have discussed these issues in a philosophical way from that viewpoint identified as Thomist or, loosely, as scholastic. Cutting across the existing border lines of the formal branches of philosophy, I have chosen a theme, human life, which runs through most philosophical fields. The questions circling about this theme deserve careful philosophical analysis, exposition, competent proof, and indications of their consequences. Many of the answers presented are very controversial outside the halls of Thomists. But as debate and defense in these controversies lie outside the chief purpose of this book, little note has been taken of rival opinions and theories. In some ways this will weaken the sense of battle for the reader. Yet unity of point of view carries its own light, while controversy may confuse. Moreover, if the evidence given in the proofs is strong enough to convince, then the principle of the unity of truth makes the sifting and refuting of discordant views a collateral but not an essential task.

Two questions basic to human living have scarcely been raised in this book. "Why do you accept God?" "What think you of Christ?" The matter of the evidence for God's existence is touched on lightly in a few places, but on the whole I assume that the reader has a settled mind on God's existence. If not, he may investigate some of the abundant literature on the subject. The problem for a philosophy of life is how God influences human life. As the other issue on Christ's Godhead is a purely theological one, its answer does not fall within the province of a philosopher as a philosopher. The writer, by God's goodness, believes that Christ is the Son of God and that He taught a scheme of living which no philosopher and no man may overlook. A non-Christian is less committed, perhaps more neutral, in regard to Christ; he is not, by that fact, more objective or more philosophical. For open-minded good will toward Christianity is eminently more philosophical than a prejudiced rationalism, which denies that theology is an intellectual study worthy of philosophical respect.

No set of purely philosophical answers to the problems of life suffices for actual living in our historical situation. The facts of history and of theology must be faced by the philosopher, for he lives in their presence. No philosopher can today roll back the ages, don the chiton of Aristotle or the toga of Cicero, and pretend to explore for truth in some make-believe universe to which the good news of Christ crucified and glorified has not penetrated. We are not philosophizing for some fictitious men who dwell in some historical vacuum.

Still, writer and reader must recognize the difference between philosophy and theology, especially in starting points, methods, and mode of proof. Although I have given only philosophical proofs, I have also presented those supplementary truths and interpretations which Christian theology offers on the same matters. This Christian supplement, mainly condensed into a separate chapter on Christ's contributions, crops out in other brief passages. It seemed too prim and mechanical always to warn the reader that he is being transported over the frontier into theology where propositions are grounded not merely on the rock of reason but on the rock of Peter. If any reader is unacquainted with the sharp line between philosophy and theology, he may take warning from the flashing of the theological signals, Christ, revelation, faith, the Bible, the Church.

May the Virgin Mother, who with the Holy Spirit is author of human life in God's Son, be also the light of our lives and the cause of our joy in life.

Contents

Chapter 1

Man Looks at Life

1. Man's Interest in Life

The Success of the baffled and discouraged Socrates began when he turned away from the maze of opinions about nature and took up his new interest in man.[1] Man's wonder about his own life is one point at which philosophy may begin. A general curiosity about human beings is probably the center of whatever notice the plain man gives to philosophical ideas. Though untrained in philosophical reflection, the plain or common man has some attitudes to his own life and to the lives of those dear to him. Life fascinates or bores him, he says. He sings of life's sweet mystery or curses its cruel woes. He has some notions of what he wants from life, what he regards as success, and what sacrifices he would be ready to make for his chosen causes. Looking ahead, he believes that death will end all life or he hopes that it will open the door to more life beyond the grave.

As living men deeply and personally involved in their own well-being, all will be mentally restless until the meaning and values of life stand clear before their intelligence.[2]

This puzzling over life, experienced by the ordinary mind, becomes much sharpened in mature and thoughtful persons. Their minds are delving more deeply into the great problems and their debated solutions. They are seeking a fuller understanding of man and of what relates to him. They want more than a glance; they want a vista, a vision of life. On such weighty themes as human nature and human worth they will not be quieted by guesses and suspicions but only by assured knowledge. They recognize a need for sound guiding principles. They acknowledge that decisions about living ought to be consistent with these principles. They are aware that they need competent intellectual methods of discovering the truths about life. They

1

appreciate the fact that one of the great rewards of education and reflection is a mind formed in a solid, tested, humane philosophy of life.

The student is often introduced to one or more theories of life and to a number of its themes in his freshman college readings of selected essays, poems, and plays. But in other studies, too, he pursues the discovery of life. In learning history and its consequences, in reliving the biographies of great men and women, in studies of foreign cultures as well as in courses of philosophy and religion, the collegian and the genuinely thoughtful person meet ideals of life, evaluations of it, and, at times, attacks on its worth.

Society expects some estimate of and teaching on life from its leaders in universities and pulpits. This social interest in life also appears in the acute party and governmental propaganda that seeks to influence people's ideas in many modern countries. *The Communist Manifesto* and *Mein Kampf* are two of many witnesses to this process of political teaching on the ends and means of living. Totalitarian governments, like Russia and her enslaved allies, with their tightly censored press and official party line, spend vast efforts to shape their subjects' ideas to their own plans and purposes and to their own ideals for man and society. Democratic governments are growing in a similar awareness of the importance of their peoples' basic attitudes, ideals, and hopes. Such governments must persuade their people rather than drive them. To win elections and popular approval, to enforce sacrifices, to get maximum national effort and harmony in pursuit of national aims, they must meet emotional forces which grow out of ingrained, cherished ideas. They must uphold or topple over old traditions and customs grounded in traditions. Governments today realize that it is not enough to have arms, power, and wealth; they must have also the minds and the hearts of their people on their side.

2. EXAMPLES OF PHILOSOPHIES OF LIFE

At this point it may be helpful to notice both some popular and some complex literary statements about life's meaning to man.

The roars of the Roman rabble demanding bread and circuses, free food and free fun, present a famous summary of what the mob wanted from life and made their rulers supply as the price of popularity and public order.

The pessimist moans that life is an ugly doghouse or a game of hide-and-seek with the undertaker or a blind ride given to man on the flywheel of the universe. The bright blown leaves, green, gold, and scarlet, of an autumn day become to his imagination the stories of human lives drifting by chance to graves on earth. The hard pressed and discouraged often hear a voice like the Tempter's in Eliot's *Murder in the Cathedral*, suggesting even to the hero that "Life is a cheat and a disappointment."[3]

Military and revolutionary movements have tried to condense their view of human existence and aspiration into various flaming slogans and popular symbols. The French Revolution chanted its "Liberty, Equality, Fraternity." The Crusaders recruited and fought for the thought, "God wills it." Communists shout, "Liberation for the masses," and, "Workers of the world, unite." The dove, the crescent, the red star tell whole theories of life and society.

In the religious field, symbols like the Good Shepherd and the cross express an ideal of life more clearly than many words. But words find their place, as in the mottoes adopted by saints to spur on themselves and their co-workers. Examples include St. Benedict's *Peace*, St. Ignatius Loyola's *For the greater glory of God*, St. Pius X's *To restore all things in Christ*, and Pope Pius XII's *Peace, the fruit of justice*. The coats of arms adopted by our American bishops at the time of their consecration frame their ideals of life in a few stirring words which indicate the bishops' dedication to a cause or their program of religious government or their personal offering of their spiritual leadership to Christ or Mary.[4]

College shields emblazon some short sayings about life to represent their founders' and faculties' outlooks on life and education. The Christophers have captured their main spirit and enterprise in one sentence: "It is better to light one candle than to curse the darkness."

A few celebrated literary statements on the issues of life give a wider preliminary view into the far-reaching power that ideas can have. The first, from the biblical Book of Wisdom, describes what the Jewish sage found among pagans and Hebrew apostates in Hellenized Egypt at his time. He has laid the blame for death in the world upon the wicked, and continues:

> Reason they offer, yet reason all amiss. Their hearts tell them. So brief our time here, so full of discomfort, and death brings no remedy! Never a man yet made good his title to have come back from the grave!

Whence came we, none can tell; and it will be all one hereafter whether we lived or no. What is our breath, but a passing vapour; what is our reason, but a spark that sets the brain whirling? Quench that spark, and our body is turned to ashes; like a spent sigh, our breath is wasted on the air; like the cloud-wrack our life passes away, unsubstantial as the mist yonder sun disperses with its ray, bears down with its heat. Time will surely efface our memory, and none will mark the record of our doings. Only a passing shadow, this life of ours, and from its end there is no returning; the doom is sealed, and there is no acquittal.

Come then (they say), let us enjoy pleasure, while pleasure is ours; youth does not last, and creation is at our call; of rich wine and well spiced take we our fill. Spring shall not cheat us of her blossoming; crown we our heads with roses ere they wither; be every meadow the scene of our wanton mirth. Share we the revels all alike, leave traces everywhere of our joyous passing; no part or lot have we but this.

Helpless innocence shall lie at our mercy; not for us to spare the widow, to respect the venerable head, grown white with years. Might shall be our right, weakness count for proof of worthlessness.[5]

The passage continues with a prophecy that the wicked will persecute the just man, the coming Messias, because of his opposition to their way of living. From a basic opinion that man dies and is no more, the wicked draw two lines of conclusions: first, the philosophy of pleasure for themselves in this life; and second, the philosophy of force as a substitute for justice, of cruelty to the weak, and of defiance even to the Son of God. The same philosophy of life as a holiday for the lucky and rich is found in the expressions "wine, woman, and song," and Horace's carpe diem, "seize the instant opportunity."

At the other extreme, the closing lines of the speech by the murderer Macbeth over his dead wife state the pessimist's theory when unrighteous might is overturned by greater might.

> Tomorrow, and tomorrow, and tomorrow,
> Creeps in this petty pace from day to day,
> To the last syllable of recorded Time;
> And all our yesterdays have lighted fools
> The way to dusty death. Out, out, brief candle!
> Life's but a walking shadow; a poor player,
> That struts and frets his hour upon the stage,
> And then is heard no more; it is a Tale,
> Told by an idiot, full of sound and fury,
> Signifying nothing.[6]

Shakespeare here dramatizes the bitterness in the heart of a defeated wicked ambition. But the suicide who pleads that life is no longer worth living or the scientist who believes that man is but one more material speck in nature and speaks of us as a doomed race chained to a sinking ship are not mere players on the stage. Their views of the tragedy of unspiritual man in a godless perishing universe have been famously stated by Bertrand Russell in a piece of majestic but fearsome prose closing his essay, "A Free Man's Worship." It is meant to apply even to the innocent.

> Brief and powerless is Man's life; on him and all his race the slow sure doom falls, pitiless and dark. Blind to good and evil, reckless of destruction, omnipotent Matter rolls on its relentless way; for Man, condemned today to lose his dearest, tomorrow himself to pass through the gates of darkness, it remains only to cherish, ere yet the blow falls, the lofty thoughts that ennoble his little day; disdaining the coward terrors of the slave of Fate, to worship at the shrine his own hands have built; undismayed by the empire of chance, to preserve a mind free from the wanton tyranny that rules his outward life; proudly defiant of the irresistible forces that tolerate, for a moment, his knowledge and his condemnation, to sustain alone, a weary and unyielding Atlas, the world that his own ideals have fashioned despite the trampling march of unconscious power.[7]

This new stoicism which casts man in the role of the hopeless yet unperturbed spectator of universal ruin makes old Greco-Roman stoicism seem a comparatively gentle creed.

3. WHAT IS A PHILOSOPHICAL VIEW OF LIFE?

A philosophical view of life implies a related set of ideas about life. Its first flower is an intellectual understanding of realities; its later fruit is a program of activity and a policy for decisions conforming to one's standards of the values of life. As a reasoned and tested body of ideas about life, the philosophical view differs from the outlook of the ordinary untrained man or even of the man of faith who lacks any grasp of the grounds upon which his beliefs rest. The plain man cannot live long and think a little without gaining some view of the nature and destiny of man. But even if his thoughts be right, they will fall short of the true philosophical view on many counts. The prephilosophical view tends to be an assemblage of bits and fragments gathered at haphazard from one's parents, friends, church, teachers, and union, from casual reading, and from conversation about people's successes and sorrows. Formed thus at random, such an outlook may be dangerously incomplete, one-sided, and very unreliable for guiding men to the total benefits of human living. It will usually be somewhat inconsistent in its various answers and unsure when challenged by difficulties. Socrates long ago noted that such ordinary thinking is an unexamined life, leaving one with an unproved, untested, uncriticized opinion, not clear in its outlines of its own truth, probability, and error.[8]

Philosophy, on the contrary, is an intellectual enterprise which studies life thoroughly by sound intellectual methods. It gathers its evidence; it analyzes, distinguishes, and summarizes; it probes into meanings and causes; it proves and tests; it discusses various proposals and gleans their partial truths; it rebuts the false and correlates all the true into a pattern of thought which is a discovery, a vision, and an insight. The knowledge of life thus gained is called a wisdom since wisdom names the excelling type of knowledge. The passing show of life, its shimmering variety of action and lusterless routine constitute the factual starting point for the philosopher's wonderment about life's secrets and its causes. The harvest of facts reach philosophical stature when the intelligence of man finds their meaning, the reasons for their occurrence, and the causes of their being what they are. In the mirror of philosophy, no less than in the glasses of literature and history, man looks objectively at life and discovers great truths about himself.

The causes which the philosophers hunt are mainly four.[9] The efficient cause or maker of life brings life into existence and keeps it in being. The final cause or purpose of life is the chief good for which it was made and which living men are capable of achieving. This cause is the main key to the meaning of any being, event, or development. In addition, there are two principles within a visible creature which give a basic explanation of its reality and nature. One principle is named form or formal cause; it is the specific, characterizing component of a being. The other principle, called matter or the material cause, is the subject or potency, which is the changeable, determinable principle common to many species of beings. The philosophical analysis of man must state all these causes of a human being.

If there be a set of causes of a being or event, the philosophical interest is chiefly in the basic or most original of these causes. Relatives and journalists are interested in one's parents and grandparents; philosophers are more interested in the first man and the first author of life in all men. Philosophy asks basic questions and typically answers by basic principles. It concerns fundamentals, but it is by no means elementary. It not only seeks to know the causes, but to understand life through these causes. Insight can follow when the mind has gone to the bottom of the truth and has seen how the basic truths interconnect. Perhaps insight is the right name to be given to a view that is both unified and expansive.

In the unified philosophical view of human life many truths and partial answers come together in a single concordant pattern. When the mind grasps how details fit into the whole, how means are related to the end, how all the causes conspire to make one total explanation, then understanding is clear and strong. The philosophical sense of order as well as of wonder is satisfied. For life then looks like something with a shape, a form, a center, and one mighty aim.

The philosopher is not content to have this basic and unified view only of his own individual human life. He seeks the expansive or total view of the meaning of all human lives. He looks for man's place in the hierarchies of life that include both subhuman and superhuman. He seeks not only understanding of some significant single days of life but also the meaning of the long span of years and of the way in which each day, each experience, and each change belongs in some right spot in the scheme of life as a whole. Both personal and social aspects of life must fall into the pattern of the meaning of the whole. The philosopher's aspiration is that of a mental map maker who puts many pieces together until he gets a spacious glimpse of the whole wide world of life. Clearly, then, such a view differs from the common, simple view.

The approaches and methods of philosophy differ also from those of faith and theology, though its conclusions should be in accordance with those of divine revelation. Philosophy discovers, compares, reasons, and tests by human intelligence, rising from the data of the world about us and within us to its own answers. Faith begins from the word of God speaking the truth to us about various features of human life. Faith is very good, but it is not philosophy. Theology, from a purely speculative viewpoint, is even better than faith because it is a systematic understanding of the faith, using tools of logic, history, and philosophical method to gain added understanding of the content of faith. But neither is theology the same as philosophy; in many ways it surpasses philosophy. Scholastic and Christian philosophers are honestly aware that reason cannot answer all questions that the mind raises; they gladly welcome the added light of revelation so that they may be better men and even better philosophers with better minds. For a good understanding of life, the best combination of abilities unites the shrewd respect for facts of the plain man, the critical probings of the Aristotelian-Thomist philosopher, and the powerful heaven-sent light of Catholic theology.

4. PRACTICAL PHILOSOPHY

A philosophy of life is known as practical rather than speculative philosophy. It thus has a kinship with ethics, the science of right human action. It seeks principles for evaluating life, its opportunities and difficulties, and offers guidance for human action. It dares to give advice on gaining life's best prizes and suggests cues for fullness of human living. The philosophy of life does not merely send its gleams into the den of the student calmly pursuing truth for truth's sake; it holds up its bright lantern of ideals to help men walking on the roads of life.

Though concerned with action, it is not itself a way of life. A way of life includes our habitual activities and our regular round of duties, burdens, recreations, and hobbies. Thus, our life may be said to be the kind of work in which we take delight, the kind of activities for which we have a bent, the things we prefer and to which we give our time, and the objectives to which we direct our whole life, as far as we can. In this sense, men lead scholarly or religious lives, self-indulgent or selfless lives, sportsmen's and politicians' lives; and we speak of the American or Soviet way of life, of free men's lives and a convict's way of life. Ways of life are part of the valuable data which the philosopher must consider in evaluating noble and ignoble ideals. A wise way of life must be grounded in a wise view of life, but the two are not the same.

The philosophy of life does not confine itself to any single ordinary branch of systematic scholastic philosophy, as logic or the philosophy of man. For — to be technical — it has a material rather than a formal object of study. Around the central object, human life, it gathers the related questions, issues, and answers that come from metaphysics, the philosophy of man, the theory of knowledge, natural theology, ethics, and social philosophy. But this interweaving of pertinent truths from many parts of philosophy gives this study a peculiar value in breaking down the needless barriers between the parts of philosophy and thereby unifying, broadening, and deepening our vision of man. With such a many-sided, picture-window view of man's life, one should be more at home in this universe and richer in one's hopes for life everlasting.

Briefly, then, a philosophy of life will be a reasoned understanding of the meaning and worth of human life in both its personal and social aspects. It must be man's own intellectual discovery of the origin, nature, and destiny of human life, of its value, and of man's principal relationships as a living being to other things, whether these be divine, human, or even nonliving. But as it is only a human answer to profound problems, the Christian or Thomist philosopher willingly accepts additional wisdom on life's mysteries from the words which Christ has spoken to all men.

CHAPTER 2

The Big Questions

THE READER may wish to start with an outline of the inquiry and a survey of the positions taken by most scholastic philosophers on the big questions pertinent to a philosophy of life.

Not every one of our human interests and puzzles about life is of basic importance. What I should eat or drink this evening, what type of auto I should buy, in what neighborhood I should live, what kind of flowers I should plant, how early I should set out on this trip, and scores of similar questions in some measure affect our happiness. But they may be safely appraised as of minor import. Other types of problems concern larger and more far-reaching issues, such as the importance of bodily health or length of life on this earth, the comparative value of different systems of government, the need and desirability of several children in every family, old-age security, and opportunity of the gifted to receive higher education. Yet these, too, are secondary in importance since they depend for a right solution upon the answers to the really big questions.

The really big questions concerning human life are those that affect the being and well-being of every person. They touch on the universal problems of life rather than on the lives of the few or of a class or on the fortunes of men in some particular period or region. The profound issues claim every man's attention and permanent interest, for the right answers can become the lasting roots of good lives and can grow in strength and beauty and control human thought, choice, and policy. The big questions have fundamental, widely branching, and long-lasting, even everlasting consequences for happiness or misery, for good or evil. The answers to these questions are the ones which the human spirit insistently desires to know so that it may understand and appreciate man, his life, his nobility, his progress, his place in the universe, and the destiny to which he is moving. The big questions treat of the supreme values and the highest goods of human life. If they remain unanswered, man does not know in what camp he finds himself. He does not know whether he is a person or a mere thing. He does not know whether to be a pessimist or an optimist about life. He cannot say whether life is a joke, a trick, a riddle, a snare, or an adventure. He is uncertain whether the universe is his friend or foe, and whether other people are his masters, equals, or slaves. Whereon shall man stand? Is he to think and act as a materialist or as one who esteems the values of the spirit? Is a man of good will to live and act and die as an atheist, a pantheist, an agnostic, or as a friend of God? Are the limits of life some years on earth or unmeasured years in eternity after a stay on earth? What shall any man live for? What prospects may a man hope for? What does God intend for man?

We may conveniently catalog the big questions under eight headings. In each instance we shall state the question, the scholastic philosopher's answer, and then the Catholic theologian's co-ordinate view of the matter. Further exposition and proof of each philosophical answer will appear in order in coming chapters of this book.

1. THE NATURE OF HUMAN LIFE

What is man? Who am I? What is human life? What would I be without life? How does human life compare with other forms of being and of life? These philosophical questions concern the internal character and constitution of human life.

The Thomist has his distinctive answers, for which he is much indebted to Aristotle, St. Augustine, and especially St. Thomas Aquinas. He claims and proves that man is one being, though a complex or composite one. This one being has one nature which is neither purely bodily nor purely spiritual; it is a natural result of the union of the spiritual soul with a suitable material body. Man is not a machine, not a mere animal, and not an angel living in an animal's body that is not part of himself. Man is one body-spirit, a person composed of spirit and flesh.

But in this complex being, the spiritual element or soul is the source of all man's life. The soul is the vital principle or the formal cause of man; the matter of the body is the material principle animated and humanized by this soul. Being spiritual, the human soul is also immortal. Although it is united with the body on earth, it does not depend on that body for its being or for its operations of thinking and willing. The body cannot live without the human soul; but the human soul, being already partially independent of the body, can go on living forever without the body.

The faith of Christ is in close accord with the scholastic philosopher's conclusions on this matter. For the Church of Christ teaches that the human soul is in some sense the form of man or the specific principle of human life and that it is naturally both spiritual and immortal.[1]

2. The Origin of Human Life

A second big question concerns the origin of human life. While the previous question led us to the formal and material causes, this one seeks for the efficient cause or agent who produces so wonderful a thing as a human soul and unites it to a body.

It is biologically certain that the parents of the individual person directly cause the body by providing the material ingredients of that first living cell or fertilized ovum with which new human life commences. All generations of human bodies on this earth can consequently be accounted for by parents until we ask: Was there a first human body and whence did it come? Who was the first human being? Was he adult or child, man or woman? Did the race start from one or many who simultaneously came into being? Many biologists have proposed the hazardous hypothesis that the human body first arose from some purely animal body, as of some primate animal. In regard to this opinion the philosopher usually admits that evolution of the human body would seem to be possible, but that evidence of the actuality of such development is very far from being sufficient. In any hypothesis, the bodies and souls of all living things that preceded man must originally have come into being by the creative act of God. If human life evolved, it did so under divine concurring action and intention.

Man's soul is not a biological question. The philosopher can prove that in each instance each human soul is immediately created and infused by God into the body prepared by the human parents. No human soul is evolved from animal matter or produced by any human or other finite agent. Each soul is a new creation from the living God, endowed with life, intelligence, liberty, immortality, duties and rights.

Christian theology also ascribes the ultimate origin of human life, of both the body and the soul, to God's creative gift. Revelation knows, too, who the first human being was. He was a man named Adam, who was made by God before the first woman, Eve. From this pair the whole human race has descended. Adam's was the first human soul, a fresh creation of God; at its union with whatever constituted the matter of Adam's body the first living human being appeared on earth.

3. THE SUPREME PURPOSE OF HUMAN LIFE

The next inquiry concerns the fourth cause, the end. If there is a set of related ends, the principal interest of the philosopher lies in the supreme purpose or the end of all subordinate ends. This purpose is the highest and most important good for which a nature exists and acts. This highest good open to human life will constitute man's perfection.

The scholastic philosopher maintains that the soul of man was not only made by God but that it also was made for God. The human soul has the ability to know and love God, to do so forever, to do so in a very perfect way, and in this endless activity of knowing and loving God to find its full and enduring happiness. At the same time this very happiness of man in the eternal possession of God is the highest glory which God can receive from His human creatures.

Each man can actually and surely attain this happiness and glory. But he cannot reach it while on earth. He prepares for it in this life, qualifying himself for endless life with God after the death of the body. And one of the biggest issues that man must solve is the discovery of the type of life on earth which can serve to prepare and merit for him eternal life. Certainly our well-being in the next life depends largely on our well-doing in this life.

In the light of the supreme goal of life, other goals pursued by men and other activities can be measured by their relation to the end. This holds for health, wealth, knowledge of science, virtues, pleasures, sports, marriage, religion, political and military glory, indeed, for any human interest, vocation, or profession. If other goals are means to the end, they are admissible to human life; if they are hindrances, they are contrary to life's purpose and are inadmissible.

All the questions about the good life for man depend largely on knowing what the supreme good and destiny of human life is. For the good leads man to God; the evil takes him away from God. Life becomes something of an adventurous exploring for and exploitation of the means to take us to God, even though their use may demand difficult and lifelong perseverance. Indeed, the very question of the value of choice of means or the value of liberty must demand an understanding of the purpose of human liberty. It is glorious to be free to be good; it is shameful to use freedom to do evil. Our rights, too, are precious, genuine, and ennobling only in so far as they lead us to God, our goal.

Catholic faith gives us a divine guarantee that this answer is true. Faith, moreover, enlarges our grasp of the meaning of this destiny of ours. The Author of our faith tells us of heaven, prepared by God and the Redeemer for the just. He tells us, too, of the restoration of the body to man in the end of all days and of the body's share in glory. He tells us that the very vision of God will be given to the good and faithful and it will be their fullest joy. Christ also made known that more than natural means are needed to gain this vision; and He has made known, promised, and provided these special means. Finally, He cautions that never ending misery and the loss of the vision will be the lot of anyone who misuses his human liberty and neglects the means.

4. THE DIGNITY OF LIFE AND PERSONALITY

A keen intellectual awareness of the nobility of the human person and of the high opportunities of human living contributes much to a spirited, humanistic, and reverent attitude to man. This appreciation of human dignity is assisted by combining the partial views gained in learning each of the four causes of human life and then comparing man with the being and life of nonhuman things.

Why is man excellent? What does it mean to be someone "a little less than the angels"? Our reply is that man's basic excellence depends on two natural and one supernatural consideration. The natural reasons are the spiritual side of his nature with all that this implies and the lofty purpose of his being. The supernatural reason is the sanctifying grace given to men by God's special love. Adding these reasons together, we describe man as the image of God. In St. John's language the graced are "the sons of God."

5. THE ESSENTIAL PATTERN OF HUMAN RELATIONSHIPS

A man realizes that he is not the only being in the world. Though an individual, he is not isolated, but is one member of a universe of beings. Every dimension of the physical world surrounds him with material beings. Other human beings stand near him and some influence him from afar. God, who made man and in whose presence man lives on earth, strongly acts on his life. The thinker is forced to ask what all these other beings may mean in his life and how he must conduct himself in their regard to achieve the best in human existence.

The pattern of the individual man's life shows a special constant relation to each of these three types of beings: nonhuman, created reality; other men; and God. Each set of relationships is pertinent to the good and happy life. Without maintenance of all three of these relationships human life becomes impoverished, inhuman, even impossible. The right understanding of these three essential relationships between man and other beings is, then, a big issue.

Scholastic philosophers regard man as better than material things, saluting him as the lord and proprietor who finds his right place in physical nature by making it serve his material and spiritual needs, his human ends.

Man at the same time is under God as essentially below God in excellence. He depends on God to be, to continue in being, and to act. He needs God to be good. He must work in partnership with God's effort on his behalf. He has every gift from God and so must use it according to His desire. The wise will of this supreme Master of man is a compass to human life; expressed in the natural moral law and in any divine positive law, it is most sacred to man. Hence, the question is most urgent: What does God want of me? How does God want me to live? How can I find God in this life and in the eternal life? The answer indicates that human life must be lived under God and for God. Only a God-centered life is truly human; a self-centered, earth-centered, social-centered life does not measure up to normal human standards.

The third orbit of these basic human relationships situates man as one among millions of people. Very much of life consists in some form of sharing with other men. Man is bound to man by many ties of need and affection, of dependence and helpfulness, of common purpose and mutual effort. In this social aspect of his nature he partakes of the common good and contributes to it, especially in those groups known as the family and the state.

Where there is society, there must be authority. Where there is a common order among many, there must be the order of laws and directives on the one hand and the correlative order of obedience and co-operative effort on the other. Human law guides and protects human liberty, but also restricts its wayward, selfish independence. Since society has claims upon man and man has claims upon society, human life on earth must be a life of liberty under law, a life expanding under the control of human authority, a life shared with other men for the good of each and all.

Christian theology agrees with the philosophers' efforts to adjust man into his right place in nature, before God, and in the company of his fellow men. In some particulars, it expands on the philosophical answers. In man's relationships with material things, Christianity insistently warns of the greater importance of spiritual values and the use of nature for spiritual ends. In man's relationships with God, Christianity shows that God has made specific revelations of religious truths and manifested His will to man in many important details. Finally, our social nature must work out our spiritual destiny in a new supernatural society, the one true Church or Mystical Body of Christ. This society, while effectively helping us, also claims our fidelity, obedience, and service to its personal and social ideals.

6. THE IDEAL HUMAN LIFE

Sometimes a fifth cause, the model or exemplary cause, enlightens philosophical understanding. When we ask what the good life is and what the best life for man is, we are searching for this fifth cause. Who is a perfect man? What does he do and how does he live? What kind of life is the fullest and richest? What ideals are the most splendid?

To answer this question the philosopher must first determine what human goodness really is and set up the proper standard by which goodness may be judged. Next, he must examine how human perfection can be attained. Is it by a life of study and prayer, by a life of domestic devotion, scientific invention, public service, teaching, or by some other way of life? The final part of the answer examines the perfect man, the ideal of human character. Who is the wise and good man who has arrived as this pinnacle of human development? Is he the philosopher-king whom Plato proposes, the magnanimous man of Aristotle's *Ethics*, the child of fortune and competent administrator like Solomon, an all-conquering hero like Alexander, the suffering servant of Isaias, or the scientific genius among Nobel prize winners?

In answer to the first part of this question, it must be said that the minimum norm of human goodness requires that man live up to his humanity. He must never violate any one of the essential features of his own nature and must impair none of his essential relationships to God, to fellow men, and to physical nature.

The inquiry about the best mode of life has to be answered, it seems, on two different levels: in the abstract and in the concrete. In the abstract, the contemplative life is superior to the active or the mixed life, since it stresses the spiritual side of man's nature. But when we answer more realistically in terms of individual human beings, their personal needs, their psychological capacities and opportunities, and their total concrete situation, we come upon a variety of best ways of life. The best must consider the real person. Vocation is relative to many circumstances, including favorable external circumstances and others' needs. The potential scholar, for example, may have to stop his studies in order to go into military service and there be permanently prevented by lack of time or by injuries and death from ever fulfilling his hopes of leadership through learning. The will of God calling men to one or another way of life deals with individual persons in the particular historical circumstances of their separate lives.

The closing consideration, that touching on the ideal man, leads to a discussion of some of the ideals proposed by the sages concerning the plenitude and harmonious blending of the virtues in human character.

Christian theology has settled the question about the ideal man. The teachings of Christ have pointed up some little appreciated virtues and have identified the supreme virtue as charity. The life of Christ on earth has portrayed the divine ideal before us. Christ is the perfect man, the ideal come to existence. The person most like Christ is the finest flower of human perfection.

7. THE CONFLICTS IN HUMAN LIFE

The truism that "everyone has his troubles" is as well known to the philosopher as to the tired laborer and the disheartened mother. What is the meaning of all these difficulties and sorrows that surround men and what is their function in human life? Do all or at least some of them fit in some way into a big scheme of life? Or are these the signs of an implacable fate or the relics of an evil demiurge interfering in human affairs? If so, who will relieve man from this harsh fate and from this power? If life is good, whose is the plan and what is its secret?

Various aspects of this problem of evil meet man. There is first of all the prevision of human death for oneself and for others. Why is there death? How can the stopping of life fit into the total plan of human life? Furthermore, on this side of the grave, men experience many physical and mental sufferings, many of them beyond their control and at times seemingly undeserved. There is the burning tragedy of man's inhumanity to his fellows. There is the repeated proof of enmity among men and of crime in word and work. Then, too, so much of life seems to be wasted in trivialities and fading pleasures, in doing unimportant and monotonous things, in sleeping, in just waiting wearily. Life is so short, yet growth is so slow. Why is there ignorance and error? Why sin and failure? Why so many wounds and broken hopes? Why so many insignificant, hidden human lives?

All these shadows thrown across the splendor of life and our human appreciation of it deserve careful attention. The main key to the whole riddle is, of course, the truth of the providence of God. All-wise and all-good, God has a complete plan into which all things on earth and all events in human life can be made to fit, with the exception of moral evils. All-good and all-powerful, God lovingly governs each individual person according to this plan. He will successfully bring each to his human destiny provided man does his own part and clings fast to God's living will or law. Every moment, every task, every joy, every pain, every burden, every fear can be aligned with the divine plan; for it is a perfect plan that is meant only for our ultimate good.

A feature of this plan is that life on earth is but the first episode in human living, while human destiny is never complete on earth.

We are ever growing up toward God. Still more, the present lifetime is a season of testing; and therefore, it is a time of trying, enduring, and waiting until God says that we have done enough. Perfect happiness, full understanding, total living, the splendor of success come only in the next life.

Religion helps more than philosophy in leading us to mental and emotional contentment with this riddle of suffering. Christian faith reads in the biblical record many marks of God's personal tender providence for good men. Faith especially presents the Son of God coming to earth to share man's lot of suffering and death, thereby redeeming us from evil and showing man that He understands. Faith points to Adam, not God, as the one who began human woes by original sin. Faith shows God combating evil and restoring men, broken by wickedness, to new favor with Him. Faith reveals the victorious Redeemer, rising from the grave, entering heaven, and there preparing for the coming of His followers. These truths, supported by the interior graces of God in the soul, can bring nearly perfect peace to the good man's heart even in the hour of greatest pain, disgrace, and death.

8. Is There Anything Better Than Natural Life?

There is a last question which even pagan philosophers have asked: Is this all? Is what reason discovers of the life and soul of man, of the reaches of intellect and will for perfection and happiness, is this all that is possible to man? Can man come somewhat closer than this to God? Or God come closer to man? Shall man forever know nature and himself and other men better than he can ever know God? Is our love of God always to be the love of One who is hidden from the vision of the intelligence and seen only through opaque premises and distant resemblances of Himself? Is the life of reason the true summit of human life?

Reason goes on to ask but is unable to answer other questions, too. Is there anything special that God may want me to do in this life over and above what my best thinking can discover of His will? Is God content with what I do? Is there something that He could tell me that I cannot learn by my merely human efforts? Is there some hope, some help that He is stretching out to me, some gift that He has for me, something more than natural life contains?

Such and related questions pierced certain pagan intellects[2] who prayed that a god would come and teach them. The wise man of the Old Testament also begged God that His Wisdom would come down and give answers to supplement the wisdom which reason can attain. This cry for God's coming is not alien to the philosophers. The better philosophers have usually recognized the incompleteness of philosophy, the deficiencies of reason, and the unfinished form of natural things. Philosophers have been particularly unskillful in being teachers of the masses and providing them guidance in the great truths of life and destiny. Some educator, some society, if possible a divine Educator and a divine society must teach and help us know and achieve essential human perfection. Even the wisest of mere men, left to themselves, end in half-answers, unsettled issues, and dim visions. In his infinite hunger for truth, life, love, and joy, the philosopher knows well that his hunger is not sated, that there is far more.

God has supplied this poignant want, Christian theology says to philosophy. God has come! Christ has come! He has given many answers and gifts, though He has not always stated the reasons for His solutions. He has come to His subjects in physical nature and by miraculous interventions shown His favor to men. He has come to the human minds which He has created and which lie open to His influence; He has mercifully instructed them by His own revelation. He has come to the will to strengthen it in pursuit of the good, inflaming it with better and high motives, and giving it power to love God in a new and more than natural way, through His actual graces. He has lifted up the very life of the soul, not only its powers, by instilling a higher form of life, that life of sonship of God and of friendship with Him which theology calls sanctifying grace. Of the fullness of the Light of God, the Life of God, the Word made flesh we have all received, grace upon grace. This proffered life will be crowned by the vision of God's adorable Trinity in God's own home, heaven.

The philosopher can merely say that some expansion to a quasi-divine level of life is possible for man. There are no limits other than the contradictory to what God can do for a creature to whom His love has given limitless spiritual capacities and receptivities. But the fact and manner of God's historical intervention, as well as the kind of gifts which He has showered on the human race, is a theological truth, not a philosophical one. This truth is attested by God's own special proofs, miracles and prophecies, and not by our own human reasonings on the data of nature.

Christ's contribution to the theory and practice of life is the manifold grace of God that presupposes, preserves, and perfects nature. All that sound philosophy has said of man and man's life is still true, but it is not the whole truth. As biology does not tell the whole truth about human beings, but needs help from psychology, history, sociology, and other studies, so philosophy does not tell us all the basic truths needed for man's life. Philosophy is a better friend and guide when she has been enriched and uplifted by theology.

As the answers to these eight questions are unfolded, they will display a true and fruitful vision of life. The fruitfulness of the vision will depend on human choice to live according to its truths. Principles can have consequences; from the seedplot of ideas grows the harvest of deeds; and deeds are deathless fruits in the case of immortal men. Around our ideas of man's origin, nature, and destiny, we map our lives, set our course, and build our hopes; according to these ideas we form our values and make our main decisions; from them as our base we steadily move forward to eternal peace.

9. Criteria of the True Answers

There are many answers to these eight questions besides the scholastic and Christian ones. In the hot debate over these issues, the beginner prudently asks for the signs by which he can discern the true from the false, the sure from the uncertain. This is not one of the big questions about life, but it is a big question about philosophizing on life.

There is a perennial first question about any pattern of ideas, any corpus of principles, any wisdom: Is it true? Any genuine philosopher is deeply concerned whether his principles, proofs, and conclusions are or are not true. What then is the mark and the measure of truth?

Principles and conclusions are true when and as far as they are conformed to reality. They are known to be true if they are objectively evident. Hence the earnest philosophical student is ever seeking the evidence which suggests, originates, supports, discriminates, improves, or in any way tests his views. It is the evidence drawn from the real that basically determines the wisdom or folly, the sufficiency or insufficiency of any philosophy. What is contrary to the evidence is false; what is not evident can at best be probable; what is objectively evident is true and certain. The primary control over philosophical thinking is evidence. By it one must judge all philosophical opinions, hypotheses, and commitments.

This over-all standard of evidence contains some particular tests. Somewhat like a judge on a bench searching for truth in a case, the philosopher has rules of evidence to obey. First, the theory or view presented must take account of *all* available evidence pertinent to the matter. The intellectual quest must weigh all the relevant facts, all the principles or truths connected with a question, and all the varied aspects which the problem may present. "With a true view," said Aristotle, "all the data harmonize, but with a false one the facts soon clash."[3] Hence, a philosophical mind must always be open to reality and not sealed in a system that is closed to new evidence or that lacks all power of assimilation and adaptation to new discoveries about nature, man, life, or God. One result of this is that many new findings of history, of fairly modern sciences like geology or laboratory psychology, and data coming from God personally in revelation may have a bearing on philosophy, for they constitute part of the evidence. Curiously enough, even the disagreements of the philosophers and the serpentine windings of their errors are part of the body of facts which must be wisely sifted for truth and error and meaning.[4]

A second particular test requires that the philosophical view must neither deny any facts it is intended to explain nor deliberately ignore any of them. This negative test is a crucial experiment in the honesty and completeness of a philosophy: what does it do with difficult and unmanageable facts? If there is not an impartial inclusion of these troublesome facts, extreme, exaggerated, and one-sided errors arise. From neglecting this test many of the half definitions of man, for example, seem to stem. Many ideologies are distorted views of human nature because they look to only one truth about man. This negative test obviously implies that no philosophical answer may conflict with other known facts and known truths.

Third, the views of a philosopher must not be derived from false assumptions, for then they lack all guarantee of their truth, even if by lucky accident they are right. Nor may they issue from any logical fallacy in reasoning badly from true premises.

Moreover, the theory or conclusion must not lead with logical necessity to any errors or any contradictions of otherwise known facts or truths. This criterion is concerned with the logical implications and the necessary connections between ideas. The philosopher does not judge people's conduct, but their ideas.

A theory, in addition, must succeed in explaining. A view is not yet philosophical when it has assembled various evidences without connecting the facts, giving them a causative interpretation, and supplying an intelligible meaning or a wholeness of view based on the evidence. Until a sufficiently complete mental vision of the whole plan of human life has been gained, philosophy has not yet risen from curiosity to its own level of understanding. Yet, while the philosophical view must throw light on the problems raised, it need not solve them all. Mysteries may remain, as in the problem of evil, but contradictions may not.

A final particular rule for evidence is that a philosophical theory, like a scientific one, must be capable of being tested. If it cannot be tested by known facts, sure principles, or some other method, it cannot become evident. It remains but a guess. To put this rule in another way: the theory must obey the principle of economy which dictates that the simplest theory consistent with the evidence is to be preferred. Otherwise, we encounter gratis, elaborate philosophical hypotheses or views which proceed from unnecessary and, therefore, nonevident assumptions.[5] Views not amenable to being tested for truth or error cannot compete philosophically with a theory that submits to the evidence presented by reality.

The practical fruitfulness of a theory is a popular test that seems to be especially inviting in regard to a philosophy of life and an ethical system, both of which are expected to supply some sense of values, some motives, some directions, and even some grounds for hope and ways to happiness. This criterion of practical consequences must be regarded as insufficient, though not useless. The judgment about truth must always precede the judgment of goodness or of utility. Hence, fruits good or bad, helps and dangers latent in or flowing from a philosophical position judge it only because they are logically consistent with it if the position is pursued to its consequences in human conduct. Such consequences are necessarily connected with the position if they are just the kind of activities that must follow when the theory is actually applied to life. Destruction of human dignity and values, for instance, is a sign to one who accepts human dignity that something important has been overlooked in the theory behind that practice; it has left out spirit or liberty or dependence on God or human equality. The theory becomes suspect and unacceptable because of its results.

The Thomist philosopher quietly proposes his views on human life as fitting all the evidence. Other views, which he accepts with reservations or which he rejects, he thinks lack evidence or even conflict with the evidence. It is the intellectual privilege of every reader of Thomist thought to inspect the evidence and to agree or disagree with him philosophically in so far as he is content with the conformity of these views of life with the reality of life's being, causes, and bonds.

Chapter 3

What Is Life?

1. Descriptions of Life

The Various uses to which people put the words *alive*, *living*, and *life* deserve some attention. As usage shows popular understanding, in it we may be able to discern the common trait which men generally recognize as characterizing life.

We speak of the biography of saint, pope, or president as his life. We regard someone's main interests as his life or lifework. A vigorous child, we say, is lively; we praise an attentive student for having an alive appearance. A butterfly on the wing or a trout struggling at the end of a line is thought to be alive. Growing things and awake, conscious animals are said to be showing signs of life. The Bible and God's perfect knowledge of those who shall be saved are called the book of life. The failure of a trapped mouse or a swatted fly to respond to any stimulus is taken as a proof of its loss of life.

Aristotle and philosophers both before and after him have noticed that movement is popularly considered as a special trait of living things. But some of the uses of the word *life* seem to be metaphorical comparisons, as when we refer to music with a quick tempo as lively and fountains of splashing waters as living. It is not merely motion, but self-motion, an internal motion of its own, which indicates life.[1] A living thing is self-active. A living man is not just pushed or pulled or thrown. He jumps by his own efforts and on his own initiative; he resists pushing; he tugs against the overpowering lurch of a bus that tries to throw him off his balance. A small boy holding a canary which has escaped from its cage will tell you how he recognizes life. To your question why he thinks the bird is alive, he will tell you: it moves; it beats its wings; it wants to get away; it sings; it eats. A little girl knows very well the differences between her doll and her baby sister in the crib. Sister cries on her own, moves her own eyes and arms, rolls around in the cradle; she is not helpless, motionless, and as inactive as the doll is.

This internal moving of themselves, this acting on themselves is the popularly accepted characteristic of living things.

2. THE TRAITS OF LIVING BODIES

Though living bodies are not the only living things, they are better known to us and more readily yield the first answers to our inquiry about the true nature of life. Plants, animals, and human bodies possess some special properties. Their chemical instability and variety is astonishing when compared with the fixity and uniformity which we see in lifeless things such as quarries of stone, beaches of sand, and pits of sulphur. More noteworthy than these chemical properties are vegetative activities possessed by plant, brute, and human types of life.

The first vegetative function is self-nourishment. Once bodies have begun to live, they take in materials from their environment as their food. This material they change into their own substance; they digest it, preparing thereby to assimilate it, that is, to make it or some of it a living part of themselves. Living things use this material partly as a fresh source of energy to replace materials which they have worn out and oxidized, partly to repair injuries, and partly for their own material enlargement in the process of growth. This second function, growth, appears especially in young living things, phenomenally in the unborn human baby, and through indefinite years in the growth of the trunk, branches, and leaves in some of the bigger trees. The living being grows its own parts and transforms the ingested food into parts of its own body. In the third vegetal type of operation, living bodies bring into life new living things of their own species. The exercise of this generative power requires that the living parent itself have developed and reached a stage of comparative bodily maturity, whereupon certain specialized living cells which it elaborates within its body as fruit and seed become capable of giving life to its descendants. These become living things distinct from their parents and continue the cycle of life.

Nonliving things, including the most ingenious machines and automatic calculators, for all their wizardry, beauty, and structure, have no trace of any of these three characteristics of nutrition, growth, and reproduction.

In addition, a living being adapts itself, within limits and according to its special nature, to external causes and surrounding forces. All make claims upon the environment for their food; some make claims for shelter, nests, and hiding places; men make demands on the environment also for clothing, sport, and art. A living thing can make itself fit its environment to some extent. It reacts not in one way but in a variety of ways under differing situations of light, heat and cold, air and wind pressure, dryness and moisture, kinds of soils, and the kinds and numbers of other living things in its neighborhood. This surprising variety can be seen in the seasonal changes of shrubs and trees, in their blooming, in their search for light, in their deep or branching roots exploring for water, in their graceful yielding to breezes. Many animals change their activities, their coats, body heat, and body chemistry with changing seasons, changing internal needs, and changing dangers. In all these changes the organism adapts itself and does so for its own benefit, not for the sake of the causes and forces in whose presence the organism finds itself. Some of these spontaneous adaptive processes in man are clearly safety measures, as the tanning of skin, the clotting of blood in a cut, the perspiration of the overheated body, the increased breathing rate to restore oxygen, and the natural immunity that follows exposure to certain illnesses. Nonliving bodies show no signs of such responses aimed at their own self-preservation and protection from damaging forces.

The capacity of the living to help themselves by adaptation is shown in the process known as irritability. This does not imply anger, but an intense response seemingly disproportionate to the stimulus that sets it off. A gashed oak tree, for example, starts a long series of actions to heal itself. The horse bitten by flies tries to remove the pests by waving its tail and scratching its legs and flapping its ears. A human baby in pain or fear explodes with cries until it is soothed. All these living reactions are highly purposeful; in all of them the organism is seeking the good of its own existence, health, comfort, or progeny. In men the response to discomforts, sorrows, and needs even reaches the magnificent achievements of modern medical education, surgical wonders, pharmacological helps, and hospital care.

One of the unique traits of human life is its very wide range of adaptability or of plasticity. Man is found in all parts of the earth at all seasons of the year. He has found ways to live in spite of extreme heat and cold and in spite of the lack of water and food in the immediate area where he dwells. He has adapted himself to nature's extremes and shortages by inventing his own artificial environment of clothing and shelter and his own methods of storing, preserving, and transporting food and water. He has the greatest range of means for keeping and restoring bodily health. He has the longest comparative period of postmaturity. Of all living species he has the widest variety of occupations, of interests, and of customary ways of living; only among the most backward and poverty-stricken tribes is there any likeness to the one-track monotony of plant and animal life. His plasticity also includes exceptional resistance to stresses; and even ardent evolutionists grant that this is not due to man's special physical strength or fitness to his contemporary milieu. Its secret lies chiefly in the fact that man has intellect and will, with which he can control, conquer, and shape the immediate world to himself, rather than in any natural fitness to be totally shaped by it as a more passive and rigid being must be.

Living bodies have a fifth distinction in the fact that they are organisms. The living body consists of organs which are special parts of the whole, each with special structures for the performance of special functions or for achieving special results by a special kind of activity. The several different organs are interrelated, and this structural relation to the whole is the organism's own splendid achievement. The organism builds its own special parts and builds them relative to the whole body and to each other so that there is mutual assistance in action. The unity in variety of parts thus achieved provides for both a big variety of activities and an integration in co-operative activity.

A physiologist might entertain one all evening with descriptions of the co-ordinating activities of the nervous system in man. But all of us without much specialized knowledge can realize that the human body, the most notable organism, has different parts with different structures that function differently and that work together. The variety of organs is obvious: eyes, ears, tongue, lungs, heart, stomach, nerves, bones, blood, glands, brain, and others. The gross differences of these organs are accentuated in microscopic study that shows numerous minute details of differences of cell structure in distinct organs. Diversity of functions in the specialized parts is also plain. The eye's acts of focusing light and sending it to the brain via the optic nerve, the heart's work of pumping blood, the blood stream's task of conveying oxygen and prepared food to every cell of the body are highly different. In all respects anatomy, i.e., structure, is related to physiology, i.e., to function, as the worker fitted to a good work. All this living action springs from within the organism and is mainly for its own good, whether to develop it, preserve it, restore it, or even to spread it into the external world and into new living beings.

This drive to its own good, this internal unity of purpose in all its many activities hour after hour of its life may well be regarded as the most remarkable of all traits of the living being. In contrast, lifeless things are most indifferent to their own self-interest. Animate bodies, furthermore, often identify the interest of their species with their own individual self-interest. They act for the sake of the continuity of life. They make sacrifices, involving great effort, health, even their lives, for the sake of their offspring's life. The mature individual sometimes loses his material identity in generating and protecting, but life goes on in young descendants. Surely, this propagation and survival of life in distinct beings also shows purpose. In man, especially, some of the greatest satisfactions of life are in the purposive procreation and provident care for the members of his own life circle, his own family.

3. IMMANENT ACTIVITY

Aristotle and St. Thomas[2] saw a common feature in the many instances and varied patterns of living action. They noticed that whether a living thing nourishes itself, maintains itself in being and health, organizes its own body, brings itself to its own mature perfection, makes out of itself a principle of life for its kind, or adapts itself to its environment, it is always acting on itself and working for the good of its own whole self or for the good of its species. This action of a living thing by itself, on itself, and for itself is named immanent action. The living thing is both the start and term of its own action. It is both the acting cause and the principal beneficiary of its living acts. The initiative as well as the first effect of action are interior to the living actor. Hence, because of this interiority or immanence of its operations, the living being is called self-moving, self-perfecting, self-benefiting.

The opposite kind of action, transeunt or transitive, can be seen in instances such as slicing bread or laying brick. The knife cuts bread; it acts on the bread, not on itself. A distinct thing, the bread, receives the effect of the knife's action. The knife is not particularly benefited by the act; any benefit is derived by the object or by those who use the bread. Similarly, whatever the inanimate object may be, a falling stone, a table moved into position, a piano that is played, a whistle blown, all act only as moved and used by another cause or force. They do not act on themselves and for themselves. A ventriloquist like Edgar Bergen performs a living or immanent action when he speaks. But Charlie McCarthy, his puppet, acts only transitively, as a being changed or moved by Bergen and for Bergen's benefit.

The induction, then, is that the universal feature of living action is this immanence in which the agent, the action, and the first good of the action are contained within the same living being.

4. Degrees of Life

Life's splendor in the universe is enhanced by the many types and degrees of immanent action, such as interior growth, seeing, imagining, sensory desires, judging truth, and choosing. It is of interest to man to learn just how high his life ranks. Biologists use certain criteria to compare the perfection of the bodily life of man to that of other animals. The philosopher's principle for grading life follows from the fact that living action is immanent activity. Hence, to him more perfect life will be more immanent; the better the immanence, the higher the form of life;[3] the greater the transience or passivity, the lower the grade of life.

Using this rule to measure life, the scholastic finds five distinct grades of living things: (1) plant life at the lowest level; (2) animal life beginning with those tiny creatures that seem to have only the sense of touch and climbing to those which have the full complement of senses, including sight and the internal senses of imagination and estimative power; (3) above all other animals, man with his added living powers of intelligence and free choice; (4) then, the angels who as pure spirits are always knowing; (5) and at the summit, God who is properly, perfectly, and totally Life.

The points in which the immanence of a being may be studied are its source of life, the perfection of self-activity and of internal determination in its living acts, its freedom from limitation, the interiority of the principle or form which directs the being in acting, and the immanence of the end for which the being lives.

Judged by these marks, man stands at the third level on the ladder of life. He mingles self-activity with transience or passivity, self-movement with received motions. He nourishes himself, forms his own body, grows, heals some of his injuries, produces bodily likenesses of himself in his children. He has the full set of senses, external and internal, for the immanent actions of sensation; he has the two sensory appetites for organic striving and desiring. He has also the much deeper immanence of intelligence and will. In addition, he guides many of the activities of his life by his own personally acquired forms of sentient and spiritual cognition. He also chooses for himself, by his own interior living act, the means by which he will pursue happiness. He controls many of his powers and activities by his own knowledge and deliberate purpose. He commands his powers.

But all this remarkable immanence has its limitations. For the beginnings of his life he is completely passive and dependent and can do nothing to get it for himself. He depends on material environment to sustain him in bodily being and health; his senses depend on that same external world for information or activation; his intellect depends on his senses; his will on his intellect. He depends on other people for help, instruction, companionship, and for giving life to his descendants. Even his main goals are totally determined by his nature and are not an object of immanent self-determination, yet he freely directs himself to these goals. The destiny of his vegetal and sentient activities and the final tendency of his spiritual nature to happiness is fixed for him. Other limitations on his life are manifest in the slow growth of his body and mind and in the fact that he measures his life by a certain number of birthdays which precede the end of bodily life.

Man's life, accordingly, presents both self-activity and subjection to outside influences. We shall never well understand man unless we understand his dependence in his distinctive human traits of life. He is especially dependent on God, as we shall see. To find the perfect mode of life we must look far above man to the living God.

5. The Essential Difference Between Living and Nonliving Bodies

Comparison of bodies that have vegetive powers with lifeless bodies reveals some similarities in material properties. Both react to gravitational, magnetic, electrical, and many chemical forces. The dissimilarities in the presence and absence of immanent actions lead philosophers to ask whether the difference between the two is one of degree or of nature. Is it an accidental difference as between the wise father and ignorant young son or is it an essential difference as between the wise father and the furniture in his home?

The scholastics claim that living beings are naturally or essentially different from nonliving things. They reason that we know what the natures of things are from their observed and known activities, for actions flow from and reveal the natures of the beings by which they are caused. Hence, comparison of known activities leads to the discovery of likenesses or differences between natures.

As a thing acts, so it is. But living bodies act in essentially different ways from nonliving ones. Therefore, living bodies are essentially different in their being and nature from nonliving bodies.

The premise contained in the second sentence above is true because the special immanent activities of living bodies belong to them alone. Lifeless things of every class have not even the beginnings or weakest manifestations of any immanent activity whether of the vegetative, sentient, or intellectual order. The difference in activities is an all-or-none difference. Ingeniously contrived machines seem to simulate some traits of life.[4] They have organization of a sort and sometimes a complex structure. But they do not build themselves from their parts; they do not organize their own structure; they are put together piece by piece by men and tools external to them. They show no internal independence or initiative in action; they act only when moved or started by their masters or attendants. The unity found in the machine does not grow from within, but is imposed on it by the mind of the inventor and mechanic who binds its parts together. Above all, machines produce things distinct from themselves, as presses print newspapers; they do not act for their own good, but for goods desired by their owners or users. Nothing closely resembles a living thing in its immanence, unity, and internal purposiveness, however much it may resemble it in material properties and in attributes of shape, complexity, orderliness, or exterior beauty.

Descartes is one of many philosophers who regarded animals as mere machines. One wonders, as the great British physiologist C. S. Sherrington[5] has remarked, whether he ever had a cat as a living pet whose numerous differences from a mechanical cat he might observe. Another scientist, the French physiologist Alexis Carrel,[6] has compared an artefact, a humanly built house, with a living human body. If living cells are bricks, they are magic ones surely. One magic brick, one living cell, without experience or blueprints, builds other cells of several kinds;

it arranges them in proper groups and places; it installs windows and openings in the house of its body, healing and cooling systems, its own telephone system between the members, its camera, its phonograph and recording systems, its drugstore and nursing services, its paint shop for coloring skin, hair, and eyes, a tool kit for many uses, a pump, elevators, reservoirs, storage bins, a cooking system, cleaning service, emergency warnings, and a variety of other services. The analogies between the parts of the human body and the parts of a man-built house are clear. But the living body did this by itself, did it before it was born, beginning with the one magic first cell of life.

Life in its wonders must be acknowledged as essentially different from anything nonliving. One consequence of this essential difference is that any change from nonliving to living or from life to death must be an essential or substantial change, a change in the very natures of the things that pass up to or down from life.

6. Essential Superiority of Living Bodies

Wondering curiosity about life prompts the further question whether the living is not only essentially different from but also essentially better than the nonliving. The sign of essential or natural superiority is a being's possession of activities and attributes which are not only totally different from but also totally better than those of another being. The better being may and usually will have operations and attributes that match those of the lower grade of being, but it will also have acts of its own that are missing altogether from the lower type of being and which are free from the limits that shut it in. In other words, perfection A in a being excels perfection B when A implies B's presence, but not vice versa.

Life's range of activities clearly meets this test. Though living bodies suppose the chemical and physical properties of other bodies, they add far more in nutrition, growth, reproduction, self-organization, adaptation, and self-directed goodness. These are totally superior operations, so that it is clearly better to live than not to live.

Consequently, there is simply no possibility that the nonliving should ever spring into life spontaneously, by itself, and without the helping action of another living being. The better cannot come from the inferior unless the better supplies what is completely lacking in the inferior. Our food comes to life within us because we share our life with it when we have assimilated it. But no lifeless material ever comes to life by its own agency, for it is an insufficient cause of such a development within itself. Spontaneous generation is a myth, for it is a causal impossibility.

7. SOUL IN LIVING BEINGS

After their search for the inner secret of these special living activities, many philosophers have named this inside source of life a vital principle or soul. Living things are said to be animated because they have an *anima*, a soul within them as some part of their being. Living plants, animals, and men are called besouled bodies. What then is a soul? What does the cow expel from the grass that it eats? What does the hunter crush out of the rabbit that he kills?

The soul is real because the living being in which it exists is real. The soul is a real source of living powers and functions. When it is present, a body lives; when it is absent, a body is lifeless. The life of the whole must somehow be ascribed to this element or principle. The soul is not the matter of the body which it animates, but it is penetratingly united to the matter of the body to make the plant or animal or man live. It is not the whole living being; it is the part which explains life and the particular kind of life that a thing has; hence, it is really distinct from, while united with, the matter of the body. Furthermore, the soul is the specific part because it both differentiates a living body from a nonliving one and distinguishes one type of life from any other type. A rose, a robin, and a rhinoceros, for example, each has a specifically different kind of soul. The soul, lastly, is a substantial part of the living thing. As such, it is part of its basic being, an ultimate principle of its nature and acts, and not merely an outgrowth or attribute of it like the special structure, figure, or other identifying external bodily characteristic. In summary, the soul is a real, intrinsic, specific substantial part of a living body, really distinct from the matter of that body, yet really united with that matter, and determining the whole thing to be alive with its own kind of life. To be human, then, means to have a human body animated with a special kind of soul, a human soul.

The same notion of soul is expressed in the shorter formula: the soul is the substantial form of a living body. Aristotle[7] expressed it in his famous definition of psyche as the "first actuality of a natural body that has life in it potentially." From this Greek word psyche, we understand that psychology was originally the philosophical study of natural bodies that have souls. The Aristotelian concept of the structure of a living thing is put in the usual terms of actuality and potency and is often called the theory of vitalism. Every living body is a substance composed of two incomplete substantial principles, really distinct from each other and really united together; of these principles the soul is the first actuality or the substantial form, and the disposed matter is the potential element or material cause.

Any proof offered for the existence of a soul is an attempt to find the basic reason for the differences between living and nonliving bodies. Two out of several proofs will here be presented. The first is based on an analysis of the activities performed by a living being. The observed living acts of anything recognized as alive are surely not explained sufficiently by the matter of the body. Matter alone is indifferent to life and death; it is indifferent, too, to the type of life which it sometimes has. If it dies, it is still matter. If it is eaten by different living beings, it becomes, for instance, seal tissue or bear meat or human flesh. What is indifferent to its various perfections and states of being cannot be the whole explanation of the various new perfections that it may acquire. Matter is also indifferent to the organization and activities of life, since it exists under many varieties of structure. That any bit of matter should have the shape of a frog, the structure of an ear, or the intricate conformation of a brain does not depend merely on matter. Some other real factor, the soul as we name it, influences the matter and organizes it so that it is this definite living structural part of a living whole.

Death provides a second proof. Death brings about a major change in the kind of being that something was before death. In dying, it lost no weight, no tissue, no bodily figure; what it lost was its soul, its substantial form that made it capable of living acts, something that was intimately in the matter but really different from it. The real and substantial change of death means that the soul has ceased to dwell in and inform that body.

We will renew this discussion of the soul when treating of the human soul in Chapter 5.

8. The Unity of a Living Man

The recognition of the distinct principles of body and life in a living thing and the observation of its multiple activities may tempt some to look upon a living body, and especially a human living body, as a sum of parts, rather than as a composite unit. A unit is something that is undivided in itself and distinct from other things. Man has body and soul as his substantial parts; he has many organs, bones, cells, and uncounted molecules and atoms in these cells. He is a composite unit, not a simple thing. Yet he is still a natural unit, not an artificial whole composed of distinct units like a suit of clothes, a book, or a typewriter. Man is not just a number of pieces, of cells, organs, or any other parts fitted together like the members of a mechanical man in a museum of health. The unity of his parts and their relationship to the whole man and to each other comes from within man himself. All parts grow from a single cell; all grow toward one aim, the formation of a unitary whole man. Two well-known criteria or signs of unity show this oneness of the human person.

Man has the internal evidence or his own immediate experience of his unity. He is aware of his body and of many of its various parts. He knows that he has different organs, bones, and muscles, hands and feet, chest and ribs, eyes and ears, nose and tongue, and others. He knows them to be distinct from each other. Yet he is equally sure that all these various parts belong to the same one self, the man. These are "my" hands, "my" eyes, "my" skull. All belong to the same one conscious being and to no one but to "me."

In addition, man's experience of his own activities strongly indicates the basic unity of their source. Each man is fully conscious that he is the same one being who now sees and later hears and again tastes and later feels hard or warm surfaces of other objects and then remembers these experiences and who likes, dislikes, or fears these objects that his senses contact and know. It is not one person who sees, and another who touches, and another who reacts. Even in his tensions within himself, he knows the struggle is due to his own unity. Likewise, the conscious man knows that distinct parts of his body in helping each other help the same one whole to which the parts belong, as when the quick perception of the eye helps the whole body to dodge some danger or the strong stance of the legs keeps the whole body from being thrown down.

Maybe the most distinct of all these experiences of human unity appears in that unified activity when a man controls his mind, body, and all his being in pursuing some purpose of his own. When I strongly desire to see a game, it is the one same being, the "I," who desire to go, make my plans, dress myself, move my body from home, drive to the park, get tickets, view the sport, and cheer my favorites. The one person with a single purpose performs a complex series of many actions with many parts and powers of his being.

Besides this unmistakable internal evidence of the unity of human nature, there is a mass of observable external evidence, which one can examine in others. There is the physiological unity of man's body achieved by its special co-ordinating and integrating systems, such as the nervous, skeletal, circulatory, and glandular sets of cells and organs which are parts that serve the whole body and connect together its structures and functions. The levels of life in man assist each other; the activities of nutrition and healing feed the sentient body and heal various ailments in the senses. The senses, in turn, act to protect and feed the vegetal powers, so that the vegetal and sentient forms of life are not opposed to or independent of each other but spontaneously aid each other. The relations of bodily and mental activities are very noteworthy, indicating the dynamic interaction of parts in their relation to the whole individual person. States of bodily well-being affect the ease, sharpness, and clearness of thinking. Mental states, as cheerfulness, contribute to health and its recovery.

Because of this unity of life in the human being, successful dealing with ourselves and with others may not stop at considering what is good or harmful to the parts. The advertiser appeals to the whole man and stimulates his action by appealing to his sense of sight and hearing and by starting various associations with pleasures dear to customers. The doctor finds that a patient's peaceful, contented mind is his best co-operator in healing bodily ills. The depth psychologist looks for a hidden purpose which will explain abnormal fears and paralysis of his client. A mother and father know very well the singular unity of each individual child. The old wisdom about a sound mind in a sound body is a popular witness to this natural unity of interdependent and interacting parts in human nature. During one's whole life on earth body and soul are natural partners, much closer than wife and husband or twins or the fastest friends. This companionship of body and soul is unique in intimacy and completeness. For each human being is one, an independent "I," a single whole, this real person.

CHAPTER 4

Thought, Desire, and Choice

1. UNDERSTANDING HUMAN ACTIVITY

THE ANCIENT sages advised man: "Know thyself." A modern man may well take this perennially good advice, since self-knowledge truly suits man and must usually precede planned self-improvement and well-directed living. Man's structure and bodily behavior shows that he is indeed an individual living substance whose life is due to a substantial form or soul within him. But it also shows that man is a sentient being, with the anatomical structure, physiological activities, and cognitive and appetitive operations that are found in animals. Zoological, anthropological, physiological, and biochemical data about man give us valuable information for a detailed understanding of his body, his health and illness, and his animal status as a member of the vertebrates, mammals, primates, hominidae, of the genus homo, the species homo sapiens, with brain unusually capacious in its ratio to body weight. It is not news that man has a body and is in part at least an animal; and these facts do not advance our basic insight into human nature. But we stand to deepen our knowledge of man's distinctive being by learning more of his unique psychological activities and the powers by which he performs his human functions of thinking, willing, and choosing.

In exploring the nature of man the investigator must begin with what man does. In and through man's acts his endowments can be known. No philosophical approach not grounded in man's observed acts has hitherto been successful. A priori theories of man do not begin with his acts but from various assumptions such as that he cannot be more than a sensing animal or that he cannot be one being with both matter and spirit united in his nature. Such assumptions or conclusions or prejudices have not had the patience to examine the data re-

38

ported by man's activities. Aristotle's philosophical way is the right technique, for it moves from facts to the analysis and interpretation of their nature, and thus to knowledge of the being, man.[1]

Aristotle looks at man in action. The Aristotelian collates, compares, groups, and distinguishes these acts. He notes that all activities of cognition or awareness and of appetency or conscious striving are concerned with an object. One sees a hat, an object; one smells candy, an object; one remembers a tune. One dreads mad dogs; one wants some coffee; one hopes for a raise; one chooses a wife. All such acts of living persons pair with objects. No object, no act. By finding likeness and unlikeness in the objects, one can find some characteristic similarities and differences in the acts. This method is accessible to each of us. It is merely refined by psychological laboratory procedures that increase the accuracy of observation, reduce chances of error, measure performance, and isolate separate elements in the rich whole of human behavior.

In the scholastic theory, typical acts which a man performs again and again, off and on, in a great variety of situations are regarded as being produced by permanent natural abilities or powers in man. Nutrition, sight, imagination, and intelligence are examples of powers. Powers are native abilities, not acquired as are the habits of man. Intellect, for example, is a power; knowledge of English is a habit. The acts manifest the existence of the power; they aid in formation of the habit. Powers are, then, constant abilities of man to act or react in regard to some special type of object. These abilities are called powers because they are springs or principles of operation; their function is to do some definite thing, as to see colored objects, to feed the body, to understand, or to love the good. They are the vital immediate instruments which the living man uses when acting.

That such powers exist in us is clear from the fact that we act in a number of specifically different ways in regard to a number of sharply different types of objects of action. The kinds of action give us the catalogue of the kinds of powers. Seeing is a very different experience from hearing; knowing is not desiring; reasoning is not choosing. The specific kinds of action are partly explained by differences in the material organs involved, if it be a question of organic powers, for each organ is adapted to only one task such as focusing rays from lighted objects or responding to sound vibrations or to flavors. But the difference is chiefly explained by the fact that the different powers, both organic and nonorganic, have an exclusive proportion or adaptation to one particular kind of object. This specialty of the object of the powers is called the formal or proper object of each. Color sent into the eye from objects is the specialty of sight; resistance is the specialty of the pressure sense; past images are the specialty of the imagination; knowable being or being as true is the unique object of the intellect; the intellectually known good is the object reserved to the will. Each power has a natural relation or proportionate capacity for its own respective object as the term of its special activities. The distinction and number of the powers is the same as the number of the distinct formal objects.

Though the powers are distinct, in the adult they will seldom be working alone, but will co-operate in many fascinating combinations. Speaking a sentence will involve powers of thought, memories of sounds of words, muscular sensations in the vocal cords, tongue and lips, and other factors. Not all of man's powers, however, need be acting simultaneously.

2. HUMAN SENSORY POWERS

Having a living body much like the bodies of other higher animals, man has the generic sentient perfections of animals. The acts of such sensory powers are known as sensations and emotions. The cognitive powers of animals with complete nervous systems fall into two main groups: external senses in immediate contact with sensible objects in the material world, and internal senses which have a sensation or one of its internal effects as their objects. The external senses are sight, hearing, taste, smell, touch which meets the hard and soft, the warm and cool, the pleasant and painful, and probably also the sense of balance. The best known of the internal senses is the imagination; but it has three partners known as the central or unifying or common sense, the estimative power which informs the animal of the sensibly useful or harmful in the objects known by the other senses, and the memorative power. In actual daily life, these senses are weaving patterns of learning, awareness, and recognition in innumerable ways and sequences of interdependent action.[2]

There are also two sensory appetites, sources of emotions, satisfactions, and conscious wants. They can act only after the animal has knowledge of objects. The concupiscible or pleasure-loving appetite is concerned with the sensibly pleasant, which it desires and prompts us to pursue, and its opposite, the unpleasant, which it spontaneously shuns. The other appetite is the irascible, the "anger" or fighting appetite, which prompts the animal to act for difficult sensible goods which the pleasure-loving appetite might make it fear as unpleasant, even though useful or necessary to the animal. The two appetites together are called sensuality.

Analysis of sensory acts leads to the conclusion that every sentient power has a twofold component, an organ as its material part and the specific sentient form that knows or seeks its distinctive object. Although the organ is not the power, the power completely depends on the organ for its operation. The principal physical part of the power is usually regarded as some area of the brain cortex. These points may be illustrated for the case of vision. The eye, optic nerve, and brain centers of seeing are the organ; but sight is the power composed of these material structures and the ability of being aware of colored objects. The eye does not respond to reflected light merely as a camera or a photoelectric cell does; the sense of sight is aware of colored things inasmuch as they seem to be colored. The dependent relations of the power of vision then are these: without the material object reflecting light of a certain kind, the eye cannot perceive color; without the eye, the optic nerve, and the brain tissue, the power cannot experience color awareness; without the power, even in the presence of the other factors, there is no knowledge of visual objects.

All sensory powers are marked by material dependence and characteristics. Their object is something material, concrete, sensible, extended in space. Because of their involvement in organic conditions of matter, all sensory powers are subject to considerable physical change, to fatigue, disease, impediments of age, material separation from the body, and finally to death together with the organism to which they belong.

There are some special psychological features of the human senses, as the acuity of human color perception, the weakness of smell in man, liveliness of the imagination, and the indeterminate estimative power with the very few kinds of human instinctive activities. The senses, though at times morally dangerous, must on the whole be regarded as the friends of man. The major importance of all the senses and sensory appetites in human life is their service to the intellect and will.

But we must first determine whether man has an intellect and a will. These are the two powers which down the centuries have most interested philosophers as marking the psychological uniqueness of man. Are they supersensory, nonorganic, purely spiritual powers or not?

3. EXISTENCE AND SPIRITUALITY OF THE INTELLECT

Four preliminary points are in place. First, knowledge is truly a form of life, for it is an immanent activity, one performed by the knower, in the knower, and for the knower. Second, by intellect is meant a power of knowing objects in an immaterial way, that is, in a manner not only different from but opposite to the sensory mode of knowing. Third, by something spiritual we mean that which is free or separate from matter in its being, nature, and operations. It has no matter in its constitution; nothing material is even a partial cause of its activities. Yet a spiritual power of a lower order of being may depend extrinsically on something material as a condition for its action, as a source of supply of sensory data on which the intellect alone will think, judge, or reason, or as helping or catalyzing action in some way. Particularly, since man is composed of body and soul, it is to be expected that sensory experiences will accompany his higher mode of thinking.

The fourth note concerns the issue and method of proof. The existence and spirituality of the intellect are proved together, since the very point to be proved is the existence of a supersensory, purely immaterial, and therefore nonorganic power of knowing. The starting point of the proof must be the activities of human knowing. We must find some spiritual acts of understanding. If found, spiritual acts will reveal the spiritual nature of the power from which they proceed. Only a spiritual principle could perform totally immaterial acts.

As there are a number of types of spiritual acts performed by men, there are a number of proofs for this claim of a spiritual intellect. It would be tedious and, one hopes, unnecessary to lay them all out in full. But as this is a critical frontier between materialism and genuine humanism, several proofs ought to be given.[3]

A promising line of evidence issues from man's power of speech. The "talking animal" uses material signs for understanding and sharing meaning with other men. The proof argues that the act of understanding language is a spiritual act. But as a thing acts, so it is. Therefore, the spiritual act of understanding language shows that the agent or power which understands is also spiritual.

The first premise, namely, that understanding language is a spiritual act, needs investigation. Obviously, the movement of vocal chords in speaking, of the hand in writing, of the eyes in reading are physiological processes. But this other element, grasping the meaning, is not physiological, but spiritual.

The use of language is so familiar that we have a tendency to overlook its remarkable character. Language is a sign or set of signs which express thought and other mental states and can convey knowledge of these to another person who is familiar with their accepted usage. Few language signs have any natural connection with the objects for which they stand or with the ideas and relationships between ideas which they present. We use many languages, and not only in the sense that we have many tongues as English, French, and Greek. Even in English, vocal language uses one set of signs, written language uses another, braille language uses a third, numerals use a fourth. We have other languages — for many mathematical ideas; the dots and dashes of telegraphic signals; semaphore flags; playing cards with their different values and relationships; traffic lights and various manual movements to express our traveling intentions; graphs indicating statistical relations and business trends; musical notation; and other sets of arbitrary signs.

Any one with hearing can catch the tones of the word *father*; any one with sight can see the sequence of letters that spell the word. That is just a sensory grasp of something audible or visible. To understand that these tones or these letters refer to a man who has a son and to understand the connotation of reverence and affection is something far different and far more. This act recognizes the sign as a sign, goes beyond the sign to its meaning, to the object signified, to the inner thought of the user of the sign, to union with the mind of the writer, and to the social sentiments clustering about the person signified.

The reading of one declarative sentence, and a fairly easy one, as language goes, reveals this knowing activity. "The President of the United States and his family live and work in the White House in the nation's capital." Here twenty signs are strung together in one whole meaning. None of them has a natural connection with the objects mentioned or the ideas involved. The reading of them by eyes and lips occurs one syllable at a time, requiring a few seconds and involving spatial movements of the eyes across the area of the line. The signs themselves are individual, concrete, black, of one definite shape and size; they are marked by matter. The writer of that sentence or its printer may be many miles away. But the reader looks and then, if he knows the language, understands. He catches the writer's meaning, his reference to definite persons, occupations, place of residence, and the relation of that place to the whole nation. In understanding, the reader fuses all these multiple signs, objects, and relations into one. All in one act he has caught the multiple intangible nonsensory connections between the signs and the things signified and the relationships behind the things signified. Here is an act which has no characters of matter, of extension, or of time. Understanding is a single instantaneous act of seizing the meaning. It is an indivisible act and not a piece-by-piece thing like the string of signs printed on the page.

Conditional sentences and a set of commands may be used to show the same thing, especially if they are so arranged that all meaning must be suspended until the last sign in a set is read. It is no wonder that the child, then, is performing a big feat in grasping this world of signs into which education in speech, in reading, in writing, and in arithmetic introduces him. He might prefer a picture of a shoe, but that is not the usual sign in our culture. He might prefer to point to a shoe or make a shadow drawing of a shoe in the air; but he must learn to speak the particular tones that grownups have long ago selected to represent this object. The child might well ask, why spell S H O E instead of S E H O. Neither has a natural connection with the object. But he will learn that if you are to live in society, you have to use the codes of signs which society has adopted for learning, exchanging ideas, gathering information, winning friends, and influencing purchasers. Some day the child will prove his spiritual intelligence by making language his own creature. He will show keen selectivity and easy freedom in using hundreds of words. He will learn grammar with its maze of combinations for signifying relations of persons, times, questions, and parallelism. He will invent new phrases, reshuffle the peculiar signs and relations of signs that will more carefully convey his meaning. He will strive for variety in saying the same old thing. He will adopt metaphors that further complicate the immediate meaning of the sign. He will perhaps become adept in ciphers and hidden languages, or even learn to polish language into intricate beauty in poetry, adorning it with rhythm, rhyme, alliteration, musical values, and a medley of figures of speech. He can be so subtle with signs because he has a mind independent of the tones, strokes, lip movements, and other merely material factors involved in the sign and in its utterance or perception.

Animals have ears and voices. They can associate some familiar sounds. Some of them can imitate human sounds. Yet they show no grasp of meaning in spite of years of hearing sounds or uttering imitations. The parakeet picks up a few words or phrases and uses them endlessly, without relevance, in a monotonous identity and with no rearrangement of the signs to express new meanings or new perceptions of its own states or new references to different objects or new relationships noted in things.

Another proof for the existence of an immaterial intellect in man was advanced by Aristotle. He preferred to show the immateriality of human intelligence by applying his principle of the relation of acts to objects. He discovered that we think of immaterial objects. Because of the natural proportion between objects and powers, the existence of immaterial objects of thought postulates an immaterial power of knowing. In this method of studying thought, the reflective person attends not to the language men use but to the objects which occupy their thinking. When one gathers and classifies the things that he observes and wonders about, he finds that many are individual, material, concrete, extended, sensible, limited to some bit of matter, and externally affecting material things or one's senses. But there is a group of other objects. It includes numerous universal objects where one nature common to many things is thought about; examples are gold, ship, man, child, school. These objects are not of any particular individual gold medal of an Olympic winner or a special boat or a given child, but represent natures common to many members of a large class that one is thinking about. One is thinking of gold — as such, of human nature — as such, not of the individuals in that class, not of the size, shape, color, and other sensible accidents of any one of them. Men also think of abstract objects such as humanity, kindness, prettiness, depth, brilliance, justice, energy, purposiveness. None of these exist in the world of material singular things; there are kind deeds and pretty dresses, but kindness and prettiness as such are nonexistent. These qualities have been separated from their concrete objects and made to stand by themselves in the intellect. Men also inquire about and think of immaterial objects which completely exclude matter, such as the spiritual soul of man, an angel, and God. Thought goes out to unlimited objects, as being, truth, the infinite, God. It attends to meanings and relationships such as those of cause and effect, means and end, authority and subject, imperfect and complete; and none of these relationships or bonds are material objects.

Whether such objects of thought exist in themselves, either in whole or in part, is here not important. The fact is that men very often think of such beings and know what they mean when they talk of them and read about them. Any thoughtful piece of prose is full of these signs of universal, abstract, immaterial, unlimited objects that have no material being, no extension, no individuality in the world of the sensible. There is nothing about them that a sense can grasp; they are quite opposite in character to the material elements with which the eye, the ear, the imagination, and other senses are concerned. In thinking of these objects, men have thought of something that has not and cannot have concrete matter with its own extension and sensible properties. The power named intellect which thinks of these objects has gone deeper into things than the senses ever go. The intellect has pierced into the nature or essence, formed a definition, struck a form, grasped an intelligible relation, broken free of the limiting material factors found in sensible objects.

Since objects measure acts, Aristotle concludes that so different and better an operation is a spiritual act. It is performed by a proportionate power of knowing named the intellect. Indeed by the very fact that a man asks, thinks, or doubts about the spirituality of his intellect he has well proved the spirituality of the intellect. For his question, his wonder, his understanding of the meaning has attained an immaterial object.

Man's knowledge of himself supplies another evidence of a spiritual act of knowing. Man makes judgments about himself such as: I know that I am thinking; I know that I am talking; I know that I am loving; I know that I am. When man reflects on himself, his mind finds his own self. The mind is an agent present to itself, knowing itself in its own acts. Here is the self-identity of the observer and of the object observed. This is not like looking at oneself in a photograph, which is an object distinct from oneself. Here the same being perceives and is perceived in the one same act of perception and without media or copies of itself. This self-identity can only mean that the knowing power here active has no parts and that the whole is perceiving the same active whole. Everything material, however, is extended and has parts. A material knower might know another part of itself or an image of itself, as the eye might see its image or one finger touch another finger. But the whole can know the whole only because there is simplicity, and therefore spirituality or independence of material pieces. Ortega y Gasset has also noticed this difference between animal and human knowledge and has commented on the animal's constant attention to what goes on outside itself and to the things about it.[4] The brute does so, not only because of incitements and dangers in this outside world, but because it cannot go within itself or reflect on itself; it has no consciousness of self, no power to contemplate itself, no capacity to examine or rest in or worry about itself. Not so man, the thinker.

Against modern Marxists who glorify the toolmaking ability of man it has become customary to point to man's invention of tools as a plain disproof of the basic Marxist postulate that man is only a special kind of matter. A tool, thoroughly material in itself, is brilliantly marked by the spiritual mind that has fashioned matter to a new form for man's deliberate purpose. In the invention and manufacture of some instrument, whether it be a stove for cooking and heating, a pen for communication, a wheel or auto for transportation, a lamp or garment for human comfort, there seems to be first a thought of human betterment and a desire and hope for modifying natural objects in some way in order to bring about an improvement. This is followed by a search for some apt means to adapt material objects to a given end, by a period of experimenting with different materials, by correcting mistakes, and, frequently enough, by the final discovery of a new tool. During the period of investigation and construction of the first model of the tool, we notice an interest in progress and a dissatisfaction with remaining in the same old rut of instinctive and traditional ways of acting. We notice human curiosity in the face of the unknown. We notice human criticism of the results, recognition of successful and unsuccessful combinations, procedures, and tests. We notice an understanding of natural operations. There is a formal perception of the relation of means to prospective ends and an elimination of some lines of search as being inept for the end. Often there are abstract mathematical calculations. Safety features are devised. The maker transfers the idea of the mind into matter. He sees in the tool the fact that it is a type, a pattern, a species, in other words, a universal. It can do the same kind of work in many situations again and again; other tools can be made according to the same specifications of the model and by the same manufacturing process. The inventor sees more than the thing before him; he sees into the thing, into its nature, into its relation to ends, into its copies. He sees the many which do not exist in the one which does exist. All this mental activity shows characteristics that sensory knowledge completely lacks.

As this spirituality of some acts of knowing is for philosophers "a line of no retreat," we may mention other spiritual acts which could be analyzed and shaped into a proof. The act of judging existence, truth and error, actuality and possibility is a spiritual act. The act of reasoning implies reaching to the unseen, a looking forward to the unknown and the future, a formal grasp of connections between antecedent and consequent. The fact that man knows matter itself and not just its singular material surface features shows that his intellectual knowledge is an act not restricted by a material organ. Many human interests and skills show man performing spiritual thinking: man as artist and gardener interested in beauty; man as moralist, lawyer, and citizen interested in immaterial goodness, in justice, in social organization, in other men's minds and wills; man as religious interested in spiritual realities and the relationships of his soul to God. Perhaps the phenomena of telepathy and imageless thought are a new body of evidence to immaterial knowledge.

We can think about anything under the aspect of being; the only thing we cannot think of is the contradictory, nonbeing. Whether the object be material or spiritual, actual or possible, finite or infinite, concrete or abstract, individual or universal, as long as it is being, it is within the mind's range of curiosity and consideration. Being then is the object of the intellect; certain material characteristics of being are the restricted objects of senses. Intellectual knowledge is accordingly asserted to be essentially superior to any sentient or animal knowledge; and the being with an intellect, man, must on one side of his nature be completely better than the mere animal.

4. The Will

In addition to thinking about objects, man likes and dislikes them. After thought follows desire for or aversion from the things thought about. Man not only knows goods, but he wants them, wishes to use them, enjoys them, hopes to have them, fears to lose them, hates evils in some of them, selects some of them, rejects others of them. He presses toward objects which he regards as in some way good for himself; he hurries away from what he considers evil for himself. As a result of these dynamic tendencies he directs his various powers both to accomplish the aims which he seeks and to remove the obstacles that prevent his possession, use, enjoyment, or preservation of the goods that he longs to have.

This kind of human movement toward the intellectually known good and away from the intellectually recognized evil both follows knowing and differs from it. Here is an outward thrust of man's nature toward the object and not an inner assimilation of the form of the thing, as happens in knowledge. Here, too, is a different vital union with the object. In knowing, the initial efficiency producing knowledge comes from the object, which creates a representation of itself in the knower, conforms the knower to its being, and makes him one with it. In volition, the efficient cause of the love or dislike is the inner power itself, while the object serves as a final cause and term of action. The power here wants to take action in regard to the object and not merely know it.

This permanent power, will, is called a rational appetite, an intellectual tendency toward goods, for it follows reason and is the partner of intelligence. The evidence for the existence of this distinct power is fourfold. (1) This power has a special formal object, any being intellectually known to be good or, by contrast, not good. (2) The intellect needs the will as a necessary complement of its nature. One must be able to do something about what he knows to be good, needful, useful, desirable, or dangerous. The intellect not only sees and speculates, but suggests action and attitude in regard to good or its opposite. Life requires that knowledge be completed by proportionate motivation and action. (3) The distinction of intellect from will appears in the conflict that occasionally disturbs their partnership. "I see and approve the better, I follow the worse," as Ovid put it. (4) Finally, a new feature, freedom, appears in these acts of desire and aversion for some objects, whereas the power of knowing, apart from the influence received from the will, is incapable of options.[5]

Acts of the will also manifest spirituality, because they follow the spiritual action of the intellect and because they seek and shun spiritual goods. This is readily seen in acts of love of God, of yearning for the universal good, of love of virtue and hatred of evil. In addition, the will's freedom reflects its immateriality or independence of material conditions and the invariable routine of physical laws of action.

Whether the will is man's highest power is disputable.[6] Certainly it is the highest appetite, far surpassing the sensitive ones; it is the specifically human appetite, for irrational animals have sensory appetites. The will has one special quality of its own, the quality of liberty in some of its acts, that is, of directing one's acts and life according to one's judgment.

5. LIBERTY OF SOME ACTS OF WILLING

With the notion of liberty we associate many things dear to the human spirit: freedom from slavery, political independence, privileges of citizenship, freedom of conscience, religious rights, sovereignty over our own homes, and our own loyalties to various persons and causes. Here we are concerned only with the basic liberty or psychological freedom of the will's acts. We champion true liberty for the human will, but only in some of its acts and only under certain conditions.

It must be noticed that the intellect and the will team together in action. The will follows the intellect. Hence, its freedom in regard to goods depends heavily on the way the mind presents them to the will.[7] Both reality itself and our way of knowing it set conditions for and limitations upon choice. Reality confines us. We cannot choose ends, but only means; choice presupposes that an end is already willed. In particular, man's natural end, the supreme good to which our nature is inevitably urged, namely, happiness in general or good in general, cannot be chosen; it is simply willed. Also, any means which we know is the only one that can effectively reach an end which we have seriously willed is not an object of selection; we must want such a unique means if we want the end to which it leads. Hence, there must be alternative means, various courses of action open to us, a situation of either-or, and competition for our favor before objective conditions for choice are given. Finally, what we know to be impossible cannot be chosen. The intellect for its part must not be ignorant of or inattentive to the alternatives; it must present two or more goods, two or more possible means, alternative objects of choice and action to the will, something that does not seem to be an altogether perfect good.

The manner in which the intellect influences the will is the philosophically best evidence of the liberty of the will. Sometimes the intellect sets before the spiritual appetite two or more objectives that appeal to the will as good in some way. With the presentation is the judgment that these are particular or partial goods, not a universal one, that they are contingent, nonnecessary or indifferent goods, which we can take or leave, at least for the present, and that all these goods are somewhat apt for our purposes but not all of them simultaneously needed. In the presence of objects of this kind and of the judgment that they are such partial, contingent, limited, and alternative goods, the will freely chooses which good it will make its own and which it will put off or refuse. The preference for one means or alternative good over another is the will's act; even if it declines to act, it has chosen to wait or to do nothing. A quarterback picking a play to score a touchdown against a determined opponent has perhaps a dozen possible alternatives, sneaks, bucks, passes to different players, end runs, deceptive plays, power plays, speed plays, some which have been successful before but which opponents know, some which have not been used and may prove to be successful surprises. No doubt, memory of practiced plays, habit, desire to win, excitement and coaching instructions, all influence him; but he ultimately chooses only one definite play from his stock. Whatever he does or does not do results from his own active decision. The objectively indifferent situation becomes settled and one good or line of action is adopted by the will; only one of the several possibilities is actualized because of the choice made; the indetermination of the will itself to pick any of these goods is removed by the will's own decision. But it is clear that both intellect and will had jointly to operate in this act of choice.

Some believe that the personal experience of freedom is a better proof, even though it gives less insight into the mind-will relationship. A person is directly aware of his free way of acting in some of his liking and disliking, desires and aversions, decisions and efforts. In preparation for action, one deliberates on a line of conduct, knowing well that one is able to choose and is responsible for the selection that he will make. If he chooses to go sailing this afternoon, he must stay away from the golf course. If he proposes to Martha, he cannot marry Lucy. He knows he can do either, but cannot do both, and so he weighs the advantages, prospects, and disadvantages. In the moment of choice, one clearly recognizes that it is he, only he, who is deciding; while motives influence him on both or several sides, nothing forces him to settle the issue in one way rather than another. Therefore, after one has chosen, he distinctly realizes that he is the author of the choice and its normally foreseeable consequences. He feels that the results of the choice should rightly and fairly be credited to him for praise or shame, for liability to reward or to penalty, and that he must mainly blame himself for wrong and take up the burden of undoing any harm that he has caused. Hence, too, the agent who has chosen usually feels some glow of joy and peace of conscience for doing well or some uneasy guilt and regret because of doing something pleasant or useful but morally evil.

In summary, the quality of freedom is experienced in some acts. Before, during, and after one's acts of choice, one knows that he alone decides.

Finally, the whole moral and legal order, which most people accept as valid, implies that men are free. Men know the interior war between moral good and moral evil, between duty and pleasure, between honor and instant advantage, between the desire to have their own way and the need of following the way of God or other authority. Men, furthermore, think that the will ought to go along the path of duty, though they recognize that they can and sometimes do evade or defy the obligations laid on them by superiors. Obligation and responsibility mean a system in which inducements to do good are held before beings who have power to direct their own actions and control their external powers according to their knowledge of what ought and ought not be done. The lawgiver appeals to the mind, presenting motives for the good course. He seeks intelligent voluntary co-operation of men of good will; he tries to deter the ill-disposed by threats of penalties before they act. In proposing motives law recognizes the physical ability of man to choose either the way of law or the way forbidden by law. The whole system of law in publication, enforcement, trial, reward, acquittal, punishment, and reform implies recognition of the fact that the good could, if they wished, do evil and that the bad could, if they wished, do the morally good.[8] Law does not treat men as trainers treat their beasts. For men are not helpless creatures moved irresistibly by forces of nature, feelings, and habituation.

In our reflections on human unity we have already noticed that the will, as man's highest appetite, has at least a partial control over the other powers in human nature and leads these, the intellect helping, to secure the will's purposes for the man. A little reflection would show how many powers and acts we put to work to carry out our wish to go on a vacation, to succeed in an examination, or to buy a home. The controlling purpose also makes us eliminate other goods and alternatives that would defeat our purpose.

Finally, the will's control can affect one's past and one's future. By freedom one can to some extent undo any evils of the past and reorder one's life. Please God, we can also change our lives for the better. By freedom we can provide for the future by forming good habits, by deliberate training for future performance, and by storing up merits for a great future beyond the grave.

CHAPTER 5

Spirit and Form

1. THE DIVIDING LINE BETWEEN MAN AND MATTER

THE LEVELS of living activity that we have found in man are vegetal like that of plants, sentient like that of animals, and intellectual unlike any activities of plants and beasts. In man then we have a horizon or meeting place of material and spiritual activities. But the horizon divides sky from earth, as well as unites them. In man spirituality divides him from mere matter. While implications of man's spiritual intelligence and freedom will burst forth in almost all phases of our study of human life, a few points call for exploration in this place.

The establishment of some spiritual activity in man may be regarded as the root from which spring the further proofs of his distinctive nature. Spiritual objects of thought are signposts of spiritual acts; the spiritual acts imply that the powers of intellect and will are spiritual. If these powers are spiritual, then the substance of man must be in some way the interior spiritual source to which these powers and acts belong. In other words, man's substance must be partially spiritual. But if part of man is spiritual, we shall argue that it should also be immortal. Spirituality defines the difference between man and everything else in the visible universe.

As spirit is free from the material restrictions that confine the senses to some specific area of objects, it is to be expected that human intelligence will have a limitless capacity to know anything that is being, an insatiable thirst for truth, a boundless curiosity about the glories and secrets of the universe, a wonderment about even an infinite object, and an aspiration to reach the infinite, a Spirit, by knowledge and love. Here philosophy enters into life since man is

54

peculiarly the Thinker, the being who is interested in everything, who wonders over the universal, seeks out reasons as well as facts. He has a spiritual hunger to get to the bottom of things, to know the profoundest truths, to see the most intimate bonds between realities, and to have a proportional view of all significant elements in the universal design. Because of his spiritual intelligence, he wants an understanding of his own life.

Religion also enters into the life of man at this point in the spirit's search for and response to the spiritual reality of God. The vast scope of spiritual action explains other human peculiarities, such as man's potentiality for personal development, his pursuit of education, his discontent with merely material things, and his uneasy striving for better and permanent things as his unbounded spirit leaps upward to the best.

Man's special capacity for society is also founded on his spiritual abilities. For human association is a unity of spirits, of minds and wills agreeing to a commonly known and commonly willed purpose. In social living men use their own special invention, language, as one of the bonds for exchanging ideas, concerting plans, and uniting in pursuit of common objectives. By language, too, both oral and written, men accumulate experience and amass truth, which they can turn over to the coming generation as a basis for future development. Hence, tradition grows, culture expands with each succeeding generation, civilization becomes broader. Truth, morality, religion, history, culture, science, and their human fruitfulness thus become not just a personal possession learned afresh by each generation; they are a family treasure of the whole human race. No doubt, this need of handing down the traditions of humanity to new generations explains two biological peculiarities of man: the long years of his premature development and education in which so much must be learned, and the long period of biologically postmature life which the human animal needs as a leader who bequeaths the whole human inheritance of knowledge and goodness to even the third and fourth generations of his descendants.

It is not remarkable that a truth such as spirituality, freighted with such consequences, should be hotly challenged. It means almost too much to some people. Likewise, the hot denials of human liberty seem to hint at a deep, intimate realization of the importance of freedom. Welcome as this truth is to most, it is a truth which some men dread. It is too daring, too dangerous, too demanding. It means that I must admit that this is my choice, my doing, that I am the author and originator of some deeds, that I am at times a captain alone on a sea who must decide my own fate and give orders to powers below me about my course and theirs. Certainly freedom puts each man on a spot and makes him face a basic responsibility for his inner life, his effects on the world about him, and his future destiny as a man. Freedom makes him answerable for his choices and their normally forseeable results. His greatest individual differences from his fellow men lie rooted in the unique or personal nature of his own choices. Freedom means a fearful inner loneliness and the risk of inner conflicts.

A free man is a responsible man, with the duty of ruling himself. Hence, he must prepare himself for the wise use of his freedom. He must plan his way, be reasonably sure before he acts, cultivate prudence, bear the burden of the advice that he gives to others. He must help himself by picking right means to noble ends and persevere in their use. God helps him to help himself, but this divine help demands man's personal response and generous effort.

At the same time his freedom is his greatest protection. It defends him from the helpless status of being a passive victim who must wait for things to happen to him and who, robot-like, must bow to every accident, natural force, physical peril, or social evil. Often he can do something to ward off these evils and even to change them. Even when he can do little, he can do much interiorly to react as he pleases to these external pressures. Freedom protects him, too, with the mantle of rights that God puts on him as a means to fulfill his duty.

Most of all, freedom is not only an immunity from evil; freedom is man's high opportunity. It gives him the opportunity for much good in his own life and in that of others. He commands and disciplines himself to be at liberty to choose the good. He co-operates willingly and gladly with the formative efforts of parents, teachers, and God in bringing his human potentialities to their fullness. He has the chance to bring charity into the world. The free man has a spiritual love life; he deliberately prefers the good, his friends, his wife, his God. He has the privilege to love truly and loyally, not because he must, like ants or bees, but because he selects. He has the chance to create good, to participate with others in advancing the good, to approach through freedom ever closer to the infinite all-lovable Good. It is wonderful to be a free man living in this moral universe where spirit surpasses the physical universe of matter, force, necessity, and impulse.

2. The Human Soul

Some persons seem to think that facing the question of the existence of the human soul is even more formidable than their meeting with their intelligence and freedom. Perhaps one feels that there is an ultimate escape from spirituality and responsibility if he denies the existence of an immortal soul to which these belong. Maybe the misgivings and tremors of the spirit on this question arise from religious considerations and from the history of philosophical opinions. Religion makes the matter of the soul's existence, salvation, security, and loyalty to God a paramount interest, reigning over all temporal and worldly considerations. This intense concern naturally evokes strong emotional attitudes, including fears for its well-being and dread at the thought of some day being alone with one's soul. Then the variety of philosophical theories on the soul reaching from the early Greek psyche to numerous modern substitutes tends to create doubts and bewilderment.

The soul is known by man in and through its acts. By reasoning from its acts we can learn its special nature. The professional philosopher puts the question of the soul's existence somewhat in these terms. Is there a substantial principle of thought (or of willing) in man? Is there within man a principle of being which puts him in the species, man, a class of beings with its own special human operations peculiar to man alone? Is this substantial principle really distinct from the human body or is it a mere complex variation of the body's elements and actions? Is it a special organ or some biotic force? Is it a mere psychological aspect of his physiological structure and activities or a special nonphysical part of man? Is it material or spiritual? Is it permanent or changeable, even perishable? If it is really distinct from the body, is it also really separate from the body or really united with it as its substantial form? Is it an essential part of man or something superadded to his nature?

To these questions the Thomistic proofs conclude[1] there is a soul in man, a principle of life, a real substantial part of him, and his substantial form. This soul, really distinct from the body, is nevertheless really united to the body as the actual specific principle of human nature. Though joined with the matter of the body, it is spiritual. It is permanent, self-identical through life, and immortal.

A glance at three ways of establishing the existence of the soul will reward us. The first is based on a study of the differences between living and nonliving things; the second on introspection; and the third on an analysis of man's spiritual activities.

We have already seen from our discussion of the inner source of life that every living body has a soul. Man, then, must also have such a vital principle or soul within his living self. As in the case of other living bodies, the human soul is really distinct from the material of the human body since not all bodies are alive. It is the specific principle of life since the distinctive life of man requires a principle of a human type as its explanation. It is said to be the substantial form, as explained in Chapter 3, for it is the intrinsic part that unites with the bodily material to constitute this flesh as a human body and this being as a human being. Man, then, is body and soul, or better, body-soul.

We can, moreover, get a direct look at our souls present in us, for we have the gift of self-reflection on our own acts. When we attend not to exterior objects as a flowering lilac or a detective story but to our own experiences, we are observing something going on within ourselves. An accurate, qualified report of this personal scrutiny finds a double object of consciousness. "I" am aware of acts of thinking or inquiring, of loving or choosing. But I am also aware of something more. I am aware of my thinking, my loving. I must report the data of consciousness by saying: "I think; I ask; I wonder; I love; I exist." The ubiquitous I is always given in this report. Both the act and the existing agent are presented to our immediate self-knowledge; both the thought and the subject who is thinking and in whom the thought or love exists are given in this awareness. We do not directly perceive this ego, this self, tagged with the name of substance or form; but we do clearly recognize that it is the ultimate interior subject of existence or action. Indeed, its existence is much more evident than that of the powers of intellect and will to which we reason and which we distinguish both from our acts of thinking and willing and from the acting soul.

Moreover, whenever I repeat this introspective act over a period of many years, it is the same "I" which comes up before consciousness. I remember, for example, my pleasure many years ago when this typewriter was given to me. I remember the fact that it was I, no other, who committed that fault which years later I still regret. I see that it is the same I who am the subject of so many conflicting desires, so many different thoughts, of so many different moments of existence, of joy, fatigue, and sorrow. Some of these selves seem years later to be almost strangers to me because the acts are long since past and the acts are so inconsistent with each other; but I know that it is the same I who acted then and remember now, and that my self is the bond between all these diverse remembered experiences. But while I am so sure of this self-identity, I am equally sure that bodily changes in me have been very considerable. I have no reason to think that these are the same bits of material substance in my fingers which were there when I was given this typewriter long ago. Indeed, scientists assure us that every cell uses energy and releases used up matter to replace it with new so that there is a total change of my bodily substance in a period of years. I have then a completely identical part of my being and a completely changing part; the two must be different principles of my being. The permanent I and the passing acts and the bodily changes and the changed body are not really the same. The permanent ego or the lasting identical part of my ego I may name my soul, for it continues to identify me as this living man. It was I, not some other now vanished person, who was graduated from high school on such a day, who fought in such a war, who signed this lease for a home some years ago, who wed my wife on such a day, who must bear the credit and responsibilities of my past deliberate deeds.

The law, too, will regard as foolish any attempt to escape consequences of legal violations by the plea that it was not I, but some former self, somebody else, who injured my fellow man or evaded my just taxes.

A third approach to the existence of the soul relies on the fact that we perform some spiritual activities. These come not only from a spiritual power, which can be only an accident, but from something that is substantially spiritual. The basic proportionate cause must be a proportionately excellent principle in man's nature; spiritual acts come from spirit. Other acts are material and come from a material part in man, the body. Since matter is the very opposite of spirit and since man's nature is in part spiritual and in part corporeal, then these two parts are really distinct from each other. The two parts may be united, but they cannot be the same.

Because the soul is spiritual, material images of it are not satisfying or helpful in understanding it. To speak of it as a fountain of life or as a flaming sun within us, to picture it as a "white-hair'd shadow" or to clothe it as one of Shakespeare's tragic ghosts can be only figurative expressions of some aspect of its being or functioning.[2] The images materializing the soul may mislead the unwary. Perhaps it is such imagery and not downright stupidity which has again and again led some anatomist to use the absence of some organ named soul, x, as a proof of its nonexistence. The surgeon before an opened body can no more contact the soul with a material knife than he can contact its loyalty or heroism. A spiritual reality cannot be seen or touched by bodily senses; it must be grasped by a spiritual mind.

3. Form Functions and Spiritual Functions

A more serious difficulty than tricks of fancy arises in trying to understand how two distinct principles, so diverse in ultimate character, can be united in one composite nature. For man is undoubtedly substantially one. The same man both senses and understands; the same man sees the moon and thinks about its distance, weight, atmosphere, source of light, and other purely intellectual problems. He needs the body and the living soul to see the moon; he is independent of the body in mentally probing the moon. Yet, the one same man does both operations. This substantial partnership of body and soul, this unity in duality will be better understood by considering the two roles played by the human soul. These are its form functions and its spiritual functions.

As man's substantial form,[3] the human soul is a real intrinsic principle of his being, a substantial coprinciple in union with the matter of the body as its correlative principle. It is present in the body and in its every living part. It is the actuality of the living body; it gives it its human life. It is the intrinsic reason why this flesh is human flesh; that is, it specifies the body to be human and nothing else. The soul shares its being with the matter; this sharing is a union of itself with the matter in order to form one natural compound, the whole man. Yet in so sharing itself, it does not lose its real distinction from the matter. The soul unifies all parts, powers, and acts of this being into one agent, one person, one man, one being having these various real parts, powers, organs, and operations. The soul is the basic source of the characteristic powers and operations of this one human being. The substantial form explains all the significant differences.

The form functions appear in the vegetative and sentient operations. For the soul as form not only gives life to the body but it is also with the body the basic principle of the bodily acts of nutrition, digestion, healing, generation, and childbearing; it is the ultimate source for the sensory acts of seeing, hearing, touching, imagining, instinctive behavior, liking and disliking. These acts are performed not by the body alone nor by the soul alone but by the animated body. In such operations of the merely plant and animal levels of life, the soul is intrinsically dependent on the body. The matter of the body, that is, is a necessary partial cause of these acts; man, the body-soul, is the complete cause.

In its spiritual functions the soul acts without the body's concurring causality. By itself, using the spiritual intellect and will, it thinks of a universal object, as mankind, and loves all mankind; it thinks of the future and desires to prepare for it; it knows God and loves God, pure Spirit that He is. Herein the active soul is independent of the matter of the body, excluding it from any partial agency in these activities. Yet even here its close bond with the body is seen in the help or hindrance which the senses and sense appetites can provide in presenting objects for thought and affection. The soul alone thinks and wills; but the senses as conditions enable it to start by supplying it with something to think about. They act as a telephone operator who opens the line while only I converse on the prepared circuit.

4. SPIRIT AS FORM

Finally, in an impressive group of operations, the soul unites its form functions and its spirit functions. Spiritual powers acting without the body and bodily powers using soul and flesh team together under the control of the soul. Speaking and reading combine such material and spiritual factors, as our earlier discussion of language showed. Of like character are tool invention, smiling, cooking, voluntary movements of the body's nerves and muscles as in sprinting to win a race, cultivation of beauty in art and horticulture, externalized religious worship. In these, spirit both unites with the body and dominates the body, which exists for the soul. The spirit functions, too, seem to dominate the form functions which are subservient to the purposes imposed upon them by the spiritual side of man's nature. Perhaps we also have some conflict of the spirit and form roles when a man rejects organic desires and sexual allurements, for instance, or when his soul leaps up to God while his body yet fears pain and death. The goods of the body bring one set of motives before the will, the needs of the spirit bring up other attractions so that there is a contest of flesh lusting against spirit, with both sides appealing to the free will to vote for them.

The student of man wisely pays more attention to the spiritual functions of the human soul than to its form functions. Yet inattention to the role of form will much lessen our understanding of man's nature, the conditions under which human life on earth is lived, and some special problems which touch man's life, but which would have no bearing on the life of a purely immaterial being.

One who grasps the doctrine of form understands why man is said to be one natural whole in spite of the unmixed antithetical components of flesh and spirit. Form names the decisive part. It states why man is not just a spirit and his body not just the inanimate home or the passive material tool of that spirit. Man is body-soul, a rational animal, a reasoning sentient body, or as Chesterton wittily said of himself, "a well-meaning hippopotamus." Man is a complete animal, for he has a complete sentient body in being and in operations. But he is not wholly an animal, for he is truly spiritual and rational as well. He is a species of animal apart from others by the majestic difference, rational. Man is neither a mere animal nor a bodiless angel; nor is he an accidental combination of animal and angel, a soul captive in a body, a rider tied to a chariot, a radiant spirit fettered to foul bones that are alien to his true nature, an angelic pilot seated in a sensitive earthly brain. Since form keeps him one being, there is no good excuse for the philosophical treatment of man as a clumsy Humpty-Dumpty whose spirit and flesh can never be put together.

Well understood, the theory of the soul as spiritual form transfigures our appreciation of the human body and affects our views on morals, education, religion, work, clothing, medicine, festivity, marriage, economics, and government. For in a whole balanced view of man both his material and spiritual sides are recognized as important, with the material element in due subjection to the nobler spiritual principle. The spiritual form radiates its own excellence to this body which has become one being with it. Man has little excellence just as an animal. But the spirit's nobility gives to the flesh a suppleness and refinement; it leaves in the nervous system a plasticity, adaptability, and responsiveness to the action of spirit, a quick ability to serve the spiritual functions. It is quite likely that since matter and form are proportionate, the soul is not only specifically but individually adapted to the body of each man so that their partnership in life may be as congenial as possible. It follows, too, that the fixed patterns of instinct found in so many animals would be altogether unsuitable to man, for there would then be nothing for his intellect and will to do and no power to control the overpowering tendencies of the nervous motor system to act in only one way.

As permeated by spirit, the human body deserves honor and care and ought not be made an object of Manichaean contempt. Furthermore, its interests are necessary, legitimate, and honorable as long as they conform to reason. Because of his unity in two parts, health of spirit and health of body are closely related, though spirit can dominate even in bodily illness. The deportment of the body and the ritual of good manners both help the soul and reveal it. The face, the voice, the hands are highly sensitive recorders of states of the mind and will. Painters have been known to dread painting faces, not because, like Communists, they preferred the anonymous faceless multitudes, but because they were overwhelmed at the task of expressing in material paint the spiritual language of the face. When a man's spirit rejoices, his body joins in by glad laughter, song, and feasting. When a man mourns, he walks in measured pace, with bowed head, and somberly clad. When man would honor the human dead, he respects the corpse as well as the soul of his departed friend. When man clothes himself, he is vesting a besouled body, and so considers not only physical protection, but looks to beauty, honor, *esprit de corps*, and charity; and these are spiritual considerations. Clothing is a gesture of the spirit and not a mere vesture of the skin.

In the light of the doctrine of the rational animal, the nobility and the actualities of the society of the family are better understood. The wedding ceremony unites not two mating animals nor two angels, but two body-souls. Wedded, they must adapt themselves to each other's mind and body; they have a temporal and a spiritual life to lead in common; they must care for the interests of both the soul and body of each other. The physical symbol of the kiss must express a fully human affection and respect for the soul as well as the body of the spouse. Theirs is a unity in dining, in physical and economic assistance, in companionship, conversation, and prayer. The family must care for and educate its young members as body-spirits who are neither little cubs nor wingless angels. Much training of mind and will must begin through the senses and sensory appetites.

Other human occupations have a distinctive character precisely because of the bond of spirit and flesh in man. Man must, for instance, worship as a complete body-soul. Therefore, acts of mind and intentions of will must often fuse with reverent bodily postures, vocal prayer, religious music, ceremonial robes, and visible sacraments and sacrifice. Human morality must consider the right order of man's powers, giving the spiritual powers priority, but not daring to neglect the true though subordinate place of the bodily activities in human living. To be an angel is quite different from being a man; and therefore it is quite different to be angelically good and humanly good. Human medicine, aware of this psychosomatic duality in man, must consider not only the body as veterinary medicine does, nor only the soul as mental healing does, but must treat the true man in whom mental and organic factors reciprocally act in illness and in recovery. Human charity, too, will have to reckon with man's full nature, practice both spiritual and corporal works of mercy, and properly relate the two. Indeed, charity will often have to meet temporal and bodily needs before spiritual assistance is practicable. Yet it is not truly human to stop with only bodily relief if more can be given without offense to the recipient of material aid. Finally, good government ought to help not only in man's material necessities but should also do its proportionate part to make accessible the temporal means needed for the cultural and spiritual goals of man.

We shall come back to this theme of the soul as form in other contexts. Now we turn to the state of the soul when its partnership with the body ends.

5. IMMORTALITY

Since man is a complete animal with a complete sentient body, it is to be expected that this body, like other organic matter, will be subject to injury, infection, aging, and other forces that lead to its ultimate disintegration. But because his body dies, it does not follow that man wholly dies. The soul will no longer function as the form of that dead body, but its being and functions as spirit are not totally tied to the body even in this life. Can it then continue to be spiritual and function spiritually if separated from a body that is no longer fit to house a human soul? Its independence in being and in some psychic activities during this present life of union with the body suggests some likelihood of continuing independence in existence and spiritual action after the union is ended. Has reason any evidence to guarantee this permanent natural existence of every human soul that has ever informed a human body? As this is a naturally due immortality, not a miraculous or supernatural gift, that we are discussing, it is a proper topic of philosophical inquiry.

Two lines of thought yield certain proof of this immortality. The first relies on the familiar principle that a good is natural to man for which he has the natural capacities, the constant and universal desires, and the constant and common needs. The second eliminates as contrary to man's nature and to God's will any of the possible ways in which spiritual souls might hypothetically cease to exist. The second way overlaps considerably with the first and need not be given here. Christian theology solemnly assures us that the conclusions of reason and the natural hopes of man in this matter are certain.

The proof opens with a look at the capacity of the human soul to survive the death of the body and even the ruin of the universe. It depends on the twin facts of the soul's simplicity and spirituality.

Being simple, the soul has no parts into which it can be broken. If it should perish, this would be not decay but simple cessation of being. Its simplicity is assured to us from its nonmaterial nature and from its power to reflect on itself.

Being spiritual, the soul does not need matter for its being nor for all of its activities. The dissolution of the body does not require parallel destruction of the soul which is distinct from and free of the body. It subsists in itself. There is no reason why the body's period of life should measure the soul's period. No blow at the body, then, can extinguish spiritual life in the soul; no dusty deathwind can blow out the lamp of life which the Author of life has set glowing. The blows and winds can merely transfer the life elsewhere.

The second phase of the proof reflects on man's constant and general desires for endless existence. Almost all men during all their lives desire to go on living. They desire more than the preservation of the body; they yearn for the preservation of the essential self, the permanent ego whom they know. The instances and sharpness of this desire are numberless. The sick and the aged in our hospitals want more life.

We all want more life for our dear ones. Who could bear the funeral of a friend or the thought of his own coffin if he believed that death closed every door? We pray for the dead and to them, knowing that they still live. Literature tells of nonhuman folk who come to earth to steal the souls of human children, for they, too, wish to live forever and adopt our human desires. Even unbelievers and hardened materialists, when forced to think of the issues of death, sometimes plead for life. Bukharin, the great Communist theorist executed by Stalin, wrote to a friend expelled from the U.S.S.R. for anti-Marxist deviations: "Tell them over in Europe to be quick and find us immortality! For if we must die one day, all we are doing here is pointless. The Revolution means nothing, Communism means nothing. We can't take it with us."[4]

Some people may not wish for a longer bodily life, though most would like it if they could have it without its great burdens. All, however, want more happiness. They crave for a longer life of the mind and for existence to fill their limitless spiritual curiosity. They hunger to give and receive more love than a single lifetime ever allows. Nobody desires simply to stop from well-being.

Such a desire, universal and persistent, seems to be natural to man. If natural, its object, more life, must be naturally obtainable, for no desire is purposeless or foolish. So genuine, deep, and widespread is this desire that only the Author of nature could have embedded it in each human soul. This hope is not a freak or quirk of human nature, not a mistake or illusion. But God treats all things according to their natures. Having implanted this desire in human hearts, He means it to be realized in an endless span of existence. He has implicitly promised His unceasing gift of life to a nature capable of living forever.

In the third feature of the proof, our need for immortality joins with human capacity and desire to provide an infallible index to nature's true intention in regard to our future living. This human need may be regarded as psychological and as moral, though the two are actually one need. Man has a psychological need for perfect happiness or the complete fulfillment of his spiritual nature. Yet this perfection of man simply cannot be reached in this life. Time, leisure, and opportunity are wanting even in a very long and most energetic earthly lifetime. The intellect needs more and better knowledge of God. The will has a related need for fuller good and for divine love. For the soul is potentially all things and potentially united with the divine Being.

But the gates to such human perfection are never wide open on earth. Nothing is ever complete. Artist and poet never achieve the perfect work. The saint has never scaled the peak of character and love for God. Without that continuing afterlife, the perfection, unity, and purpose of man's life, together with the glory of God, fall short.

The moral aspect of this human need for future life is even more urgent. If the soul perishes when the body dies, why should one be moral, especially in heroic circumstances? Why should one sacrifice pleasure or even life for the sake of moral good, for moral principle, for God? Heroic parents, heroic soldiers, heroic martyrs, innocent ones who break their hearts and lose their noble blood because of the carelessness and cruelty of other people must have a season of reward for their great deeds. Those who give up earth for God's sake are candidates for immortality. Moral standards, virtue, justice, the common good, and the Lawgiver's sovereignty cannot be vanquished both in this life and forever. For there is no immediate sufficient advantage in this life for virtue or evident immediate penalties for much vice. A competent Lawgiver of a rational universe must effectively sanction His own laws and restore the balance of order by immortal victory for the good and eternal losses for those who have given up God for the sake of earth. Violators of divine law and of the great rights of their fellow men cannot have all the riches, power, and fun that they wish now and yet escape the consequences of their misdeeds merely by the accident of death, suicide, or legal ruses. Justice, decency, the majesty of the law, and proportion clamor, then, for more life after death lest loyalty, goodness, truth, courage, and love of God and men end with a man's last breath.

God, then, can have no intention of discontinuing His conservation of the soul which He has made with both natural capacity and desire for immortality. It can live forever; and God wills it to survive forever.

The argument may be more cogent for immortality for the virtuous than for the vicious and weaklings, though these have the same human nature with the same capacity, set within the same framework of divine law. In a sense William James's remark has genuine point: "The best argument I know for an immortal life is the existence of a man who deserves it." It is a still better argument that an all-wise, all-good, all-holy God gives endless life as a part of the inalienable treasure of the human soul.

The melancholy view of life which can see it only as a procession of "golden lads and girls" marching to the dust of nothingness violates all humane sentiments and much sound reason. A meditation on a skull may lead the unspiritual to adopt the creed of hurried pleasure before the moment of fate: "Let us eat, drink, and be merry, for tomorrow we shall die." But the merriment of St. Thomas More awaiting martyrdom is the right fun, for it looks forward to eternal merriment with God. Bertrand Russell in tragic mood sees man perishing in the wreck of the universe; but the poet, Thomas Campbell, triumphantly presents his *Last Man* challenging the universe to slay his imperishable spirit. The Communist who talks of immortal hopes as opium is going to find beyond the grave that the opium that deadened life was his own materialism.

In this discussion of immortality we have looked only to the prolongation of life after death; its quality, its type of activity, will be considered in the later treatment of beatitude. But enough has been said to give us a glimpse of the splendor of this truth of our immortal existence. No one, as Pascal said, can be indifferent on this issue. "The immortality of the soul is a question of such moment to us, touches us so nearly, that a man must have lost his senses to remain unconcerned to know whether or not it is true."[5] This golden truth of our living perpetuity gives every thoughtful man a morning vision of a wonderful future. It presents a limitless fresh perspective in which to view our present life as a part of a nobler and greater whole, whose full story is never told in any biography of one's years on earth. Man belongs to time for only a while; his soul is not restricted to time but is made to dwell in a future without clocks. Man is made to live in two worlds and two media. He is a sort of amphibian of body and spirit, of time and eternity. His nature and destiny can be well understood only if it is considered to belong to both these worlds. That the life of the soul and its endless future is the greater life is a simple matter of arithmetic. In fact, it is not even a good wager to live only for earth since no one can disprove his immortality. One is reminded of the repartee of a hospital nun to an unbeliever protesting against the sacrifices of her life. "If I am wasting my life, I am wasting only a few years on earth. But if you are wrong, you are wasting an eternity."

This solid hope of everlasting life is one of the most decisive, energizing, and enduring of all motives for right living, for paying the price needed for our souls, and for helping others to gain the same tremendous prize. This interest in the human soul also determines the primacy of purposes and efforts in all truly human education. Though body and soul must both be trained and education for temporal life is part of education, yet "the soul of education is the education of the soul." At death we leave the spent body to the earth; we carry with us to God all that belongs to the free soul.

CHAPTER 6

The Source of Human Life

PHILOSOPHICAL CURIOSITY, not content to know the wonderful nature of human life as described by its material and formal causes, goes on to the question of the beginnings of human life, and particularly of the soul's life. Before discussing the origin of man, we would do well to reflect on the origin of any kind of life on our planet.

1. THE ORIGIN OF LIFE ON EARTH

We have to bear in mind two sets of physical facts and one philosophical truth. The first set of facts, coming from much collated scientific information, makes it clear that all life was once absent from our earth. Terrestrial heat was so intense that no known form of life could exist or propagate itself on earth. Atmospheric conditions also made life impossible; either there was no atmosphere or a very thin one or one full of noxious gases or one lacking the specific chemicals — nitrogen, oxygen, carbon, and carbon dioxide — which plants and animals require for maintenance of their life. Under these conditions water, too, may have been missing. Light, an indispensable factor in photosynthesis for plant nourishment and growth, was wanting, for the atmosphere for long periods was so dense that light could not penetrate to the land. It is, then, not surprising that geologists can find no traces of fossil life in the oldest igneous rocks. The earth had not yet developed to a state where it could support life.[1]

The second set of facts concerns the actual existence of many forms of plant and animal life on our earth today, with uncountable individuals in the species that cover the world. Qualified scientists say that there are at least one-and-one-half million species of plant and animal life, with varieties within these species. This teeming pageant

70

of living bodies is something to be explained, not merely to be accepted. Where did it come from or, better, from whom did it come? When life, whether nonsentient or sentient, first appeared on earth, it was something completely novel.

The philosophical point is that this new reality, something living, had to have an adequate cause. The nonliving materials of earth supply the matter, the chemicals, but not the life itself, for life is essentially better than the nonliving.[2] No scientific minds synthesized that life because no scientists were alive at the dawn of life. Mere bombardment of some organized protein molecules by ultraviolet rays could not produce something essentially superior to any combination of rays and molecules. No meteor could bring it, for how could it support life and whence did it get life?

There is only one source left who can originate life from nothing. The Creator of life is the living God, all-powerful, in control of earth, able to introduce this new form of being into this planet, inform selected materials of earth with it, and give these new living things powers to grow, to multiply, and, at least probably, to vary into many branching species. This being, in whom life as well as every other wonderful attribute is perfect, is the generous original Author of life and the only possible first source of it. If He did not make plant and animal life simultaneously, He had to intervene a second time to produce the animal or sentient type; for, as the animal is essentially superior in nature to the plant, it cannot evolve its sentient form and powers from a plant soul and a plant structure. The exuberant riches, fecundity, structures, powers, varieties, and movements of plants and animals eloquently witness to the immense life and inventive genius of the one living God.

Once plant or animal life is started, it can go in an endless chain through a number of methods of reproduction. How far living types may diverge into new species from the latent powers in older types is more of a scientific than a philosophical question; what disasters eliminate all representatives of some species is likewise a scientific problem. Alongside the unending sequence of life runs another endless cycle of food, of assimilation of inorganic material by plants and of organic material by animals. To maintain supplies of food, air, and water, the earth needs the exchange of gases between plants and animals, and all the factors that renew inorganic supplies and soil, purify the air, circulate water, and scatter light over the face of the earth.

Astonishing co-ordination, timing, and balancing between many physical systems of light, heat, planetary axial and orbital movements, air and water circulation, watersheds, respiration, assimilation, organic elimination, soil building, and fertility factors are needed to make possible this incredible renewal of food and perpetuation of life. We live among so many wonders that they are commonplace; but that they are so numerous and so sure as ever to become commonplace is the greatest wonder.

2. THE ORIGIN OF HUMAN LIFE

To man the important phase of this problem on origins is that of the beginning of human life. Historically, this has been an important religious question, particularly in the Jewish and Christian teachings of Genesis[3] on the origin of Adam and Eve. Here our interest is chiefly the philosophical question. It has three aspects, the origin or formation of the human body, the origin of the human soul, and, finally, the union of the human soul with a fit body so that human life first began.

There is no reason to doubt that the material components of the first human body contained the same chemicals of carbon, oxygen, hydrogen, nitrogen, water, sulphur, and others that our twentieth-century bodies have. The immediate source of these was the earth; the ultimate source was the Creator of all being. How God may have elaborated these chemicals for organization into the human form, no scientist or philosopher is really sure. The record from the past is by no means adequate to answer this; and the examination of possible methods of preparation for the coming of man onto the scene reveals two chief possibilities. God could have prepared the body of man through many thousands of years of biological changes until some organism reached a borderland between apelike men and true men and was at last all but fitted to become the body of a higher class of being, man. Or God could have fashioned this human body suddenly, coming to His own world, taking some of its material substances needed for human organic life, and all in one step fashioning a human organism from this selected matter.

Geology, physical anthropology, and philosophy have no demonstrative proof for either the hypothesis of evolutionary development of the human body or that of instantaneous change from lifeless matter into human flesh. Theology leaves the question open. Biology warns us not to underrate even the physical uniqueness of man. There is much to be said for the opinion that the spiritual form required for a thinking and choosing being could suitably exist only in the type of body that belongs to man, a body, namely, that is multicellular and sufficiently large for brain and head, with skeleton, limbs, breathing apparatus, blood system, and sense organs. Even if the geological and burial record of transitional forms from brute to man were complete, even if the homology between man and animals approached identity, and even if the present kind of human body is the only terrestrial sentient organism that can house a spiritual soul, yet mere succession in time, closer and closer homologies in structure of bones, jaws, teeth, and brains, and the unique suitability of a particular animal for human living do not prove descent. Descent means that one of the prior animal forms was a producer of the bodily being of man or of animal life in a body into which God at some time infused a spiritual soul.[4]

The origin of the body of the first man is still a riddle as far as its method goes. Whatever the method, the providential power of God guided and regulated the process toward the origin of a truly human body. In man's total nature there is an all but infinite gap separating him from brutes because he has a spiritual principle of life that performs spiritual activities.

Whence does this spiritual soul of man originate? This question is the same for the first man who ever lived and for the last man who will be born on earth. Michelangelo in his *Creation of Adam*, which is often said to be the greatest of all paintings, has caught that golden instant of omnipotent power and man's surprise and spiritual awakening to the Being who made him. What is the philosophical evidence for this creative act of making and infusing the soul?

Any proof for the immediate creative act of God must move by ruling out other attempted causative explanations as impossible. As naturally excelling matter, the soul cannot come from some pre-existing matter or pre-existing bodily life. In addition, the soul cannot spring into being by breaking off from some previous spiritual substance, for example, from its parents' souls, and growing apart from them. Spiritual substances and forms, as simple, have no parts and cannot give away a seed, a breath of the spirit, or fragment of themselves to their young. It remains that the only possible origin of existing human souls is total production of them from nothing by God. Religious history relates that God created a human soul for the first time when He made a soul for the first man, Adam, infusing it into the prepared body. But His creative act goes on every day as new human beings are conceived.[5]

A minor point is here asked about the precise moment when the rational soul first exists. Does the individual's soul date from the moment of conception or from some later hour in prenatal development of the human child? One hoary theory based on insufficient and poorly interpreted anatomical and physiological evidence believed that the human being first had a plant soul in the maternal womb, then came to have an animal soul, and finally at the time of the "quickening" in the womb (when, as we now know, the foetus begins to move and stretch its limbs), a rational soul was created and infused by God. This opinion of a succession of souls in the unborn human child has a few eminent sponsors[6] today, but for quite different modern reasons. One reason is that the theory believes that nothing truly human is in the womb until a human brain is sufficiently formed; an organism is not suited for a human soul until there is a suitable brain. Another reason is that this view of succeeding souls fits in with the scientific desire to see some phylogenetic evolution or recapitulation of the evolution of the race in the evolution of each single human being from its own stage of plant life, to brute life, to human life.

The principle of economy suggests, however, that this series of three vital principles is quite unnecessary. The one soul that can perform spiritual, sentient, and vegetative functions in union with the extrauterine body can also perform all these necessary vegetative and sentient functions in the womb.[7] We also know that the whole development of the first human cell is continuously directed toward the formation of a human body and no other type of being. It seems, in summary, that God creates the soul at the moment of fertilization of the maternal ovum by the paternal sperm.[8] In the same instant He infuses the newly created soul into this inherited bit of human protoplasm, thus uniting the biological material component supplied by the parents with the spiritual principle supplied exclusively by Himself. God and parents are co-causes of the new human person that has just begun its life within the mother's organism.

3. Heredity and Likeness to the Causes

This causal role of God and of parents suggests many reflections. In view of the philosophical truth that every agent produces a being in some way like itself, we naturally look for a resemblance of the man to God and to his parents. His bodily heredity from the parents leads us to expect some composite likeness of both parents. Many of his physical traits, however, such as tone of voice and mannerism, are learned by imitation and are not inherited. Nurture plays perhaps as large a role as nature. The human soul is a likeness of God in its spirituality, its immortality, in intellect and will, and particularly in the capacity of these powers to know and love God, now and in eternity. We shall return to this notion of man as image of God in Chapter 9.

A second reflection on our double inheritance indicates a dual lifelong debt of gratitude to both the divine and human sources of our being. Life, the first and in some respects the best of all gifts, the one which no one can give himself and which makes all other blessings possible, is the fruit of an act of love of God and an act of love of parents. It is a more precious favor than the saving of our lives by some hero or protector in an hour of great danger. We can hardly do too much for or duly thank benefactors who have given so much so freely. It is a thrilling thought to know that this once happened to "me."

G. K. Chesterton has somewhere remarked: "When we were children we were grateful to those who filled our stockings with toys at Christmastime; why are we not grateful to God for filling our stockings with legs?" Our debt of gratitude to God is far greater than that to our parents. God created our parents; through them as His agents He supplied us with a body; He created the decisive part of our nature, our spiritual soul. We take the gift of life so much for granted that we often fail to realize that we are creatures who recently were nonexistent. We may also fail to recognize that the same almighty love that gave us being must keep us alive by His conserving causality, must help us or concur with us in all our activity, and prepare for our future. We fail to see our dependence on His constant care of the world about us and of the people in that world for our preservation and development. Divine government keeps up the supply of oxygen without which we die in a few minutes;

divine power prevents the few seconds of erratic movement of the sun or planets that would bring disaster to earth and its atmosphere; divine energy controls the specks of atomic energy that could disintegrate our bodies, the germs that could permanently destroy our life, the people whose neglect, bad example, and bad judgment might turn even the life of our spirits into disastrous misery. Only God's watchful eye over men and things makes life possible or relatively secure for each of us. As Father Frederick W. Faber said: "The Creator's hand is the creature's home."

4. MAN, THE SERVANT AND STEWARD OF GOD

God is our Maker and, therefore, owns us body and soul. He has a maker's full rights over us, as much as we would have over a chocolate bunny that we would make out of our own foodstuffs and by our own work in our own candy kitchen. Because of His rights over us, His will is all-important for us. Why did He make us? What does He want from us? What kind of service does He wish? His will is our law. What does He will us to do with our lives? The finding of God's will for one's life and the carrying out of that known will must be a main concern in each one's life.

God is sovereign over the totality of our lives. As our Creator and as the sole end of human life, He has supreme, unlimited, and exclusive dominion over the whole being, all the powers, and the life-long activities of human nature. Man is necessarily God's servant during his total life, in his bodily and spiritual nature, and especially in his human acts of which he is the free author. God makes each man a caretaker of a divine property, his own humanity, and the responsible manager of years of human living. God has given man power, freedom, and moral control of his members and acts. Since the servant or custodian must manage the divine property according to the divine Owner's wishes, he must learn the Master's will and lovingly serve that will by directing his activities to realizing the divine order in human affairs. In the words of the ancient axiom: man must know God, love God, and serve God, and thereby glorify God on earth. Whoever does so is the good steward to whom the Master has promised this praise in the last reckoning of accounts: "Well done, good and faithful servant, because you have been faithful in a few things, I will place you over many."

5. THE RIGHTS OF LIFE

As each man has received from God the gift of life for the definite purpose of knowing, loving, and serving God, it follows that each has from God the complementary precious gift of the right to live.

A right is an inviolable moral power to do, possess, or claim something as one's own. Where God imposes a purpose demanding our human efforts to realize it, He gives us also the moral powers as the needed means to accomplish this purpose. Without life we cannot accomplish the purpose. We have, therefore, directly from God this moral power, the right to live. The grant of the power is sanctioned by God Himself as the Lawgiver and is hallowed under His protective justice. The same point about the divine source of our rights is clear if we recall how necessary our life is to perform any duties, whether of religion, justice, charity, or other virtues. A man must be living to do anything God requires him to do. Once again, the right to life is an essential means to the life of virtue.

This right to life is a personal gift of God through the natural law. It is a connatural right, say the ethicians, because its title is the very fact of our human existence and human destiny. It is a basic right since all other rights and their exercise require that this right be safe. Who takes life takes away all our rights and all further opportunity to serve God on earth.

The right to life belongs to the class of perfect rights. In these rights one has a supporting right or accessory moral power to use physical force against unjust actual or imminent attack against the right. When life is unjustly and seriously endangered, God empowers man to use what force or violence may be necessary to stop the assailant. If there were no right of effective and proportionate self-defense, the sacred right of life would be nullified by the wickedness of others, good men would be helpless victims of criminals, justice and order could not prevail as the normal conditions of living. The right to life given by God to each human person is violated chiefly by the major crimes of suicide, murder, and genocide. The state is the normal defender of the right to life in organized society; yet instances are still occurring where people must flee for their lives against the injustices of their own governments and conquerors.

In addition to his right to life and to its defense, a man receives from God the right to all the means essential to the preservation of life, as the right to use the earth for food, shelter, and clothing, the right to earn a living, the right of access to property for the sake of maintaining life, the right to healthy living and working conditions, and cognate economic rights.

A final important life right is that of the duly married to transmit human life to their children and to protect and foster these new lives in the family. The Creator's interest in human life induced Him to bestow upon men and women the remarkable powers of sex by whose use the race of men on earth is continued (and heaven eventually filled with the number of the redeemed). In marital activity men and women fulfill a fundamental divine purpose as co-operators with God in the production of life. The lifelong association of one man with one woman in marriage is the life-giving institution. The family home is the house of life on earth, into which God enters to create human souls, in which human life is begotten, nourished, developed, protected, matured, and perfected. Because life is so important, the family will always be important. Because life is important, all attacks upon the family and the rightful use of sex and the stability of the home are attacks against human life. It is no wonder that the Son of God, the Author of life, so strenuously campaigned for the safety, purity, and dignity of the family.

CHAPTER 7

The Supreme Goal of Human Life

1. THE DISCOVERY OF PURPOSE

THE SUPREME purpose or highest good obtainable by man is the biggest of all questions. The answer to it forms the main frontier on either side of which stand philosophies that maintain a temporal or supratemporal end for man, a material or spiritual goal, a worldly or otherworldly purpose, a low and limited or an absolute and quasi-divine end for human life. Once philosophies of pessimism, skepticism, materialism, and merely natural humanism are defeated on the issue of the supreme aim of human living, they can hardly lay serious claim to the loyalty of men except on a few secondary issues. The victory of human dignity, liberty, and happiness on the philosophical battlefield depends much on this determination of man's destiny.

Acceptance of different ends for human life must affect profound differences in human activities during life. Different businesses, having different aims, greatly differ in their operations. Different professions as medicine, law, and education have different objectives and correspondingly different training, methods, and ways of acting. Even games with their different types of goals or points for victory must differ considerably from each other, as racing, bowling, and basketball do. Similarly, our ideas about the goal of life and about its standard of success must make an immeasurable difference in almost all our other ideas about ourselves, about our activities, about people and things. What we expect from life, what we ought to expect from it, what we desire most to get out of it, what we strive most persistently to achieve in life, who our helpers and antagonists are, what we rejoice and grieve over the most: these pivot around our cardinal view of the ultimate meaning or highest good of life.

Both the practical man and the metaphysician recognize this centrality of purpose. For the end or purpose is the good for which something acts, comes into being, or exists. In a scheme or scale having several ends, the supreme is the end of all lesser ends; it is the highest good to which all other goods are pointed and under which they are organized. The end is also the cause of the other causes, and so explains them. An agent would not act except for an end; natures are built with their matter and form and their special tendencies to their own definite ends; and all their powers operate to achieve their end as far as they can under the given circumstances. This primacy of the end is applicable to human life. God would not have made us except for some end that He intended for us; nor would we ever stir unless motivated by an attractive end. Moreover, our natural inborn end is the reason why we have a body and a spiritual soul and why from this constitution flow the powers and properties peculiarly human and specially adapted to reach the due good for which man principally exists. All subordinate goals, means, and steps are judged by their suitability, sufficiency, and timeliness for our nature and for attaining the supreme good of our nature.

Aristotle's *Nicomachaean Ethics*[1] supplies a guide for the discovery of the supreme purpose of human life, though it fails to give all the answers. Aristotle begins by noting that all things have a purpose and that the dynamism inherent in them is purposively directed to a definite kind of good. Man, therefore, who is the best thing on earth, must also have a purpose which belongs to him as man and not merely as artist or farmer with a special occupation. There must be some good for which the human being as a particular species of being in the universe exists and which is peculiarly man's own end.

Many goods come within the scope of man's action. People may mistake which is the supreme natural good of their human nature. Reason has, however, certain indicators of what is the highest good to which man's powers, tendencies, and needs are by nature oriented.

One indication of the right answer lies in man's distinctive nature, higher than that of subhuman things. As a higher or better being, he is capable of higher good, and must therefore have a nobler end than they. Since the end and the nature are proportionate, it is to be expected that the end of human nature must be somehow connected with man's spiritual powers and that their object must be some spiritual good. Moreover, since man's soul is immortal, it is to be expected that his highest good and best state will be immortal.

We also notice an unusual characteristic of the human end in its personal quality. When the mind will have discovered the end of human nature, it will know the end for which each human person is made. For all members of the same species act for the same intrinsic good; they all have the same basic powers, basic movements of nature to their own good, and the same basic needs for the same kind of good. Similarly, to all members of the human species with the same fundamental nature, the same natural goal is accessible. There are no class privileges here for the intellectual, the rich, or the mighty. This is particularly true in man's case since, as a spiritual being, he has a personally immortal life and an internal independence of others which enables him personally to choose the means to reach his end even if other men refuse to strive for it. Each personally reaches his end and not merely en masse as a bit of the species or a link in the human race. It is true there may be individual differences in the degree of achievement, for there are differences of choices, works, virtues, and merits which measure this human development.

It does not seem to be a sufficient answer to the problem of human purpose to say that man, like other creatures, is made for the glory of God. This glory is an extrinsic end; it concerns the relation of human nature to God. What is looked for in the present discussion is that good attainable in human nature itself by the highest maturation or perfection of man. This supreme human condition is usually associated with the concept of happiness, of living in the best way.

2. Happiness and Beatitude

Nearly all the answers to the inquiry about man's destiny speak of happiness and perfect happiness, though happiness is interpreted in widely different ways. An analysis of the goods or content of happiness and then of the state or activity of the happy man is required before making a decision on the genuine goal of human life.

Human usage of the word happiness tells us something about it. Parents are happy about their children's progress in school; Joe is happy that Billy is his roommate; Ellen and Allen are happily married. In these and many other instances happiness means satisfaction in something good for a person, myself or others. It means conscious contentment in having this good. Awareness of the presence of the good is there; contentment, which is more than laughter, fun, or thrills, follows this awareness and appreciation. Wherever there is happiness, there is a pleasant or agreeable experience of some sort since every human power derives some pleasure from having its appropriate object. Possession or even mere hope for the good brings with it this sweetness of contentment, satisfaction, or completion. For we are aware that we have or will soon have what we desire or need, and we are not troubled by something evil, harmful, or undesirable.

The chief interest of the philosophers, however, is perfect happiness or supreme human perfection. This state they name beatitude or blessedness. The definitions attempted by many philosophers rather commonly agree in maintaining that fullness of goods and absence of all evils belong to beatitude. The essence of it seems to require the full and enduring possession of the supreme good for man. This key idea in much Western thought deserves detailed explanation. The notion of *possession* means the personal holding of the desired object as one's own, though not necessarily as exclusively one's own. Possession implies more than the desire for the good, more than the hope of obtaining it, more than waiting for and progressing toward it. Hope gives only an imperfect happiness; beatitude fulfills hope. Possession here means an interior living activity, a vital union of one's powers with the good object. Some one else may own or even be the good object, as a museum may own a Madonna; one is happy to possess it vitally by viewing and admiring it. Possession means an awareness of having this good. Hence, one is not happy when asleep or forgetful of the goods. Mere nearness to the good is not enough, as flowers in heaven are not happy since they cannot know that they are in that land of eternal goods.

The possession that is proper to blessedness is *perfect* or *full* possession of the good. Such completeness is primarily proportionate to the basic capacity of human nature and secondarily to the individual capacity of each person. In every instance, however, the completely happy person is brimful of the good and can enjoy no more because he can possess no more. This wholeness or finality of the status of beatitude would not be achieved, of course, unless the chief human powers were replete and the specific intellectual and voluntary needs of man were met.

Furthermore, beatitude must be *enduring*. Perfect happiness is a constant and uninterrupted act. This implies that the happy being must continue to live forever, that the act of possessing the good must go on immortally, and that the good possessed must be imperishable. The beatified person will have to know that his status of well-being is secure and perpetual; any doubts or suspicions that it might ever end would leave him without complete peace of mind and will.

The definition of beatitude also noted that the object of this full and eternal awareness must be the *supreme* good for man. Intellect and will are necessarily related to objects; their best acts must be related to the best objects. This object, the famous *summum bonum* of so many philosophical treatises, must be the supreme good for our human nature or the ultimate object of every heart's desire. It can be the highest end and supremely perfecting good only on these conditions: (1) it must really exist; (2) it must befit our human nature; (3) it must be the best of all goods that human nature can attain; (4) it must be a good which is necessary for us and for which all other goods together cannot substitute; (5) it must be a pure end, in no way a means or a good that is secondary to some other which man can reach; (6) it must be in no way evil or the occasion of evil; (7) it must be perpetual; (8) it must be a good within the reach of all men without exception. Such an object clearly would meet the aspirations of the human spirit and bring it the keenest delight. In possessing it, man would be performing that beatifying act which differs from all others in completely and forever satisfying him. This act would be the highest personal perfection of man's nature, the peak of his well-being, the attainment of the final goal to which all human existence and activity is principally directed. There is nothing better, higher, more perfect for man. Summing all this up, St. Thomas Aquinas says that the final end of man consists in "the best activity of the best power on its best object." Here, then, the concepts of human finality and beatitude reach a junction.

3. Perfect Happiness, Man's Supreme End

A good philosophical route to the conclusion that man is naturally destined for the possession of perfect good begins from our knowledge of human nature and rational activity. We know the specific end of a nature from the good for which it has specific capacities, constant and universal desires, as well as constant and common needs. Has man such specific capacities, desires, and needs for the perfect good?

His special human powers of intellect and will have such a capacity for the perfect. Their object is a universal one; they can know and love all being under its aspects of truth and goodness. They are capable of a universal and total good, not just a particular or limited good. The weariness, lack of interest, and disgust that we have with particular goods means that nothing but the best fully pleases us. The universal and unquenchable desire for the good, the flight from evil, and discontent with the incomplete and impermanent are well-known traits of human nature. Day by day every normal person feels his nature springing toward more good, incessantly hungering for happiness, seeking it sometimes in very strange ways but, nevertheless, eagerly pursuing it. Evil is never desired for its own sake; it is fought against. Even where moral evil is sought, this follows some misjudgment that some advantage or pleasure, passing goods, can come to one by selecting a physical good that is contaminated with moral evil. The phenomena of unrest in whatever goods that we have, the search for security, the passion for greater things and bigger opportunities, the urgent desire to grow and to rebuild, to know and to love more, to move faster, to have more intense experience, to gain more complete control, all express this world-wide human tension toward fuller good. Solomon, Alexander, St. Francis Xavier, Napoleon, Cecil Rhodes are merely unusually clear examples of this universal vaulting ambition and hope for the best. Lastly, man has a psychological and moral need not only for endless life, but for that type of life which is perfect happiness. Nothing imperfect or limited ever gives full or lasting contentment and silences our fears and misgivings. The moral need for happiness is clear from the demands of the moral law that men and women suffer long and deeply and make boundless sacrifices of temporal happiness for the sake of defending their country or preserving their faith or cherishing the will of God. The heroic dead of the nations, the saviors of their countries, selfless parents, martyrs, and cloistered contemplatives are among these witnesses to the demand of the human soul and of the moral law that nothing less than perfect happiness can be the recompense for surrendering such precious temporal goods. This is an objective worthy of all efforts that need to be expended to gain it.

4. IDENTIFYING BEATITUDE

It may come as a surprise that among the philosophers who set the end of human life in happiness there is a vast spread of views about the kind of good which they regard as king of goods and the kind of life which they identify concretely as the beatified life. We may come to our own decisions by applying the Thomistic dictum about "the best activity of the best power on its best object." Aquinas, like Aristotle and many others, draws up a check list of the best objects proposed by men and of the best proposed activities. More successfully than most, Thomas sets up his signposts for recognizing the best; and then he measures the proposed best objects and best activities by these criteria.[2]

The list of ends and goods that have been seriously proposed for human life includes wealth, economic power, and the temporal welfare of the masses; political power, military glory, and honor; pleasures of the senses or of the mind; learning and the contemplative life; moral goodness or some form of it such as justice or friendship; the good of one's family; the good of one's nation or "race"; and God. There are also various groupings of these goods and variants on them as the life of the artist, the life of the philosopher among his friends,[3] the career of a doctor.

All these we can test by the eight criteria of the supreme good mentioned a few pages back. All of them have some good about them; many have an immediate attractiveness. How many, on the other hand, are lasting objects? How many are really necessary for all men? How many of them are accessible to all men merely on the basis of their human nature? How many of them are not subordinate as means to better goods? Which of them is not wearisome and an occasion of struggle, worry, fear, and other cares? How many of them suffice to fill the powers, satiate the desires, and meet the deeper needs of man? Of all objects in the catalog, only God is a perfect good, a necessary and sufficient object, accessible to every intellect and will, an everlasting being, a pure end subordinate to no other, one whose perfection can gratify all desire and fill up every void in the soul. God Himself, not our thought or image of God, is this perfect object. The drive of human nature is toward the absolute, the infinite, the one and only best, and to nothing less than Him. On this point all Christian philosophers are agreed.

All also agree with the Aristotelian view that happiness must be an activity or living function of man. For structure is related to function, being and powers are for action, capacity is made for achieving. As we see in the case of the body's organs and parts as the heart and fingers, and its powers as sight, these things do not exist for themselves but for their perfection in activity. But there is no unanimity of opinion about the best power of man and about the best act of that power. This is the famous dispute about formal beatitude, that is, about the special activity in which beatitude actually consists.

We must first try to determine which is man's best power. There is sunny concord of views that the best power must be one of man's spiritual powers, for these alone are better than matter, are specifically human, are immortal, and can attain a spiritual reality such as God. But is formal beatitude an act of intellect, of will, or of both powers? In a sense, the answer is not too important, for if it is in the intellect, the will's love and delight spontaneously follow the intellect; if it is an act of will, this must have a preceding perfect act of knowledge; and if it is in both powers, the same total result of perfect knowledge, love, and joy follows as if the beatifying act is formally in one or other power. St. Thomas, true to his Aristotelian bent and his intellectualist spirit, had no doubt that beatitude as such was an act of the intellect, since the intellect acts more immanently and is, therefore, more fully alive than will, and since it has already attained the perfect object before the will can begin to love and rejoice in it.

Which act of the intellect is its best act? Again Aquinas draws up an inventory and eliminates all but one act. The list of proposed acts of intellect includes acts of the practical intellect, as in knowledge of the arts and prudence; acts of the speculative intellect, as some scientific or metaphysical contemplative act; acts of knowledge of God, either popular knowledge of Him, reasoned philosophical knowledge of Him, reasoned appreciation of God by knowing angelic likenesses of Him, faith in God on divine authority, or the vision of God.

The only likely contenders for the best act are faith, reasoned knowledge of God, and vision. Faith, however certain it is, is too obscure; the believer does not know God as He is in Himself, but what God says about Himself; faith cannot be the best act. Reasoned knowledge of God gives us only indirect and analogical knowledge of God; we know Him in His created effects and distant likenesses, not in His glorious Self. Even if this reasoned knowledge is heightened very far beyond our present abilities to infer His essence from His creatures, it still is knowing the books and not the author, it is too incomplete and too much shadowed by a knowledge of what God is not. What we desire, what will fill our intellects is not just a knowledge that God is and that He is a cause and somehow better than His effects; we aspire to know Him as He is. This means direct, unhidden knowledge. Such an immediate viewing of God immediately present in our minds is called vision; it is the best act of the intellect.

This attractive conclusion of St. Thomas bristles with difficulties. Has it failed to distinguish between a natural happiness which can never be perfect and, consequently, never reach a vision of God, and the supernatural happiness which alone is truly perfect because it alone reaches the vision? Some think that the position claims too much for the natural state of the human intellect by giving it a natural desire, however ineffective, for seeing God. St. Thomas, of course, never said that man has an active ability of his own, apart from the special gift of God, to have this vision. Man does not lift himself up to this vision; God's grace and the gift of glory are necessary. Man also has no natural need for a supernatural good; only graced human nature requires it as its proportionate best act.

Yet it does not seem likely that so rigorous an analyst as St. Thomas has slipped in his teaching by giving a revealed answer to a philosophical problem on beatitude or that he contradicts himself by insisting on both a natural desire for the vision of God and a total natural inability to realize it[4] or that, in spite of his keen perception of the distinction between nature and grace, he has here not merely bridged the two orders but fused them. Many suggestions have been made to clarify St. Thomas' position. One set of critics would like to distinguish between a perfect natural beatitude in a lofty rational knowledge of God and a perfect supernatural beatitude in a vision of Divinity. They would like to qualify the best operation of man as the best absolutely and the best possible and proportionate to man merely in his natural status. Only this latter would be within the province of philosophical determination. A great measure of happiness would well up in man from a knowledge of God based on vast knowledge of the wonders of the universe and an insight into the divine perfection as source, model, and end of these wonders. But it is one thing to know the photograph of one's friend and another to live with him daily; it is one thing to see a travelogue on film and another to have the firsthand experience and adventure. Similarly, there is a vast gulf between knowing God in His works and seeing Him in Himself. Could the spirit of man be naturally satisfied if it ever suspected that the vision of God is a possible way of knowing Him? Or would this suspicion, this question ever occur to a merely natural intelligence unless God had already given the secret impulse to or the open revelation of supernatural beatitude? The Christian philosopher need not settle all these thorny matters and the related interpretations of St. Thomas' text. Theology has settled the main issue by assuring us of the fact that God intends to give us the vision of His infinite loveliness.

Genuine, unreservedly complete happiness must be a supernatural happiness, an attainment of a supernatural good in an exalted supernatural act. This beatitude is called the salvation of the soul, eternal life in heaven, supernatural glory, the face-to-face vision of the Blessed Trinity. Our knowledge of this destiny, our power to receive it, and the means of gaining it are part of the treasure which Christ has contributed to human life, as we shall later see. For the present we note that all natural perfect happiness is totally absorbed into supernatural beatitude in the actual historical providence of God over us. Man's natural gains all stand, but they are immeasurably enriched in the beatifying act of seeing the living God.

From the fact that God is the required and the only sufficient good that will fill every recess of the soul it does not follow that He is the only blessing which the beatified possess. For beatitude is the perfect state of a being who has human nature and not merely spiritual powers. God will generously bestow whatever else besides Himself may help to make us happy. Perhaps the human soul retains a natural capacity and even a natural wish for life within a body. Shall we be fully human and perfect without a body? Will our soul be altogether perfect unless it functions again as a form reunited to a perfected human body? It does not, then, seem to be hoping for too much if we look forward to some bodily restoration but under conditions that will never again bring sorrow because of bodily aches and needs. We shall probably retain our interest in human friendship; if so, God will give us suitable human companionship. Our scientific, artistic, and philosophical longings may remain; if so, they will find their perfection in the next life. All these are accidental, incidental, or secondary favors that follow upon the possession of God. Whatever we need in these respects will be given, for nothing that contributes to complete happiness will be wanting. None of them will be enough without God; none of them in our perfect state will displace God. Philosophy, however, can give us only probable assurance of the presence of these objects and activities on the principle that God always governs us according to our natures. Revelation guarantees the actual presence of some of these secondary blessings in heaven when it teaches us of the resurrection of the body and the society of the angels and saints.

5. APPRECIATION OF BEATITUDE

The gladdening vision of God is, then, the chief purpose of human life. The splendor of this truth deserves intense intellectual pondering. Full realization must obviously wait until we see God, but better insight today may come from some reflections.

We notice, first, that as will follows intellect, a perfect act of love of the object follows a perfect act of knowledge. Furthermore, since every power finds its proper pleasure in its own activity, perfect operations of the power bring a complete pleasure. The pleasure proportionate to perfect knowledge and perfect love is spiritual joy. In knowing God perfectly and loving Him as fully as we can, we will have all-satisfying joy in Him. This delight of the human soul is what Dante called the peace surpassing every gladness.

We notice, second, that knowledge is a source of joy for us, or that "happiness is a joy in truth," to borrow from St. Augustine. We may tend to regard love as the immediate root of joy and neglect knowledge. Yet love waits on knowledge; and love may be but a delusion unless it accompanies knowledge of the good. Many common experiences show us that knowledge can be a source of joy.

An autumn scene on a highway may bring us much pleasure. The colors, forms, and fragrances of spring flowers lift up the heart. Theater plays gladden us by entertaining the mind. News about a baby's birth or the recovery of an ill relative brings shining happiness to human faces. Many have sipped the joy of discovering the answer to a tough problem that has long beset them. We know the joy of sharing in the knowledge that scientists have found new remedies against some dreadful disease. Gifted men sit spellbound and delighted as a communicative astronomer answers their questions about the size of the universe, the theories of the birth and growth of stars, and the newest knowledge of the far distant galaxies. We hear of the victory of a favorite team or of personal success in an examination and are elated. The shepherds rejoiced exceedingly on Christmas night at the newscast of the angels who informed them of a Saviour's birth on their own hillsides. In all these instances knowledge causes happiness. Aristotle justifiably said that happiness is a contemplative activity.[5]

As knowing is a garden gate opening on love and delight, so ignorance, error, and lack of access to knowledge immensely handicap human life and lower the level of human joy. Ignorance is bliss only in a world of fools. Think only of how inability to read seals the mind from knowing history, from getting information and affectionate remembrances in letters, from thrilling to the beauties of poetry and the marvels of science as recorded in print. Think, too, of the happiness that we would miss were we ignorant of the truths of theology. Knowledge of God, the supreme object, would especially throw wide the doors to our happiness; ignorance of Him essentially bars us from happiness.

Third, the knowledge and love in beatitude is perfect. Probably we have never had the experience of perfect knowledge or perfect love even of relatively little things. Beatifying knowledge does not entail, as does our knowledge during life, laborious inquiry, the effort of study, restless mental search, and straining to prepare examinations and lectures. Perfect knowledge is not sensory knowledge, limited to a grasp of only the appearances or accidents of merely material reality. It is not a dark, partial, distracted, hesitant, or variable possession of the perfect, spiritual, unlimited, divine object. It is sure, clear, constant, complete, filling the soul's whole capacity. It is the highest act of our intelligence, the wisdom of a person-to-person knowledge between one's soul and God. With it goes a peace of mind conscious that this radiant intellectual possession will last forever without ever fading in clearness or ever losing its entrancing wonder.

Accompanying the knowledge is a commensurate act of perfect love of this divine object. The union of the beatified will is far above the plane of the sensible emotions which beat, grow weary, and conflict with other feelings. The union of the beatified will with the good is without effort or anxiety, without the tension of desire and the straining of eager hope, without any intruding flaws of unworthy selfish love.

It is eternal peace and boundless contentment in possession of the beloved object. The whole heart, the whole soul, the full strength of the person is fixed on God in a glowing, victorious love of gratitude, in gracious good will to God, and in perpetual friendship with Him.

Fourth, we must try to appreciate what it is to know a perfect object and love it, for knowledge and love are better in proportion to the excellence of the known and beloved being. Who and what is that infinite Good to whom the blessed are united?

The human mind must stretch itself to its fullest limit and try to raise its dimension of understanding by dim analogies in order to get some better insight into the meaning of union with a boundless good. For the infinite Good, the object of intellect and will, is every perfect thing in every perfect degree in which being can exist. God is all this, all in one, and all at once. He is the one source of all other good things, their model and their cause, and He Himself contains the being of all other lovable things in a supremely nobler way. One who possesses God possesses something far better than all other things. Some comparisons may lead to a richer appreciation of this concentration of God's infinity. White light includes all hues of the rainbow. America includes the scenic, economic, scientific, educational, and political wonders of all the world. So, in God are united all the power of ocean and atom; in Him is the prudence of the statesman, the invention of the scientist, the beauty of the artist, and the wisdom of the theologian; in Him is the loyalty of the patriot, the tender constancy of the mother, the faithful love of the father.[6] In the simple diamond point of divine being are gathered together all radiance and loveliness, all truth and wisdom, all ability and glory, all charity and peace.

Whoever, therefore, knows God well in a sense knows everything, for God is excellent above all other things together. He who loves God fully in a sense loves everybody, for God is more than everybody. He is like Adam when he walked with God in paradise, like Moses before the burning bush, like Peter before Christ transfigured on Tabor. But all this is but a fragment of the truth; no mind has begun to conceive what God's final gifts mean to those who love Him.

6. BEATITUDE DELAYED

In this explanation of the supreme goal we have often observed that it is an immortal and unchangeable state of human perfection. While it is sure that each man can reach beatitude, it is equally sure that no man can reach it in this life on earth. The conditions for human perfection clearly cannot be found in our present course. The needs and weaknesses of our bodies, the limitations on our souls, the shortcomings of society cannot exclude every evil or guarantee perpetual good. The many spinnings of the wheel of change within us and in persons and things about us bring little goods into our lives, but then whirl them out of our grasp. We have to contend with illness, aging, the prospect of death, and death itself. Our troubles increase; our peace is often disturbed by worries; temptations to evil again and again trap us; wild emotions need stern management. We are held down by the slow growth of our minds and by our forgetful inconstancy. We are hemmed in by dependence on others for economic, domestic, and political security. Our best knowledge of God is so slight; our time for philosophical or religious contemplation is brief, distracted, fatiguing. Our deepest faith leaves us with a heartsick realization of the distance that still separates us from perfect knowledge and love of God. The best life on this earth is far from being paradise.

During this period of our pursuit of happiness there takes place a twofold action in the direction of its attainment. We are hunting for God, the object of happiness. In all our efforts to make any good our own, we are implicitly trying to make ourselves like the supreme good. But God, too, is pursuing us, wishing to give us happiness immortally with Himself and wishing to give us in this life many helps and some degree of temporal happiness as a present sign and a promise of His eternal kindness. God seeks His glory in all our activities; and God's formal glory is precisely our knowledge and love of Him. His glory is best achieved when we fulfill our purpose in the radiant vision and joyous embrace of God. There is, then, a movement from creature to the Creator, for our hearts capable of the divine are restless until they rest in Him. There is an even mightier movement, so to speak, from the Creator prompting our yearning and seeking to slake that ardor for the divine which He burnt into our spirits. What we gain is God's gift. Until His image is complete in us, the divine pursuit goes on. This likeness to God is at its finest when man is seeing God as He is and loving Him in His seen presence. Perfect likeness to God is the creature's end, his beatitude, his splendor, and God's glory irridescent in our souls.

Because God governs man in order to bring him at last to perfect happiness and puts upon man the mandate to pursue this happiness, each man has straight from God the inalienable, nonforfeitable right to pursue his own greatest good for the glory of God on earth. To the philosopher the right to pursuit of happiness will principally mean the person's liberty within the state and on earth to act in a way that will bring him personal eternal union with God. All powers and acts of his human nature, the earth about him, the family, political and other institutions must either immediately or indirectly contribute to the immortal success of man's soul. Even death must pay its levy to the eternal gladness of man. We speak, therefore, of a happy death, not because of its painlessness or swiftness, but because it starts an eternally happy life. The whole point of human living may be said to be its perfectly happy and unending ending.

CHAPTER 8

The Purposes of Life on Earth

1. THE MEANING OF THE PRESENT LIFE

THE FORESEEN splendor of future beatitude decides one of the biggest questions. It sheds radiance into this world and uplifts the human heart. But it does not quiet all the mind's inquiries, for man asks what other connections there are between the life of that other world and the life of this world where mortals now find themselves. Does this life in time and on earth have a meaning of its own distinct from that of its relation to beatitude? Is it without any value? Or does it draw its worth wholly from its relation to man's immortal destiny?

Thinkers have proposed many different views about the significance and excellence of the present life. The right answer must depend on the end or goods which the present life can achieve. A thing's purpose explains what it is for and what it should act for; the end specifies the nature and the acts proportionate to that end. Purpose, in other words, determines the meaning in things, their intelligibility to men, and their right use.

The Thomistic and Christian point of view accepts the present life as the first part of man's whole life, but seeks its meaning in its design within the whole. Life on earth is a period of active preparation for that future life, not merely a passive waiting, as of plants dormant in winter. This is the time of beginnings, of seeding and ploughing for a proportional harvest in the next life. The activities of the present are the means to successful beatitude.

What reasons support this claim that the present life is a means to the end?

One line of thought showing the means-to-end relationship of this life to our well-being in the next relies on an argument from exclusion.

The present life is either an end in itself, a means to an end hereafter, or it is altogether meaningless as being neither an end nor a means. The last alternative, accepted by pessimists and some existentialists, makes man's life and aspirations a freakish accident of existence. It supposes, of course, that the universe is irrational and man but material in this irrational material universe. It excludes all ends, plan, and divine care over men. In a purposeless universe there is no point in asking questions about life, for there are no answers. Nor would we think of asking for reasons in a reasonless order.

The first alternative that this life is an end in itself cannot be held consistently with the truth that man has a nature destined for perfect happiness, which cannot be realized among the manifold imperfections of earthly existence. If this life were irrelevant toward immortality, it would be a mad puzzle, almost as though it had no purpose at all.

It remains then that this life is a means to our future life with God. Like a good overture, life now must contain the main themes of that coming complete performance. It must be of a consistent pattern with that life hereafter. Man is made for a divine destination. He has already started on the way to immortal perfection with God. He is an apprentice called to heavenly happiness who is laboring in the workshop of this world to make the fortune of his soul.

Besides this argument from exclusion of alternative explanations, other considerations indicate the same truth that this life is a means to beatitude in the next. First, the excellence of the perfect good requires that we appreciate it and give some proof of our appreciation by doing our part to earn it. This requires deliberate love of God and His goodness and of all that pertains to His goodness. By a life of glorifying God and doing His signified will on earth, we merit proportionate eternal glory for ourselves. Our choices then become a partial cause of that glorious effect; the good deeds that we do for God return to us hereafter in God's abundant gifts in beatitude. Second, the dignity of man, unique in his freedom, demands that he rightly use his noble liberty and direct his own will's activities to the fulfillment of the will of God. It is fitting that the supreme good come to man not by force of circumstances, sheer luck, or the automatic consequence of existing, but that it belong to man because he chose to pay for it the noble price of service of God. Since man is free, it is solemnly important that he decide for himself whether he prefers the transitory goods of the creature to the eternal good of his Creator. This must be a personal option, not a decision forced by the fact that death cuts off all creatures. Third, the immortality of the soul suggests the same relationship of time to eternity. For our soul is already immortal. When at bodily death the soul leaves its material consort, it does not interrupt its own life. It goes onward into the next life, itself intact, freighted with its spiritual gains, its habits, its merits, its faults, and its demerits. Its spiritual merits become a sort of admission ticket to beatitude; they are the bond between our status in one life and the next; its standing demerits set up the soul's self-made barrier against entrance into happiness. There is, then, a continuity not only in living but in the moral quality of life now and then.

Finally, God's wise and holy government of this world must ordinarily require deliberate human service as the normal route to beatitude, at least for adults. If men could reach beatitude no matter how grandly or criminally they might have lived, earth would be a sorry place and human life spiritually sluggish. Beatitude for every man on his own terms would mean no honor to God on earth, no splendor or heroism in human nature, no great love of fellow men, and few glorious achievements on this earth. Needless to say, life would lose most of its luster, drama, and delight.

The relationship, then, is between moral goodness now and perfect happiness hereafter. Philosophers, unfortunately, have no way of knowing what adequate preparation is. They know there must be an alliance between the human and divine will in embracing the good and in opposing evil. But how complete a reform of any moral evil in one's life, how high a degree of moral goodness, what additional specific requisites God may have historically decreed for man's preparation, only Christ could tell us. His word is that the minimum required to please God is death at a time when the soul is in the state of sanctifying grace. As we sow, so we reap.

2. Viewing Life as a Means

The labors of man and particularly his use of liberty have abundant significance. Insight into this relation of present to future throws light on many of the rules, needs, and purposes of daily living. We need to make our evaluations in this means-to-end pattern and guide our choices by measuring them against eternal blessedness. "What has this to do with eternity?" asked St. Aloysius. This norm of the Saint should be used by any thoughtful person who is making his choices, picking a career, initiating some project, or weighing its genuine degree of success. How much does it count for eternity? Will the proposed act or way of living help or hinder the realization of the great promise? If it helps, it can be fitted into our lives. If it does not, it should be excluded. But it should first be evaluated, then chosen; not chosen, and then forced, if possible, into the mold of living well. Sin, of course, is sheer waste of life both because it is the principal source of temporal unhappiness and because it has no value whatsoever for beatitude. Sin clips a whole period out of life and renders it simply worthless. But apart from sinful acts, other earthly careers may sometimes help and sometimes hinder. Their utility for spiritual success and not their instant satisfaction is the standard by which they should be taken into our lives. Health may help, but so may illness; success in financial, political, or military careers may help, but so may failure; marriage may speed us heavenward or may betray us.

One must keep an eye single-mindedly on the great end and then pick the related means promptly, exclude the unrelated or opposed, and use the right means sufficiently to accomplish the purpose. Man is like an autoist making a difficult trip to a far city in a limited time. He cannot afford to make mistakes and dally time; he must have a good car, good maps, good fuel, good roads, and he must steer by his maps. He must make everything bear on safely reaching the journey's end.

Intention or desire of the end has primacy over the means used. A good intention binding all to the noble end is especially valuable in the selection of the morally neutral and trifling things of life and in bearing the things that happen to us by fortune or misfortune but without our previous choice. We raise all these to high moral significance by right purpose in using or bearing them.

Steadfast attention to the true connection of means with the end will more and more develop a proportional view of temporal goods. In addition to this prudent mental balance, man needs a balance of will, ready to choose what better conduces to the end. To win such balance we need not cultivate a contempt of the things of this world nor a Stoic apathy to all passing events. What we must cultivate is detachment of our will and affections from the things of the world, so that, even while we use them, they remain our servants and never rule us as masters. We must be willing to use them when, where, and in so far as they help us to reach our end and to forego them whenever, wherever, and to the degree that they impede us. Such a tension of perfect poise between conflicting attractions, such a ready control of our mere likings for pleasant and dislikings for painful things is a proof of great sincerity in seeking only the good.

The mind, then, must see that only one thing is worthy of the will's enduring and total affection and that health, the body, careers, honor, family, country, and all other goods are secondary. The will must follow by choosing them in proportion to their ultimate importance as ordered to the supreme object of our loyalty and love, God's goodness and will.

Since life is a season of preparation for eternal holiday, or better, a time to prove ourselves worthy of beatitude, it is not surprising that it is a period of testing our worthiness. We win beatitude only under certain conditions; we can miss it by not meeting the conditions. God gives it to baptized infants and idiots who die with grace but without a chance of being tested or meriting their own eternal happiness. The rest of men must meet the test of virtuous activity, choosing the good for good reasons, shaping their souls for eternal union with God by union with Him through obedient love now. Since it is such a time for testing, it is not to be wondered at if some severe tasks are put on us and that the great Examiner includes some hard questions and difficult experiments in His test. But hardships and sufferings are also means to the end, and they may be very apt means for sorting out the better candidates for beatitude. All these troubles vein our lives whether we see their meaning or not. The wise man learns to transform them into tools with which he builds his ladder to eternity, making each moment an experience of enduring value.

3. Interest in This World

The attitude that we must live in this world but not merely for its goods does not discourage interest in the world. By insisting that the present life is not the only or the chief value, it enfolds the purposes of time in the grander nobility of man's supreme purpose. Time thus becomes more precious; earth is exalted as an instrument of the spirit. The careless charge has often been made, of course, that persons interested in the next life neglect their duties and opportunities in this life and that strongly religious nations are industrially backward.[1] Holy men in India with their Oriental outlook that breaks all connection between the present life and the life to come may have this apathy. Plato's philosopher-king reluctantly leaves contemplation of justice to descend to the world of shadows to practice justice among men. The fathers of the desert withdrew from the world and spoke of it with great distrust and disdain. But history bears out the fact that in general Western otherworldliness does not damage interest in this world. It does imply less interest in worldly opportunities for their own sake; it discourages avarice for this world's goods; it concentrates on treasures in heaven. But it knows that such treasures are amassed by good deeds done now. It knows that God has given us talents to be used now. It never excuses defaulting in any of one's duties. The true paradox seems to be that wise vision of the subordination of the present to the future life adds to the Christian's zest in the present, strengthens his devotion to his tasks, sharpens his discontent with temporal conditions that block the spirit, whets his eagerness to better civilization and thereby glorify God. The man dominated by the otherworldly view is always trying to do his best since everything counts forever. Perhaps most noticeable is the charity of the otherworldly man and woman, interested in people who have the same profound problems and spiritual destiny as themselves.

Saints, we remember, were dynamos of energy in their external occupations. Yet many of them wanted to die; they were restless to meet the God for whom they lived, who was the biggest interest in their lives. But they wanted to come to His company laden with the gifts of good deeds and a personal record that would intensely gratify His good love. In this otherworldliness of motive lay the secret of their immense forcefulness in temporal pursuits.

4. THE QUEST FOR TEMPORAL HAPPINESS

The suggestion that life is a testing period may make one wonder whether God intends us to have any happiness in this life or whether He reserves it all for the future. Is the interest of the human and the American heart in the "pursuit of happiness" a complete illusion?

It is true enough that our greatest contentment in this life will never be fully satisfying. What happiness we have will not last so very long. It is never as completely essential as moral goodness is. If life is a garden, it has its thorns and frosts. But though partial, changeable, and mixed with troubles, happiness on this earth may be deep and substantial.

One may say that it is the will of God that we be happy for the most part. He has put into our nature the capacity for some temporal happiness. It surely is also within the power of people about us and the world that surrounds us that these provide us with many fine things and bring some measure of satisfaction to our days on earth. The eyes were made in part for joy, the lips were made for laughter, the voice was made for song. Moreover, there is a genuine practical need for some contentment in the lives of most people; without it, they can scarcely meet the issues of life with psychological normalcy and moral loyalty. Unhappy families tend to become bad families; unhappy nations tend to be plagued with moral problems; slums and prisons are not the normal soil for human holiness. It is normal to desire and to have some measure of temporal happiness. What is abnormal is the craving for instant perfect happiness in this life or the expectation of finding it mainly in the material advantages of this life.

Accordingly, the capacity, the interest, and the need of human nature show that the will of God means some gladness for us now. St. Augustine had a somber view of this present life and of the deep shadows that lie on the earth and in human hearts because of original and personal sin. Yet he recognized the beauties of earth which God must have meant for our enjoyment as well as for our instruction and use.[2] The hues and forms of mighty trees along a stream, the cheering songs of birds, the fascinating beauties of the changing seasons, the merriment of children, human kindness and friendly loyalty, the peace of the family's love are all signs that God is at work in the world to bring to us good things which will give us present satisfaction. The quiet of a good conscience, the cultivation of the fine arts, the security of life in a well-ordered state, and the services of science add to the sum of human happiness. Even the comforts which the senses experience are certainly normal and a normal part of nature.[3] What is wrong is not the pleasure, but its excess, its use under wrong conditions, and the preference of it to more important goods.

The pursuit of temporal happiness, then, is ordinarily not a will-o'-the-wisp. Yet it is a secondary consideration that must be adjusted to the pursuit of eternal happiness. Life will provide enough heartaches that we will not be spoiled by the bits of happiness which this world provides. The unessential character of immediate happiness can also be seen in God's way of dealing with His friends, the saints. He often lets them endure a particularly rugged and difficult life. His own Son had a bad time on earth. His Mother bore extreme sorrows. His Mother would not promise Bernadette Soubirous happiness on this earth in return for her generous services. He has often called heroic souls to endure bitterly unfair deals and to choose sternly penitential lives rather than bask in sensory comforts and worldly successes. For them He reserved a happiness deeply hidden in the soul that was conscious of doing His will and sure of His love. To them He gave brighter glimpses of a glory tomorrow and vivid hopes of that afterlife with God. These deep acts of the human spirit, hope in God and love of Him, are undoubtedly the sweetest and the most constant of all fountains of joy.

Have the philosophers any suggestions for increasing our temporal happiness in ways that God will approve? They have understood our human hunger for happiness, our frailty in chasing it, our improvidence in filling our souls with it, and our poignant need for it. The philosophers, in the explorations that led to the definition of happiness as conscious contentment in what is suitable for human nature and powers, have given their better hints on roads to peace of heart.

Contentment, they have told us, is a conscious act or state. This implies that we must be mentally aware of the good things that are present in our lives and that are opening up before us. But we can fail to notice and appreciate familiar blessings in our lives. We may, for example, be little thankful for our health until we see someone else suffer. We miss the grass by worrying over the dandelions. We do not hear the canary singing its heart out because we are deaf. Life is a song — for a spell — but we want sadness. We may be at fault for inattention while God fills His world with goods. We will not be happy even in heaven if we ever forget that we are there.

Together with these grateful dispositions we must control unreasonable desires for things that are impossible to attain or not good for us, smother our fears, and face the difficulties of reality calmly and patiently. We must quench irrational discontent, for it befogs vision of the many advantages present in our lives. We must multiply the goods in our lives more by cultivating many sides of human nature than by adding to the sum of physical possessions and sensory thrills. We must uproot evil in its sources and not merely soothe its consequences.

Other approaches to greater temporal happiness will be discussed in Chapters 10 and 20.

5. HUMANISM AND HAPPINESS

A characteristic outlook of the humanist point of view is that man may legitimately seek and expect a fair measure of temporal happiness. Sound humanism recommends that we seek happiness for all men, that we do so in a truly human way, that we cultivate all the many sides of human nature to their due purpose and in due order, and that we emphasize the development of the higher powers of man, the nobler pleasures, and the long-lasting spiritual successes. Two points of this humanistic attitude deserve attention here, of which the first is the concept of the greatness of human nature. Truth, goodness, and beauty are all of interest to man; truth and beauty especially take many forms. The happy man who has enriched his life with good things would seem ordinarily to need a wide cultivation of intelligence, clearness of conscience, a firm development of his virtues, and good taste for all that is genuinely lovely. Inability to use some of the powers of the orchestra of his nature will mute many happy voices and make the melody of life less colorful. Peaceful and genial social living will also contribute to an abundantly happy temporal life. The application of technology to the relief of man's acuter material necessities will provide more leisure for spiritual and higher human activities. Not least of all, the practice of religion fulfills one of the deepest needs of human nature, namely, its need for hope and its ever unslaked thirst for the perfect, for God. Without hope, without God, what man can turn a smiling face to the future?

Another major lesson of humanism teaches that the dedicated and the unselfish are the happiest people but that the selfish, like the wicked, are unhappy. The soul, because of its unlimited capacities, can never be satisfied just with one's self. Man hungers for something immensely greater than the self. Hence, those who give themselves to a great cause, to the service of God, to the help of the sick, to instruction of the young, to generous kindness to others enrich their own lives with many benefits. The giver is more blessed than the receiver. Happiness like goodness is expansive; it flows out in love to others and returns in joy to oneself. The servant of God and of the needy escapes from the prison of the ego and enters a wide land overflowing with the hundredfold abundance of happy living.

The subject of humanism will receive longer treatment later in this book. At the moment let us caution ourselves against counterfeit humanisms which so glorify some one side of human nature that they will not lead to happiness in eternity and can lead to considerable unhappiness even in this life. One of the less offensive of these spurious humanisms is that current of thought and sentiment for bettering man's lot that has come to be known as humanitarianism. This movement has had some sparkling successes, particularly in the nineteenth century. The people connected with it added mightily to the forces of society that labored for the abolition of slavery and the end of the slave trade, for the betterment of prison conditions and more sensible laws for debtors, for child-labor and women's-work laws, for the improvement of hospitals and the extension of hospital care, for the establishment of the Red Cross and control of brutality to prisoners of war, and, in general, for the application of science to human health and comfort. Although humanitarianism did not accomplish any of these results alone, it enlisted may people in the causes which other organizations and Christian thinkers were already powerfully supporting.

Humanitarianism, however, often degenerated into a materialism exclusively interested in the welfare of human bodies and in the relief of human pain and suffering. In refining the sentiments and in appealing to them to arouse action for better conditions, it lost its head and forgot the spiritual dignity of man and the probationary character of earthly life. The result has been that humanitarians now sponsor many objectionable causes: no medical experimentation on animals even for the sake of improving human health, mercy killing for the incurable and the aged, birth control to prevent suffering for the poor, elimination of the biologically unfit, sterilization to prevent certain types of human beings from ever being born to a life of pain, and some ultrasocialist measures. The bodily well-being of the healthier and wealthier classes has become a supreme purpose in living. Comfort without compromise has come to outrank almost all other considerations. This present life has become the whole span of human life. The economy of suffering in human nature is denied. The brotherhood of man becomes a kinship of healthy animals. To that viewpoint, the life of beatitude hereafter and the glory of the cross of Christ are foolish nonsense.

6. LEGITIMATE SECONDARY PURPOSES OF LIFE

Although the main purpose of this life is to merit our rewards in the afterlife, this preparation for beatitude is not the only purpose of the present life. We resemble mountain climbers trying to conquer Mount Everest. While the goal at every stage is the peak, they have limited objectives along the way and pitch camp at selected sites along the difficult upward slope, but there is progress ever upward. We, too, may have many immediate objectives in life other than beatitude. These are quite legitimate provided they are directed or can be directed to the supreme end. Such immediate or partial objectives are ends in one respect, it is true; but at the same time they are means to the final goal. Even an explicit intention that directs these various secondary ends to the primary one is not always necessary, though it is always good. A habitual or implicit intention in desiring and using these other things suffices for single-minded pursuit.

The very conditions of human life and the will of God approve of this concentration on secondary goods as part of the fulfillment of the big total plan of life. Our daily efforts in the good use of our human powers, our search for health, friendship, knowledge, self-control, and virtuous improvement may be pursued without adverting to eternal happiness; yet they are worthy objectives relatable to the supreme one. Life imposes certain courses of action on us, to which we must give considerable attention and devotion. The fulfillment of these dutiful actions, the use of our talents, the success in our vocation in life are certainly legitimate aims. In fact, most of us need such immediate stimulation to action as the desire to give our children a good life or relieve our neighbors' bodily and spiritual needs or serve our nation or contribute through science and law to a temporal development that is in proper subordination to man's eternal end.

Moreover, not only are the apparently big deeds and vocations in life desirable objectives, but the little things also fit well into a life that is shaped toward God. The hundreds of daily small acts, our dining, reading, and chatting, our golfing, laundering, and traveling, our human affections and domestic pleasures, not less than our worship of God and sharply felt sacrifices are pieces that belong to the full pattern. Right order keeps all such things in life, but holds them in proper subordination to the realization of the supreme good. We are always on course, directly on the beam to the eternal landing place if we point them by good intention and hold them as lower objectives. To elevate these lesser goods to the status of the main aim is a very serious mistake. But to neglect these lesser goods is often a squandering of opportunities and may be even a neglect of duty. The chances for doing good in little ways must be hoarded for the sake of the heavenly riches which they amass.

What figure, then, best portrays man's brief life? Is man on earth a conqueror, a happy warrior, or a captive? Is he laborer, guest, or master? Is he a native living in his homeland or a stranger traveling in a foreign country? Is he creator or spectator of the drama of life? Man may be pictured as the cheerful soldier fighting for his soul's welfare. He is certainly a laborer earning his way to heaven and toiling for eternal recompense. In the phrase of many poets, he is a pilgrim in this world who is marching to the true shrine of his heart in the afterlife. In the word of philosophers and theologians, man is the wayfarer who has gone forth at the command of God and is journeying from his native land to the land where all divine promises come true. Fatigue, trouble, and pain are part of the pilgrim's natural status; but his journey has its joys as well as its penitential experiences. On the last day of his journey death comes to pry open the gate that bars him from the eternal home where all meet who have been faithful in the quest. Meanwhile, the pilgrim daily keeps his eye on the goal and is ever in good heart that with the divine power and kindness assisting him he will arrive at the blessed vision. Man, the wayfarer, is his own biographer. Each by his choices is writing the adventurous story of his own life. He must so write his story that it will have a happy ending in his meeting with God.

CHAPTER 9

The Dignity of Human Life

1. THE HUMAN PERSON

THE INVESTIGATION of the causes of human life has led to the conclusion that a rational animal is constituted of a spiritual soul that informs a material body, that a man is made by God and is destined for Him, and that he resembles his divine Maker. As man is a unique being higher than other visible creatures, he bears a unique distinguished name. Man is a person. "Personality," says St. Thomas, "means that which is the most perfect thing in the whole of nature."[1] Man is the best. Therefore, the saying of the Stoic Seneca has ever been dear to the Christian thinker: Homo res sacra homini, "Man is a thing sacred to man."

We desire to probe into this excellence and sacredness of every man. But first we should recall the scholastic description of a person. A person is a substance, not just an accident or a bundle of attributes and operations. A person is a rational substance, a thinking and willing being, and so distinguished from any mere thing, lifeless or living. Personality belongs to intelligent beings only; others can at most have some individuality. A person is always an individual rational being. Groups of persons have only a legal personality in their common association for a common end; genuine personality belongs only to the individual person whether in or out of the group. A person is a whole being, a complete substance, not a part. His completeness is said to be uncommunicated or unshared. His being is his own, contained within himself, and not a part of some other being. A person finally is self-possessed; he belongs to himself; he has an end and rights of his own; he is, in short, said to be sui juris, a subject of independent being or a holder of his own rights to the exclusion of others. These attributes of

106

a person sum up to the definition that a person is an individual intellectual or rational substance, complete in itself, uncommunicated, and self-possessed.

To claim dignity for man is to assert rational grounds for a special goodness or higher worth that is his. Every man has some knowledge, as part of his general philosophy of life, that he is somehow superior to the earth he walks on, the food he eats, the car he drives, and the clothes he wears. But he may be unable to put into words the reasons why he feels that some special honor belongs to him as a man. Irrelevant and insufficient grounds for regarding man as specially noble must be put aside if we are to have convictions; and the solid titles for the value of the person must be brought into sharp focus by a philosopher.

Certain prominent accidental features and individual differences are often advanced as the reasons for human dignity. But mere rarity or difference is not excellence. The fact that man is an animal with an erect body, with a better brain and nervous system is of little relevance. Nor can we defend human personality on the basis of some attainments which pertain only to a few, such as the fact that one is physically more powerful or mentally more gifted than another. Facts like these are not radical, universal, or permanently important characteristics of all men. St. Thomas Aquinas gets us to something fundamental in his beautiful treatise on God's providence in *Summa contra Gentiles:*

> There ought to be some special kind of providence for intellectual and rational creatures over and above the care given to other creatures. For they excel other creatures both in the perfection of their nature and in the nobility of their end. They surpass others in the perfection of nature because only the rational creature is master over his action since he freely moves himself to operation, whereas other creatures are moved to their specific activities rather than act of themselves. They surpass others in the excellence of their end because only an intellectual creature reaches the supreme end of the universe by his own act of knowing and loving God, whereas other creatures cannot attain the ultimate purpose except in a distant participation of its likeness.[2]

To these two basic reasons for human superiority we may add a third one based on God's supernatural gifts to man, which no lower creature receives. We have in man's nature, end, and supernatural status the three fundamental titles to his dignity. Clearly the eminence of man is found to lie in his formal and final causes and in the supernatural elevation of both of these, but no notable uniqueness comes from his singular efficient and material causes. The God of nature has made all things, not only man. His creative touch has put goodness in all things, yet a special goodness in man. As we have elsewhere seen, the material cause of man, his body, borrows its dignity from the soul.

2. THE EXCELLENCE OF HUMAN NATURE

All the marks of a person indicate superiority in some respects. As a rational suppositum, he is a substance. Substance is better than accidents, appearances, and operations which exist in and for the sake of the substance. As an individual being, honored by his own proper name, the person is a real being. He is not an abstraction, not a universal, not a logical class. He is a complete being in himself. But the goodness of the whole surpasses the goodness of the parts and members considered separately. This excellence of the whole is reflected in the well-known axiom that the parts, powers, actions, passions, and accidents all belong to and are attributed to the person.

In this whole human nature, the spiritual soul must be singled out for its special worth. As form, it is the principle of life and, therefore, the reason for the superiority of the person over nonliving creatures. Because it is spiritual, it is the noblest of forms, having that independence and wide scope of activities which characterize spirit and enjoying a more immanent life than vegetative and sentient things. As immortal, the soul excels anything material which must be perishable, temporary, and subject to loss of its self-identity. This immortal self-identity of the human soul also shows one facet of its superiority to human societies and institutions, which are impermanent and can claim only a moral identity of purpose and structure, together with an ever-changing membership.

Spirituality is the foundation for that intelligence and freedom which best indicate the uniqueness and essential superiority of man.

For many reasons intelligence is a wonderful possession. It is the most immanent form of life because of its spirituality.[3] While matter confines things within their own being and restricts them to one place and one form, spirit breaks free from many of these restricting bonds and is open to other realities and, as it were, enters into them by understanding them and makes them its own by representing their forms in its own knowledge. Besides leaping beyond the shell of the self, the intellect also pierces beneath the material surfaces and phenomenal accidents of bodies in its immediate environment. Man knows the nature or essence; he can know the universal and immaterial; he roams over past, present, and future; he can penetrate to the unseen and the causal, to the actor and meaning and purpose behind the visible deed; he grasps the rhythm of reality and the laws by which it acts; only God the unlimited is the limit of his mind's scope.

Moreover, he can know himself; he is conscious of his own being, and not merely of his acts. This is a better way of possessing one's nature than unconscious existence or lack of knowledge of one's own existence, nature, and destiny. "The proper study of mankind is man" — though not only man. Through man there enters the universe that understanding which we try to describe as light and victory, as the expulsion of the darkness of ignorance and the conquest of error. The world within and without is all opened up to the comprehension of intelligence. With knowledge, as we concluded under beatitude, happiness comes into human life in a way that surpasses all lesser pleasures of sentient existence.

Having the ability to relate experience with reality, to unify things and their parts, to classify and find the pattern, to bind event with event, effect with cause, means with end, part with whole, present with future, the intellect has a capacity for novelty, invention, and improvement. Visions of order and original developments take shape before its glance. Intellect, joined with other powers, can retrace the history of one's own life, correct its mistakes, supplement its deficiencies, profit by repeated experience. Spiritual intelligence invents language, puts its thoughts on record, accumulates human traditions, consciously imitates other human beings, organizes ways of learning, and shares its experiences and discoveries with others. Through intelligence culture enters the world with all its splendors of the arts, the tools, the schools, the sciences, the economic and social institutions, the laws and the religious activities which are monumental triumphs of man's uniqueness.

By the presence of man on earth physical space becomes transformed into a moral universe. Thought makes possible and actual this moral realm where man explicitly knows the purpose of his own life, forms his plan for achieving it, guides himself, develops his habits by the influence of reason, illumines his interior life and motivation by conscience, and recognizes the ideals of law. In this same moral realm man shares rights and duties and the interior life of the spirit with other men; he helps and is helped by them in leading the good life.

"How infinite in faculty!" said Shakespeare, "in apprehension how like a god!" Scoffers at man may compare his bodily size and strength with the huge and countless worlds that burn in his telescopes. But is size significant? Only man is the thoughtful astronomer who knows of these worlds and is so curious about their secrets. "He is made a little less than the angels."[4]

Intellect's companion gift of free will reveals another aspect of man's singular worth. This power working with intelligence performs acts of consent and of choice. These acts of the two powers are called human because they are distinctive of man's special endowments of intelligence and liberty. In these acts man reaches a special peak of perfection, for here he is his own master, lord of his own activities, able to acquire for himself many deliberately desired goods which his intellect makes known to him.

Man is free to rule over himself and his own life and to pursue his own purposes, always of course with God's assistance. His freedom has bounds, to be sure. Moral constraints try to channel his choices toward the good. Physical needs, motives, habits, and other factors affect him. Yet where he finds alternatives, he can make his own preferences; where he discovers better ways to his personal goals, he can initiate action to follow the better way and get the finer result. He can over-rule his own passions by not consenting to them. He need not be the victim of his own feelings, no more than he need be the captive of circumstances and the slave of his historical fate. As a master who controls by insight, choice, and command, he can organize his powers, and direct his own intellect, senses, motor nerves, and muscles to work for his own good. He has power to change his goals and his courses of action, to modify his own mental and voluntary habits in many ways, and even partially to undo his own mistakes. Man breaks clear of the prison of environment and the web of his own past even more by liberty than by thought.

With will and freedom, spiritual love enters the world. Man loves whom and what he wishes to love; and among people he selects those whom he will love well. His love he directs to his family, to his benefactors, to the needy, even to his enemies, and most honorably to God. At last, after geological aeons, in a free man God's formal glory exists on earth; someone knows God, admires Him, thanks Him, and loves Him. Knowing God's will, someone on earth now voluntarily obeys God and strives to grow in loving service of the source of all goodness and love. Man's love is his own gift; no one else can give it or force it.

Endowed with intelligent freedom, the person is a moral being. He is the subject of moral law, guided in his choices not by physical compulsion but by moral obligation. If he follows the known obligation, he becomes better and ever freer to do better and better things. Since man foresees consequences and unconstrainedly does the good which he chooses, he is in a true sense author and owner of the good that he accomplishes. It is his personal achievement, a good which would not have existed unless he had chosen to do it. Hence, it is credited to his praise and may give him a title to a reward. Free action is a form of causality; it is productive of good; it is a loving way of enriching reality. It deserves to be regarded as one of the glories of a man. When he serves God by his loving willingness to follow God's commands about the good, he is exercising a royal prerogative, he is acting as a ruler who creates and gives the good. Hence, it is said that to serve God is to reign.

Being free, the person has the wreath of personal rights to protect his autonomy and give him the opportunity to keep his own goods and improve them. We shall return to this theme of rights. One of these rights is that of choosing his associates and uniting with other persons in willing and well-ordered co-operation for some common advantage. Man is not driven in social situations by mere instinctive herd impulses. He freely joins his fellows and retains in society the dignity of his liberty-loving nature. Marriage is the free gift of personality by the lovers. Political institutions, which free men set up, do not close the door to rightful personal liberty, but rather protect and enlarge it, control and humanize it. Indeed, the political order of law, duty, and right, binding men in common tasks for common goals, is itself one of the greatest achievements of human liberty. Liberty rules itself for the sake of justice and the greatest good of all within the state.

Having some insight into nature's operations and into his own nature, and being free, man has some measure of physical control over his own nerves and muscles, and through them and human tools he reigns over the external world. Liberty thus presents a double relation to the realm of matter: a measure of independence of mere physical forces and a measure of mastery over these forces for the good of men.

It is wonderful to be a person and able to determine the very attitude or spirit with which one acts, works, loves, and lives.

3. THE IMAGE OF GOD

The spiritual nature of man is the justification of man's noblest name, the image of God. The Creator, like any other cause, made all His effects resemble Himself in some degree. Other visible creatures have so distant and slight a likeness to God that they are called vestiges, traces, footprints, so to say, of God's infinity. God, however, is Himself an intellectual and free being. He copies His own style of being in making man. He endows man with knowledge, freedom in his decisions, and power to be a principle of his own works by his free acts. Built according to God Himself as the model, man is an image, analogously like to God Himself. No measure of dignity could be greater than its degree of likeness to the infinite dignity of God. Everything is rated in proportion to its likeness to God and to its principle. According to these two standards, a human being deserves a very high rating; and his rating improves the more his good deeds and his merits draw him closer to God. St. Thomas distinguishes the image of nature, the image of grace, and the image of glory as successive approximations to the divine Original. In all these levels the best reason for claiming a godlike quality in man would seem to be man's own act of knowing and loving God. Here man's activity is akin to that adorably perfect act whereby God eternally knows and loves Himself.[5]

4. EXCELLENT IN END

The possession of God, we have seen, is man's destiny. He is made for the same end for which God exists and acts. This is not only the best possible end that a creature can have; it is also one's own highest good, meant for each person, and measured by the degree of merits and graces of each. No other end lasts forever. Each individual person is permanently sacred to God, made for his individual immediate possession of God in return for his immediate service.

The person then, unlike a mere thing, exists primarily for his own welfare. No one but God owns man. Having or being an end in himself, man is not a mere means to another's welfare, a tool of a superior, a toy for another's entertainment, a cog in the state machine, or a mere link in the chain of life of the race. Man is a part of the universe and of its total perfection; but he is not subordinate to the universe.[6]

5. The Crown and Lord of the World

This many-sided superiority of human nature and destiny makes man worthy to be referred to as the jewel of the world, "the paragon of animals," the masterpiece of the visible universe, and the master over material things of every sort.

Man, the prince of space and time, has been named a microcosm or tiny universe for several reasons.[7] His nature combines in one being the perfections of all levels of being: material, plant, animal, and spirit, though he has not the fullest perfection of some beings at each of these levels. He is then both a representative of all types of beings and a sum of them. In mind and will, too, he is a microcosm for his is the capacity to possess the forms of all by knowledge and to unite himself to all of them by appreciative love. The order of the universe of being is reflected in his mind; a bit of the universal harmony is mirrored in his grasp of the size, the structure, and operations of nature. To some extent he impresses the order of his mind on things by his power of controlling matter to his own purposes; the useful and fine arts both bear witness to this influence. The beauty, too, of all creatures finds a special integration in the human body and face and in the human soul which both has its own beauty and captures the beauty of other things by contemplative admiration.

Being the crown of the world in his nature and in the development of his powers, man is also in a position to be the rightful crowned head who rules the inorganic, plant, and animal kingdoms for his purposes. As less perfect, they are properly servants of his needs, both bodily and spiritual, and instruments for his whole human development and higher perfection. They have no individual and absolute end of their own; their special part is to help man well. While man is not the measure of truth and cannot modify the truth of nature, yet he is the measure of the value of natural or artificial things. It is part of his lordly office that he has been constituted by God as His helper in caring for the earth, in better adapting it to human use through science and invention, and in producing more goodness and spreading it more widely over the earth.

6. Object of Special Providence

St. Thomas, mindful of this topmost position of man in the hierarchy of nature, wrote two magnificent chapters in his *Summa contra Gentiles*, in which he draws out the fact of God's special care for each rational creature. To God each man is important; each may be said to be "God's darling." God governs man for his own sake since He made man for his own good. He governs other things for the sake of man and shapes them toward man's welfare. St. Thomas also insists that the personal acts of each human being are *individually* governed by God. Of all visible creatures, only rational animals are capable of being directed in their actions not only in matters suitable to the species of which they are members but also in matters immediately pertinent to their personality. For man has intellect, whereby he can see the varied ways in which a certain thing is good or evil in relation to various persons, times, and places. His is not an instinctive, uniform pattern of thinking and acting for his good. Each individual human act is something unique, personal, immediately relevant to man's last end. Hence, divine government of this action accommodates itself to the individual or personalist character of each act.[8]

While in mere matter the mass and its collective action are important, in the case of spiritual beings the single life and the single human acts are important, for each act can be an immediate loving tribute paid to God and for which God will be eternally thankful.

7. SUPERNATURAL EXCELLENCE

The third basic title to dignity is a supernatural one which must be presented here for the sake of a complete view. Catholic theology teaches that God offers and gives sanctifying grace as a gratuitous endowment to men. Men can refuse it or lose it. But those who have it are more than mere human beings. By this grace they become adopted children of God, His friends, brothers of Christ, and heirs to heaven, which is their Father's estate. They become a much more intimate image of God. The gifts of grace transform their human nature, healing, improving, and uplifting it to a divine plane of being. Without losing any good natural endowments, graced men are "sharers in the divine nature."[9]

At the same time all the ignobility of original sin as well as of serious personal sin is removed from graced souls. New powers are conferred, of which the chief are the habits of faith, hope, and divine charity for God and for men. The believing intellect is opened up to a fuller world of religious and moral truth. The will obeys with filial freedom. Powered by grace, human acts done in God's service merit supernatural rewards and properly prepare man for beatitude. The more grace now and the more excellence now, the more reward hereafter. The social nature of man is expanded through living membership in the Mystical Body of Christ, Christ's own Church. The precious gifts conferred on the soul also enhance the body's dignity, making it the temple of the Holy Ghost, a sacred place. It is consecrated by contact with the Body and Blood of Christ in Holy Communion.

Proportionate to this immensely greater supernature is a new and higher end for man. The redeemed and graced Christian nature is able to enjoy the beatific vision of God and life with his Father forever in heaven. The human body, too, is to rise in glory, partake in the graced perfection of the soul, and copy the glorified state of the risen Body of Christ.

To give this sanctifying grace and its retinue of favors, to remedy the degrading evils of sin, to share in man's lot, and to teach man to know his own worth, the Son of God became man, uniting in Himself Godhead and the human nature of Mary's Son. In His personal tender interest for each person, God sent His only-begotten Son into the world to make us aware of divine esteem for us by paying the great price of His sufferings and death for each of us.[10]

8. Reverence for Man

A vision of human dignity is one of the capital prizes of philosophy. By this sense of honor to himself man should measure his conduct also to others. One of the main norms of culture consists in the degree of men's esteem for human nature. Men can, it is true, profoundly exaggerate their own importance, overrate their abilities, and overlook their moral faults and other shortcomings. We need the balanced view of both the grandeur and the misery of man, of native nobility and individual defects.[11] But failure in self-respect is as serious as failure in humility. One of the worst miseries is not to know, not to care, or even to falsify the high position of man.

Many ideologies today have a low regard for man and abet current inhuman practices. One factor that is often charged with leading to intellectual depreciation of man is the so-called Copernican revolution which has made us realize that the earth is a pigmy planet. But only a materialist should feel that bigness and physical centrality are conditions needed for spiritual greatness. Another intellectual current, the Darwinian reduction of man to animal ancestry, has tended to wash away much belief in man's descent from God. The Marxist contempt for the individual, while protesting the excesses of individualism, cheapens the person and glorifies the mass. Literary realism with its emphasis on sin and crude vulgarities has helped to villify man. Together with these, we have the adulation of the omnipotent state, the Freudian definition of man as a bundle of not so honorable pleasure-loving and pain-avoiding drives, and the dusty relics of the pagan disrespect for woman as principally a sexual object or animated toy who is not a human person fully equal to the male.[12]

Modern action far too often shows a revolting brutality toward human personality. The totalitarian regimes have been the principal offenders with their degrading police methods, invasion of the home, concentration camps, abuse of prisoners, collective guilt, mockery of legal procedure, scorn of opponents, deliberate promotion of war, and complete neglect of honor in dealing with their own people and other nations. In addition, we find in many parts of the world and in wide areas of action more than a little desecration and persecution of minorities and various underprivileged castes and races. Less common but sufficiently symptomatic are the indignities of hazing, harsh dehumanizing of military recruits, and mistreatment of hired help in some types of labor. "A man's a man for a' that," said Robert Burns. We stand to gain much in joy in life if we heed St. Leo the Great's famous cry: "Christian, recognize your dignity." One may well agree with Mr. Frank Sheed in his *Society and Sanity* that the recovery of reverence for our fellow men is one of the great needs of our times.

Reverence recognizes the dignity of each man, even of the infant, the poorest, and the sinner, all of whom may have those same basic natural goods which we honor and love in ourselves. Reverence for personality would respect both the person and his rights; it would eliminate injustice and cruelty; it would respect liberty. Respect for others would give them much contentment, and this would redound to better industrial peace and more cordial relations. Reverence would cure us of our materialistic myopia which sees live human beings only as hands forced to fit into the economic system, as statistics in a census table, as tools geared to the whims of political powers. Reverence would be fruitful in more general sincere chastity in dealing with the bodies of others. Regard for the sacredness of persons would deepen our sense of the sacredness of the family. Then two old rules of Christian manners would flourish once more in society: "To see the image of God in each person and honor him accordingly"; "To feel interiorly that each person is my superior and to show him due exterior honor and deference." To be blind to this divine image and to withhold this honor in the very presence of God is like despising a masterpiece before the face of its author.

The restoration of dignity, rights, and decency requires first of all, as the American bishops[13] have indicated, a recovery of our reverence for God. Honor to Him will flow more and more into true honor to men who are loved by God. There must be a general and genuine spirit among men that men's rights are as sacred as human personality and that the main practical expression of respect is regard for the human rights of others. Progress in government and in international relations today must have the recognition, defense, enrichment, and hallowing of human rights as one of its great aims. Hence, the United Nations Universal Declaration of Human Rights is a most important forward step, as it outlines some of the major claims of personality that any government should have at heart. The United Nations' action to defend these rights by diplomatic and other pressures is also much to be desired. The increased activity in American jurisdictions to clarify and protect rights in sound labor laws, fair employment practices acts, civil-rights legislation, and judicial decisions against discrimination are most encouraging. We also need clearer, constant education on these issues of the dignity of man, the close connection of liberty and justice, and the daily use of our rights in a social system that deprives no one. The popular confusion shown in discussions of academic freedom, loyalty oaths, congressional investigations of subversion, the privileges of the press to publish obscenity, and related issues indicate that liberalism and totalitarianism together have clouded many minds on true human dignity.[14]

A right is a person's moral power. It is a means granted by moral or civil law for the sake of a human good. As man has an end of his own and exists for his own good, he gets from God the needed rights to realize his own destiny and perform his duties to God. He is *sui juris*, the holder of his own rights. He is no one's property; he is not an object of common or public right, a being belonging to the state or to some group with loss of all autonomy of his own and of all means of protecting his liberty and all guarantees to just treatment. No one but God has a right over his being and destiny. The corpus of human rights must include the morally and legally protected power to possess, retain, and claim such natural goods as his own conscience, his own life, and his entire body; to use his mental and physical powers to support and improve life, and to associate with his fellow men for good and peaceful purposes. As man has also a supernatural destiny and the obligation to fulfill certain supernaturally revealed duties, he has added supernatural rights. These latter God-given privileges include, among others, his right to worship God as a Christian, to receive the sacraments, to have a religious education, to obey his spiritual superiors, to prepare religiously for death, and to care for like spiritual needs.

The dignity of man extends to all these rights. The practice of dignity implies full regard for man in the exercise of all his rights within their law-given limits. Liberty and equal justice are the daily ways in which we hold our fellow men as sacred. Because men are better than things, persons must precede things. Because no man is a thing, no man may be treated as a thing. He is the equal of every other man in the honor of personality.

Chapter 10

Growth in Living

1. The Starting Point of Growth

GROWTH Is one of those characteristic immanent activities which belong to living beings on earth. The growth of the human body, mind, character, and personality is fascinating. Man begins with so little; he can ascend so very high. At conception he is a microscopic one-cell body with a soul. The most marvelous development of all the structures, parts, and organs of the body has been completed by the time of his birth. This vegetative growth continues in the expansion of the body and in the improvement of the nervous system, bony frame, and sexual characteristics, both primary and secondary, until sometime between the sixteenth and twentieth year bodily maturity is reached.

At birth, however, human infants are still the most helpless, ignorant, and incomplete of living things. They have a few instincts, no habits, and no knowledge, whether sentient or rational. Yet coupled with this initial imperfection, they have astounding potentials. The human young have the liveliest desires to expand, grow up, and become strong. They have extraordinary vitality. They are boundlessly curious; all children by nature desire to know, to see for themselves, as they say. Playing is learning for them, and most learning is a delightful game. They love almost every aspect of life. They want to become acquainted with new things and make new friends. They like to experiment. They show energy and ambition. Often, they aspire to leadership. They display an almost fierce pursuit of happiness, willingness to love anything that is good, a ready adaptability and docility which support the process of growing. Even their dislike of going to bed in good time may be but one form of the eager appetite to live more by being awake longer. The young usually manifest a serene confidence that life is very wonderful. In their period of growing, youths clearly show that man is not perfect but that he is perfectible and is powerfully urged from within as well as by the world without to improve his being and life.

This fervid enthusiasm for growing must be rightly organized in the direction of suitable human maturity. It must be preserved from injury and any factors that may stunt or distort it. First, we ask what maturity is and then, how it may be reached.

2.   The Term of Growth, Human Maturity

Biological or organic maturity is relatively easily achieved by good health habits, parental care, and protection from physical injury and disease. Although muscular and neurological skills can be continually improved for a good many years after bodily maturity has been attained in the late teens, the adult's problem in regard to the vegetative and sentient powers is mostly a matter of maintaining their well-being against decline.

But the spiritual powers distinctive of man are the chief perfectible factors of his nature. They seem to be capable of unending growth as long as poor health and aging nervous system do not handicap them. As God is the term of the powers of intellect and will, their full term of maturity must be the same as the end of human life, that enduring possession of God by knowledge and love. But earth should see some beginnings of this spiritual maturity in men's character and good habits.

It is not only because of the immaterial boundlessness of the soul's faculties, but also because of the number of his powers, the variety of habits possible to man, and the scope of needs to which he must fit himself that the human potential for growth is so very vast. The human person is like an orchestra with many instruments, each of which must learn its own part and play it well in concert with the other voices. One horn and one drum and one practice session do not make an orchestra; one power and a few habits do not make a human life. There are many areas of growth: bodily health, muscular strength, healthily working senses; there are memory and imagination, mind and will. There is need for ability to earn a living, moral formation, professional training, religious growth. All powers must grow together, in proper harmony with each other's functions, for all the main needs and opportunities of life.

In the encyclical on *Christian Education*, Pope Pius XI mentioned this need of attention to the complex nature of man in the processes of educating. Then he summarized centuries of Christian thought on the ideal of human maturity in a celebrated sentence.

> The product of Christian education is
> the supernatural man who
>   thinks,
>   judges, and
>   acts
> constantly and consistently
> in accordance with
>   the principles of right reason and
>   the enlightening example and teachings of Christ.[1]

This epitome of the goal of human growth in mind and will deserves some comment here and later in this book.

The mature mind must know all the necessary and important principles or truths for living; it must have considered the evidences for them, appraised their value, and learned to relate and connect them together. The mature mind is reflective, possessed of truth, and able to think with ease and accuracy. Such a mind is not only well-stocked with information, but it is a formed mind, possessing intellectual habits of wisdom, prudence, and the specialized kinds of knowledge that it needs in its own way of life.

The pope also tell us that the mature mind can judge well. Using principles as its guides, it can readily apply itself to solutions of ever recurring problems. The judicious quality of intellect is shown in a correct, calm, clear conscience that controls a man's moral decisions. It is also shown in a fair and tolerant judgment of others' views and conduct. It is a mind which can judge for itself, for it can move from principles to new conclusions and defend truth in new battlefields with the standard weapons of principles. Such a grown-up mind reads and forms its own judgments of what it reads, determining for itself whether the content is evident or not, proved or not, true or false, certain or probable, good or bad, settled or tentative. It can read a newspaper without being regularly taken in by propaganda, slogans, partiality, suppressions of fact, and sentimentality. It sees a film and often sees through the film. It does not have to lean on others' opinions, always drifting in its views. The highest and rarest form of good judgment appraises people on their objective merits and not by their position, flattery, or shade of skin.

Both in thinking and judging, the mature man should have a constant and consistent mind. Anchored in truth and in reality, a mature person adheres to truth even in the turmoil of clamorous passions about him. He can fit truths and facts together in a pattern of harmonious wisdom that stands the test of time and of the beating waves of prejudiced error and intellectual fads. The mind of such a man is unconfused on the essential issues of life; it is not disposed to compromise on truth; and being constant and consistent, it is not gullible, disloyal, fickle as a weather-vane in its allegiance. This steadfast equanimity is part of what we mean by balance of character.

The supernatural man, we are told, also acts constantly and consistently in accordance with principles. This maturity of action is the fruit of maturity of will in a person with a love of right values, needed moral habits, steadiness of spirit in fulfilling his responsibilities, and strength of purpose to do the will of God in all his acts. A person of this sort we recognize as having good character, stability, and dependability. He keeps on an even keel and pursues a steady course in most situations; his emotions are not forever puffing him about like gusts haphazardly veering a child's sailboat in many directions. Faithful to truth and principle, he does not run away from reality, but faces it as it is, with its troubles, with its novel demands, and with its opportunities that signal the time for new growing. The man of mature will recognizes that achievement is born only of effort and sacrifices; he is ready to make these to gain the genuine and long-range good. He is also rightly motivated, not just by a fear of evil and failure, but by a love of God and loyalty to all legitimate authority. An interior spirit, a willing love, a convinced loyalty marks his religious practice; he is very far from the man who merely conforms outwardly to rubrics and practices which he neither understands nor appreciates. Perhaps best of all, with an orderly mind and a will directed to the supreme goal of life, the mature man leads a life of good order. With order most good things come into life, and one of these is the ripe fruit of steady growth.[2]

As a social being, man also must progress in his ability to live well with others, to guide and help them, to be just and friendly with men, and to be unselfish in ordinary dealings with his fellows. One of the blessings of life is society's help to man in achieving maturity of every kind.

This little may serve for the present to show the many-pointed ideal of the maturation of all human powers. There is also more than one kind of human growth in these powers.

3. KINDS OF GROWTH

Two kinds of growth, the extensive and intensive, or the horizontal and vertical, are open to our higher powers. This is the same as the difference between bigger and better, between more and finer. We may illustrate by two gardeners. One of them is interested in growing more roses on his bushes; he is interested in extensive growth, numbers, plenty. The other is interested in better flowers, a hardier stock, a more colorful variety, a longer-blooming strain, a blossom with a more intricate pattern; he is interested in qualitative or intensive growth. So, too, in the arts and virtues of the spirit. One person desires to learn more subjects, to read more and more books, to work more and more problems, to offer up more and more prayers. The other desires to learn his subject better, to grasp deeper levels of meaning in the great dramas, to move on to more complex and original problems, to pray with better motives and fuller surrender of spirit.

This latter type of growth is preferable. One reaches a limit in the quantity of work done and the number of acts performed, for time and strength are finite. One can scarcely find a limit to qualitative improvement. In intellectual development of great distinction, limited man must at some period of life, perhaps not later than his twentieth year, devote himself to some specialty, suited to his talent, that can be finely trained. If specialization begins too early in life, it may result in narrowness and in that "pinpoint man," who is criticized in much educational literature. Too exclusive specialization may give us an expert in his field, but a person who is less human for being an expert. Charles Darwin,[3] who gave up his interest in music and literature for science, confessed to the mistake of being too preoccupied with his scientific generalizing. But besides stopping growth, specialization sometimes defeats itself. A physicist who neglects the result of atomic fission on the human body may disintegrate himself as a reward for his curiosity. A clergyman whose interest in theology keeps all knowledge of human economic woes out of his mind may find himself preaching to empty pews and himself plunged into economic woe. Accordingly, some breadth of interest and some continuing extensive growth should parallel intensive improvement.

The difference of growth toward the good and toward the humanly evil, improvement or decay, is another mode of growing. More important for our present purpose is permanence in the development achieved. This leads us to the theme of human growing through gradual acquisition of desirable qualities of mind and will and of other powers subject to the guidance of reason.

4. GROWTH OF HABITS

It may not be too much to claim that of all youth's opportunities the most golden is the chance to form good habits. Men have no habits, good or bad, to begin with. They have the eagerness to learn, the energy to act, the plasticity in their powers, the adaptability of their unformed state, and the years before them to grow habits. The preciousness of their opportunity may also be estimated by the advantages which habits confer on man.

Habits are permanent or comparatively stable dispositions of the different powers of man to act in a given way.[4] A single power may have a considerable number of habits and team with other powers in habitual action. Once a good habit is won, it remains long, and, if exercised, remains for life. Because of this perseverance of habits they continue for years to promote good activity by a person and to make him secure in the goods that come from this habit. Moreover, habits make for facility in action. This ease saves effort, economizes our energy and time, helps us over the hurdles required by the effort to begin something and carry it out well. Because of this saving of time, effort, and decision, a person is freer to do other things and grow in other ways. Good habits free us, bad ones bind us in chains to what we would prefer to be without. Because of the grip that habit has on nature, a good one more or less permanently resists the lure of undesirable evils and thus gives some measure of guarantee in the continuing pursuit of good. As nature always acts in the same way, habituated powers tend always to act in the same way so that habits are often spoken of as second nature. Therefore, Amiel[5] has remarked that habits count for more than maxims in the conduct of life, for they are maxims come to life and existing in the flesh and substance of life. The person with a habit does the right thing with a certain pleasure in its performance; and pleasure is always an asset in carrying out duty. Habitual action, then, is more regular, more accurate, better done, and more satisfying in its results.

One may check these qualities and advantages in some examples like the habits of typing, good piano playing, correct English pronunciation, or courtesy to women.

We need many habits in life; the more good habits, the better for us. We need health habits, study habits, work habits, communications habits, social habits, prayer habits, and others. We need habits specially fitted to our needs, duties, personality, and sex. There are some habits, however, that everyone needs just because he is human.

Habits are not inborn, but are the products of growth. They begin with a disposition or a capacity to form the habit, if you wish. Some of them grow easily, none of them grow automatically. All require activity or exercise of the initial disposition in the power. Hence they are children of practice and are products resembling the acts that produced them. Like acts form like habits.

Several of the laws of practice are well known and are common to habits of many classes. One rule is that the practice or performance of the act must be correct and increasingly correct, if possible. Many hours of using the typewriter do not develop the habit of satisfactory typing unless there is correct practice or correct technique; incorrect practice at most develops muscular strength, and at worst, habits of bad typing. A second clue to formation is that the more intelligent the practice, the better. Intelligence thinks out the problem of habituation, selects the right means, strives for correct technique, finds opportunities for practice, and in general commands the powers of man that must co-operate to develop the new permanent quality which we call the habit.

The gaining of moral habits or virtues requires practice accompanied by the right motives. This is so, not merely because we will not persevere in practice unless we have clear and strong motives, but also because any moral virtue — prudence, justice, courage, or any other — must be a habit of performing morally good acts. An act is morally good only if it is done for a worthy motive. For example, the habit of praying or of attending Mass must arise from repeated acts together with the motive of pleasing and honoring God or of doing one's duty to Him. It is not formed by someone, however often he prays, if his motive is to be praised by parents or to avoid trouble or merely to conform to the customs of those with whom he is living. Without the right motive the moral virtues do not grow. Even if their acts have been frequently performed, the routine or seeming habit dies fast when the false or inadequate motive disappears from life, as when praise is no longer given or conformity is no longer demanded.

Another help in building habits and in ensuring their permanence is to combine them with other habits. Such an integration or interconnection of habits is seen in family life. Here a whole set of habits of affection, respect, care, thoughtfulness, conversation, companionship, and household routines are bound together in the happy relation of husband and wife. Similarly, the moral virtues are interdependent and tend to grow together. For example, every act of kindness to a child must be marked by doing the right thing to the child at the right time, by moderation, and by at least a little courage in the effort to be unselfish to the child. All virtues require some prudence, some self-control, and some love. Hence, the development of one moral virtue often involves some, even if less, development of associated virtues. The intellectual virtues show a similar clustering. A great pianist must cultivate memory, imagination, sympathetic feeling, keenness of hearing, understanding of composition, exquisite nervous co-ordination, concentrated attention in spite of audience distractions, and other gifts. A great scientist must simultaneously be a keen observer, a good mathematician, a clever manipulator of specialized instruments, an expert in detecting relationships, and a good critic of his own and others' ideas in his field of study. Naturally, such high organization of many abilities gives a unity to life, experience, and action which is one of the finer rewards of the efforts that create such a symphony of the powers of human nature.

5. SOME CONDITIONS FAVORABLE TO HUMAN GROWTH

It cannot be too strongly stressed that human growth is a rational process, not an automatic one like instinctive responses in animals. Man must make himself grow, particularly in mental and voluntary traits. He must create his own psychological and social personality by using his own intelligence and freedom, God's grace helping him.

In this sense his maturity or immaturity, his human perfection or imperfection, is his own doing; he may be said to be a self-made man. Though others can help him, he must do the main part by wise choice and prudent persistent action.

He must recognize and guard against some of the factors that prevent growth. These include inaction, sheer drift on the wave of one's feelings, self-complacency, narrowness of interests. At all costs man must keep his own interior world from growing small.

Good sense in finding interests and attempting to develop one's self in a particular career is commendable. One's many interests must be made interlocking where possible. A time comes when high-grade development demands a simplification of interests and a concentration on doing what is best for the individual's talents and opportunities and dropping lesser interests into proper perspective.

Growth is usually faster and surer when it follows a good though flexible plan. That is why some rule of life helps to much progress in monastic groups. A regime of life suitable to our vocation and status will include a schedule of work, activity, recreation, and prayer, and an expanding body of means to be used in self-training. Then there will be regular practice and less waste of the opportunities that come to us. An orderly growth implies, too, some devotion to the rule of order in action: Do the necessary first, then the useful, then the pleasant. Whoever does not do the necessary fails. Though not all of life is serious work, yet its main tasks deserve our first and best efforts.

There will be no fidelity to a rule of life and plan of action unless there is constancy of purpose. One of the major secrets of success is firmness in pursuing the same noble aim over a long time. If the goal is grand enough, it is worth the patience and perseverance of learning and gradually improving. Inconstant wills do not arrive at human maturity, for they are volatile in the use of means. Persons of this sort have a disorganized life, confused and conflicting objectives, and a lack of central purpose. Psychological studies of disordered personalities show this hopeless inconsistency of purposes in such people; and suicides have a bad record of lack of intention and of dispersed purposiveness in their lives. Stable personalities have clear, direct, and usually fairly exalted aims that are well understood and harmonized with their way of life.

The inner spring of growth is desire, continuous aspiration, especially for the big prizes of life. High aims evoke high desires and strong efforts. While low, petty, trivial, selfish aims will stunt our growth, and while easy satisfaction with self will warp personality, a big, noble, fruitful view of life and its possibilities will fecundate human powers and energize activity.[6] This never-ending stretching for the ideal is immensely quickened by a vivid personalized ideal. A living model of excellence evokes our social and imitative instincts and brings our feelings and our will's affections into the struggle for growth. A beloved mother or dutiful father exerts such a creative influence in a child's life. A friendly scientist, musician, or ballplayer has summoned up unguessed powers of human development from an admiring young heart. Above all the people of our own times, above all the heroes of history, the supreme personality of Christ stirs the idealism of young, growing hearts and supplies a permanent inspiration to reach the highest peak of human perfection.

It has often been said that the crucial test of growth is how one fits into reality as it actually touches his own life. We must live in the world, with other people, and with ourselves. We must live with our environment, with our heredity, with our own needs and shortcomings, with our own possibilities and our own obligations. In this real situation in which God's providence locates us, we prove ourselves mature or immature, equipped with the needed habits of living happily or wanting in these. To flee reality is to retreat into failure, to invite decline, to stop growing, to start decaying. Since we must live with reality, we can grow only if we keep ourselves united to God, for He is the most real of the real; to ignore Him or separate ourselves from Him is to lose the full splendor of living. One of the troubles of many sinners is that they have never grown up.

The need of fitting into the scheme of being as it is also shows us our need of absorbing the best traditions of our family, our church, and our civic community. In our real lives we belong to these several real social spheres. We receive from these societies an inheritance of truths, values, and ideals. As new needs arise in our own lives, we go forward with these traditions as our companions and advisers; we solve new problems; we do our part both to preserve, to strengthen, to add to, and to hand on the tradition to the young of coming generations. A man without traditions has little food from the granaries of the past on which to nourish himself. If he is not only without traditions but hostile to them, he will be a chameleon, an opportunist, a man unable to grow because of no constancy of principles and of values.

These suggestions on growth must include a comment on the social nature of the young and on our chances to help them grow. The young need an atmosphere of affection, encouragement, and right example if they are to grow well, fast, and straight. They need wise and kindly guidance that understands them personally. They need an atmosphere of freedom in which they are not too confined, forbidden to act, and prevented from finding themselves or exercising their own free wills or discovering their own talents. An atmosphere of force, impersonality, and dislike does not foster that personal responsibility and confidence which their future adult lives will demand of them in self-guidance, self-mastery, and self-propulsion to the good. As social beings, all of us in one role or another are giving example, directions, helps, or hindrances to those younger than ourselves. But we ourselves are growing as we help youth grow. That is one of the reasons why a growing family is a constant schooling of character and virtue for parents and even grandparents.

Specific attention to opportunities and means of growth will be given in coming chapters on the intelligence, on the will, on the life of grace, and on union with God. As we grow, our human dignity increases. Since the real maturity that lies ahead for the good man is eternal union with God, this end dictates the main line of human growth and the chief means to the end. It convincingly establishes that the growing life is ever ascending to God. The saints are so humanly mature and perfect because they have made that ascent. If you want a human runt, look among sinners; if you want a full-grown giant, look among the saints.

CHAPTER 11

The Intellectual Life

1. THE LIFE OF THE INTELLECT

OUR EARLIER studies on the intellect have shown it to be a living spiritual power capable of performing many kinds of acts that are naturally superior to sensations. Intellectual activity is a chief feature of man's happiness on earth and in beatitude. Reason accounts for much of man's special dignity. Intelligence functions in union with the will and with it controls man. It is the face or window of the soul that looks on the world without, to man's being within, and to God above. The intellect, ignorant at birth, must learn everything and form its own habits.

Like any finite living power that is still growing, human intelligence needs its own nutriment. Reality is its "food," as truth is its life. The mind is well nourished and stores up truth when reality measures its judgments and the mind responds to the stimulus of reality, not by changing reality, but by conforming itself to objective being. Truth arrives in the mind when the intellect says what being is or what it is not, just as reality in itself exists before its presentation to the mind. This feasting of the mind on reality is frequently described as a possession of the other as other, for it gives something new to the mind and gives reality a second presence in the knowing power though the object keeps its own being distinct from the mind. Somewhat as a child's hand when it imitates the motion of an airplane remains a human hand and yet becomes a moving plane, so analogously the cognitive mind remains itself and yet captures in itself the being of the known object. Once the mind knows, it stores its truth in memory and habits. Its capacity to grow is unlimited, for everything is real and God, the unlimited, is real, while the mind's object is simply whatever in any way is.

As reality is important, truth or knowledge of objective reality is important. Truth makes us human and makes us be more completely ourselves, for it is the fulfillment of our distinctive human power. Truth keeps us sane, for it sees and accepts reality as it is and anchors our life and reasoning in evidence. Truth colors life for good or for bad. Right ideas, valid judgments, and large views glorify man's mind and lead to the most valuable results in life. Truth makes us free, as the Bible suggests. It frees us from the barriers of ignorance, the perils of error, and the disasters consequent on foolishness and falsity. It liberates us from much unhappiness and mere animality and lifts us above a barbaric level of mere subsistence in our struggle with nature. It strikes down the tyranny of superstition, banishes fear of the unknown and the illusions of dream worlds, and unseats the bitterness of bias. By transporting us to reality, truth attacks a self-centered attitude to life. Truth invites us to progress. It throws its beams ahead of us, showing pathways to better living and lighting up our road to God. Truth is even the beginning of charity.

"Not by bread alone does man live," Christ said to the tempter. It is the influence of true ideas on human life in time and in eternity which makes the vocation of the intellectual a highly significant one.

The intellectual is a person whose time, efforts, and way of life are largely taken up with the finding, contemplation, and teaching of truth. The object of his life is truth; to gain it he leads a life of study, research, and scholarship. In a teaching capacity he sows the good seed of truth in other minds.

That the world and the Church need intellectuals is nearly self-evident. Our need of experts in many lines of human endeavor is known. Our clamor for scientists is heard over the land. The power of intellectuals in the field of communications is widely conceded. The influence of great teachers has been lauded by the Church in the title given to her doctors as St. Bernard, *Doctor vitae*, the teacher of life, the man bearing life-giving words to men. The community rightly gives a high prestige to intellectual leadership both because of our human dependence on truth and because the life of the intellectual demands much courage, generosity, and arduous preparation. The worldly returns of the intellectual life, lean as they usually are, are no measure of the importance of this vocation.

2. INTELLECTUAL VIRTUES

Many excellent tips on the formation of an intellectual as an apostle of our times can be found in books such as A. D. Sertillanges' *The Intellectual Life*.[1] Here we shall discuss a few of the intellectual virtues in order to deepen our understanding of the character of the intellectual life.

Although we come into the world ignorant, we do have the senses and the intellect as powers to start us knowing. These powers, but particularly the intelligence, have a magnificent initial asset, the gift of curiosity or wonder, the native desire to know and understand. All men love to see; when well, they love to travel to new places; they want to know how things work and why; the child drives parents to encyclopedias by his eternal questioning, "why?" This curiosity is spontaneous, not learned, but needs to be directed and kept alive.

From this germ of curiosity and natural interest in reality human minds grow gradually until good intellectual habits, firm and unerring capacities of knowing and judging special categories of objects, are established. There are a good number of such *intellectual virtues*, as they are known. These good habits of the intellect include the many different human arts that are concerned with rational skills for doing and making things well, the various sciences, each with its special area of investigation and its peculiar methods, the wisdom of philosophy, the practical judgment of moral values and issues, and the theologian's wisdom about God's revealed truths. With care a person may develop one or several of these intellectual gifts or virtues. When he has done so, he is, for example, a qualified painter, a keen logician, a chemist, geologist, mathematician, or metaphysician.

But whatever intellectual abilities mature within him, the intellectual needs several traits of character to assist him in his enterprises of learning. These traits we call docility, love of truth, and studiousness.

Docility is teachableness, the readiness to learn, the humility to heed any true teacher. Its presence in children helps to explain why they often learn faster and better than adults. An intellectual would abuse the nature of the intellect were he to close it against sources of truth. He must be willing throughout life to learn from the wise, from the great books of our civilization, from the great teachers of faith, and from reality itself which is the basic teacher of them all.

The life of study and teaching demands also the love of truth, a desire for the objective vision of reality, single-minded sincerity in looking for truth and in accepting it. An intellectual living for power over nature, for wealth, for influence over rulers runs the risk of betraying truth to ambition or comfort. The Baconians, Machiavellians, and Marxists are not servants of truth but of a willed cause; they are all sophists who make man or their own wishes the measure of truth. What do even the great religious ideas matter unless they are also true, unless they are presentations of objective facts and objectively founded principles? The whole man must go out to truth without reserve, honoring it somewhat as he loves God — with all his mind and all his heart.[2] This sincerity has also a special reward in an easier discovery of truth, for the Irish proverb about merciful consideration of others applies also to truth-seeking: "Sure, and it's easy to see when you look with your heart."

A third characteristic required for the intellectual life is studiousness.[3] This habit of studying would seem to be a habit in the will, controlling the mental and other activities of a student in several ways. Studiousness moderates the eagerness to learn evil or even to learn good in an evil, nonhuman way. It tempers proud search for things beyond our abilities. It helps to check the peculiar dangers of a student's life, pride, prejudice, self-opinions, fondness for the merely novel, and the faults of wanting to win an intellectual quarrel rather than reaching and spreading truth. At the same time studiousness goads the student to apply himself correctly and constantly to the objective, to be diligent, attentive, and thorough. It assists him to the discovery and employment of right methods of study and right techniques in his particular field of learning.

3. The Contemplative Life

Devotion to the life of the intellect is an ancient ideal espoused by the great Greeks, the fathers of the Church, and monastic orders long before modern universities began to make the life of truth their major glory. Plato's philosopher-king[4] knows the anguish of the competition between contemplative delight and the active duties of ruling justly. Plato's dying Socrates looks forward to a pure intellectual life beyond the grave. Aristotle[5] came to a conclusion consistent with his intellectualism that the life of knowledge surpasses the life of the moral virtues; and his God is one whose life is thought about thinking, whose essence is self-subsistent thought.

Christian thinking owes something to this Greek tradition. But it has been prompted mainly by an episode related in St. Luke's Gospel.[6] On one of Christ's visits Martha attended to His needs while Mary sat near, feasting on His conversation and presence. Upon Martha's protest that Mary was not doing her share, Jesus defended her: "Mary has chosen the better part which shall not be taken from her." Our thinkers have explored the reasons why our Lord not merely defended Mary against a charge of idleness, failure to help her sister, or carelessness in hospitality, but praised her for choosing the better part. Why was it better?

The two Jewish sisters have been regarded as examples of two types of life, contemplative and active. Mary, the contemplative, is content with the company and teaching of her Master. Martha, the active one, is troubled with many details of housekeeping, of material welfare, of getting things done for others. The contemplative person gives his time and efforts chiefly to the contemplation of truth, and especially of the truth about divine things, for they are the highest. The active life is engaged chiefly in exterior works and has for its main spiritual concern the practice of the moral virtues. Between the two are many grades of what is called a mixed type of life, partly contemplative and partly active, such as the life of a teacher of religion or of a nun caring for orphans. In any of these ways of life as practiced by a Christian, charity for God and men is the motive and root of the meritoriousness of that life. In all these types of life we also notice that the intellect is busy, but the contemplative exercises the functions of speculative intellect that seeks truth as its sole aim, and the actionist employs the practical intellect which is interested in doing and making, in finding means to ends, or in applying truth to practical necessities and opportunities.

Why then is Mary's role preferred to Martha's? Why is it, in the abstract at least and apart from the individual's ability and vocation, the better? St. Thomas[7] assigns a number of reasons, most of which he picked up from Aristotle and the fathers of the Church. (1) Contemplation is a life of the intelligence, which is the best thing in man. (2) Contemplation can last longer than exterior activities; it is a less changeable life; and change is a mark of imperfection. (3) It provides a greater feast for the spirit and gives more peace. (4) As Aristotle taught in regard to the happy life, the contemplative life is more complete, for the person needs fewer things for the pursuit of such a life than does the man of affairs and of good deeds. (5) This life is more of an end in itself and loved for itself. The active life on the contrary is not for its own sake; it is pursued for the sake of another end. Hence it has the character of a means and subordinate good. (6) The greater leisure and rest of the contemplative life put it in a higher rank than the comparatively servile life of action with its infrequent periods of thought. This aristocratic notion may not appeal to us much today, but the seventh reason is important. (7) The contemplative life is ordered more to divine than to human things; and excellence may be gauged by the object of human activities.

This analysis of St. Thomas in the *Summa Theologiae* is expanded in some points in a lyrical way in the praises of the life of wisdom which open the *Summa contra Gentiles*.[8] Fortified by Aristotle's paean to wisdom in the opening of the *Metaphysics* and exalted by a chain of scriptural statements about wisdom, St. Thomas proclaims that the pursuit of wisdom is more perfect, more sublime, more useful, and more pleasant than all other human interests. It is more perfect because it approaches the beatitude of man which consists in wisdom. It is more sublime because it brings man to a closer likeness to God, the all-wise Creator, and thereby leads man to love God more and be more beloved by God. Its greater usefulness consists in its power to draw man closer to his immortal home. It is more delightful, for wisdom has no bitterness or weariness but only gladness to offer its friends. It is this joyousness of knowledge of the great truths that eludes the appreciation of those with little experience of the intellectual life. This joy seems to have three phases: the joyous wonderment of curiosity about reality; the great joy of discovery; and the lasting joy of contemplating the discovered truth. Before reality and especially the divine reality we are like children before a Christmas tree: the joy of anticipation of the promised beauty of the tree, the joy of finding the tree and their gifts, and the simple contentment of looking at it, admiring it, and rejoicing in it again and again during the holidays.

Newman has been the major modern exponent of the ideal of liberal education, of knowledge as its own end, of pure learning, of disinterested pursuit of truth, especially in his addresses in his *Idea of a University*.[9] Other modern philosophers, not under Mary of Bethany's inspiration, have given some attention to the same theme of the merits of the contemplative life. A peculiarly urbane, sophisticated analysis has been offered by Bertrand Russell.[10] He points out the fact that much theoretical knowledge turns out later to have indirect utility, as pure science so often becomes applied science. He recommends the contemplative ideal as something of a remedy for bad features of the modern world: its ruthlessness, the coarseness of its leisure occupations, and its imprudent inability to see larger ends and secondary effects because of excessive concentration on an immediate gain. Contemplation would help us to think before acting; it would have favorable influence on character formation; it would add some humor to life; and (Russell returns to his pessimism) it would afford some relief from the pain of living, for which no technical knowledge is an antidote.

At the very least the contemplative life is an ornament of humanity, and forms with flowers, music, and swinging on the lawn a part of our *joie de vivre*. It also has the great merit of not being power seeking, asking only to be free to find, relish, and hand on truth to those who seek it.

4. THE INTELLECT IN THE PRACTICAL LIFE

Perhaps the contemplative life is for the relatively few. But the life of the many still must make generous use of the intellect; and the more the use, perhaps the better for our human success and happiness. Training and expansion of intelligence and a willingness to rely on reason more than on force are among the objectives that almost all of us seek from education. Two areas of intellectual occupation deserve attention from every thoughtful man. The one is the role of the intellect in the conduct of the moral life. The other is the part of intellect in a cultured person's life.

Ten functions of the intellect in moral living merit our notice. To begin (1) with the human act. Only human acts have an ethical quality of goodness and merit. They proceed from knowledge, deliberation, and free choice, combining intellect and will in their performance. The will completes the act as human, as one's own. But knowledge must precede and guide the will in these moral acts. The clearer and surer the knowledge, the better for the will.

In other moral affairs the guidance of the intellect is also needed. (2) The intellect discovers the norm of morals, making the distinction between right and wrong, between one virtue and another, between one vice and another, and finding the reasons why any class of acts conforms to the moral standard or not. (3) The mind also guides the moral life by discovering the obligation resting on man to act or abstain from acting. It discovers the precepts or rules of the natural moral law, sees the prudential wisdom of obeying the law for our own good, and honors the duty of fulfilling the law for the glory of God our Lord. (4) It is to intellectual beings alone that added positive laws for human order are given. These, too, man will learn and follow, thereby intelligently co-operating with authority and the other members of society for the common peace and prosperity of human life.

The intellect again must be active in (5) conscience. Conscience is an act of the mind judging the morality of one's own proposed conduct, applying the law to one's own case, urging that this act is good and necessary for me now or that another act is here and now absolutely forbidden to me, or that a third course of action is good, permissible, but not binding on my present performance. After one's choice and action, conscience again witnesses to one's merit or culpability. All the names that we give to conscience show its intellectual character. It is a guide, a monitor, a judge, a witness speaking to us of good and evil in our personal daily pursuit of moral perfection.

The development of (6) the virtues is another work of moral reason. For the intellect discovers the good and so supplies the will with motivation and reminders of motives. It discovers goals, finds methods of practicing virtue, and marks out the line of the golden mean between excess and deficiency in moral action. The intellect itself is perfected by (7) the moral virtue of prudence, which is a controlling virtue for the finding and use of the right means to worthy human aims.

Prudence, in turn, is our great counselor to help us in forming the moral life of others, in wise advising, in deep insight into individual needs and concrete situations, in far-reaching perspective of consequences of proposed action, in catching the vision of the real issues in others' lives, and in inducing them to set aside immediate impulses, feelings, whims, and near views in favor of noble ways of living.

One prudential function of the intellect helps both ourselves and others. For we must teach ourselves by reflection how to profit from our experience. We need to estimate our successes and mistakes and something of the reasons for both. We need to be receptive to the lessons of our own and of others' lives, to the lessons of our own times and of past periods. Experience without reflection does not suffice for understanding experience and gaining moral profit from it.

The intellectual occupations of a cultivated mind can also be (8) a great help in the battle with temptations to do foolish and wicked things that would sour our lives. The fuller mind has many varied interests that can keep it busy and check its fall into idle meddling with evil. It has a quicker capacity to turn its attention to something interesting and safe and to concentrate on worthier objects of thought and affection. It is also armored against undue incitements to evil by the very fact that mental development usually brings with it a refinement of taste and choice that is spontaneously averse to coarse and worthless things.

Another mental activity which is a basic asset for leading a good life is (9) the habit of prayer. Prayer turns the mind to God and engages it with spiritual realities. It lifts the mind above the level of the worldly. Intelligence has an important part to fulfill in good praying, by presenting objects of spiritual love and resolution, by controlling attention as one ponders religious truths, and by deepening appreciative understanding.

Finally, (10) the crown of the moral life, the winning of beatitude, is an act of perfect knowledge.

A moralist, a practical man and not a contemplative, may well repeat the exhortation of St. Augustine: "Strongly love your intellect."[11]

5. MARKS OF A CULTURED PERSON

In addition to the part played by intelligence in moral growth, its functioning in any cultured person's life deserves some reflection. Culture in the personal sense, not in the social sense of the anthropologists, is practically impossible for some people. Grinding poverty, barbaric lack of written language, preoccupation with the struggle for physical existence, the heavy troubles of war times and of persecuting governments will impede cultivation of the intellectual life, of the arts and sciences and their many manifestations. But those who have some leisure and talents can in ordinary times become cultured men and women. They do not have to be highly trained intellectuals; they have something more than suave manners and social ease. They have the interests and attitudes, convictions and values, taste and good judgment that broadly characterize the superior person.

Their interests are not confined to bodily and material things and to the pursuit of bodily needs and pleasures. They will feel bodily sensations as keenly as other people, yet for them the enjoyment of food, clothing, sports, and sensory spectacles is a minor interest. Neither is their time and thought hemmed in merely by their business affairs and their workaday world. Their conversational gamut includes far more than talk of engines or production records, of bond markets and the high price of coffee, of ballplayers' averages, fashion's newest frills, and the latest scandal about Betty and Bill. If an educated man is one who thinks more than is necessary for survival, a cultured man is one who frequently thinks about something more than is necessary for his bodily entertainment and financial success. It must always be remembered that in some way we become the things that we know and love. To become better, we must know and love the better.

The cultured person has a wide-open mind with many interests and a spirit that delights in nobler things. He enjoys using his mind, for he is interested in truth and likes to keep on learning. He has a taste for ideas, not merely for information and news. He thinks that reading and discussion of humanly important issues is a regular part of life. He reads weightier and meatier literature, reads for insight into the human heart, for expansion of mind, and for renewal of guiding values. Books no less than groceries are his staff of life, and expenditures for both he regards as normal and essential. Because he is interested in ideas, he judges truths not persons, and so keeps himself from petty faultfinding and enmities.

Beauty, too, is a part of the cultured person's life. With breadth of interest all forms of beauty will attract him; and constant interest will lead to finer and finer taste and deeper appreciation of subtler forms of beauty.

The cultured person tends to grow intensively in intellectual gifts by pursuing the better things and the nobler values. Better books, better pictures, better and more functional household articles appeal to him. He prefers Shakespeare to the Cisco Kid without losing his capacity to appreciate the Western, the art song to the drinking ballad, the biography of a saint to a detective thriller, the secrets of the human heart written in the Bible to the confessions of the latest movie starlet. The cultured person also possesses a keen sense of humor and proportion, but is simply bored, if not disgusted, with the coarse and bawdy substitutes for humor.

Perhaps the attitude to truth and beauty and the things of the spirit is best told in the old proverb which counsels: "If thou hast but two loaves of bread remaining of all thy worldly goods, sell one and buy hyacinths to feed thy soul."[12]

Since the cultured intelligence is interested in spiritual goods, it is normal that intellectual life be highly compatible with holiness of life. A person may have one without the other, but culture and holiness are by no means competitors. The mutual helpfulness of intelligence and devotion and their very wedding can be seen in the doctors of the Church with their genius of intelligence and of sanctity, in St. Thomas More, prince of humanists, great lawyer, devoted father, spiritual writer, and martyr, and in St. Francis de Sales[13] and his circle in the early seventeenth century. God's children are the finest gentlemen and may have the finest minds as well as the most ardent hearts.

6. The Rights of the Intellect

If the intellectual life is to be cultivated to a degree worthy of man, it must be given opportunity, encouragement, help, and protection. Knowledge is not merely the gate to a better life and a social necessity in a democracy; knowledge is an indispensable necessity in any status of life humanly lived. To know God and glorify Him, to know his duties and obey the law, to understand his various obligations, and catch some of the fundamental spirit of living, man must use his intellect. This moral duty implies the minimum right that man may learn these ends, laws, and duties pertinent to his minimum human perfection. All men have a natural right to pursue such essential truth, to think, study, and be educated in these duties, to have access to the fonts of truth, to be helped by their family in acquiring truth, and to be protected from neglect and error on the part of those who can influence learners. The right to knowledge involves the right to be educated, and that involves the right of communication between men and association with those who know the truth and are capable of handing on the tradition of human perfectibility through intelligence. Hence, there must be guaranteed freedom to teach and to learn so that truth may prevail.

But freedom to educate and to be educated, as all other rights, has the usual limitations which arise from the purpose of the right, its title, and one's other duties. As the purpose of the right is acquisition of truth and man's personal and social perfection, error, prejudice, scandal, and falsehood have no rights to spread infection to minds and wills.

A person's other duties may properly limit his opportunities to learn, since all rights are operative within a framework of our duties and others' rights. One may not, for example, acquire a better education by neglecting his family or by stealing his tuition. Nor may one pry into private or public secrets to satisfy curiosity. One may not use magical means rather than natural ones. Nor may anyone learn out of sinful motives, for example, from a desire to make counterfeit bills. One may not defy social authority by violating some reasonable code of censorship, such as the Catholic *Index of Forbidden Books*, merely on the pretext of learning. But unreasonable restriction of means of communication whether through speech, press, radio, television, assembly, schools, and pulpits is a most serious political error and injustice. Only a clear evil or clear present public danger can justify authority in diminishing such rights. For such restriction again denies human dignity and flaunts our status as men with minds made for truth. It removes one of the stronger guards of our liberties. It is one of the tyrannies of a totalitarian state with an official ideology mandatory on its people. A government's rightful modest part is to provide means of knowledge to those who need them, and, therefore, to construct schools, set up library services, assist cultural institutions such as permanent museums, and finance scientific research in the public interest. Whether it has a duty to provide topflight education for all capable of intellectual leadership may be debated.[14] It seems to be a worthy political ideal to have a citizenry educated to its capacity.

CHAPTER 12

The Good Life

1. COMMITMENT TO THE GOOD LIFE

THE VERY fact that we are alive involves some love of life. Because our wills are made for the good, we love the good that we discover in life. Since our nature is built for happiness and happiness blooms from possession of the good, our being craves the good life. But human opinion widely differs on the constituents of the good life. Does it consist in exterior or inner goods and in which of these interior goods? Does it consist chiefly in the morally good life?

Any continuing type of experience, pleasant activity, or abundance that suits human desires or tastes wins the commending phrase: "It is a good life." For some, the good life means economic prosperity, a well-paying job, adventure or exciting travel, carefree carousal; for others, it means the life of a free people under a free government with morally sound objectives. The home life of an affectionate family that is not burdened with great poverty or illness is regarded as one of the finest of these temporally good lives. Aristotle's[1] description of temporal happiness as activity of soul in accordance with virtue, in a complete and fairly long life, attended by a sufficiency of fortune is another famous view of the good life. This is a life chiefly of the spirit, but stressing the intellectual virtues more than the moral ones, it would seem. St. Thomas seems on the whole to require three factors for a good and contented life: the absence of pressing physical wants, some intellectual life and especially the exercise of prudence, and the practice of the virtues of the will.[2] "A good life consists in good deeds."[3] Good deeds require good will and good habits; and both need the steady guidance of prudence.

The kind of human goodness which wins most human praise is

moral goodness, sustained action according to right choice, or excellence in character. Men prefer the right to the bright, the noble to the smart if they cannot have both intellectual and moral gifts in another. They may praise a great actress for her beauty and her versatility, yet pity her for her personal jealousies and immoralities. She is a good actress, but in their opinion she is not a human success because she is not a good woman. The financial wizard may be admired for his acumen and be despised for his ruthless methods. But men do not pity a virtuous mother because she is not a good actress, nor a patriot because he is not a scientist. They think that the chief form of goodness is moral goodness and that there is no substitute for morality in human life. Some elements of this good life will be considered in addition to those which have been previous topics of study.

2. "Man" as the Standard of Goodness

We need a standard for judging moral goodness and evil far more than we need a standard of weight for groceries or of power for our fuel. All men draw a line somewhere between good and evil; but there is considerable diversity of opinion about the right place at which to draw the line on the map of morality. Some men put certain acts into the zone of good which others locate in the zone of evil. It is important to know which human judgment in these moral issues is correct, for error may lead to serious consequences for one's self and others. Right living seems to presuppose knowledge of the right standard as a prerequisite to right choice. Parents, teachers, and lawmakers who must guide others to the good and keep them from evil must know the reasons why one act and its object are good and another act and object bad. These reasons are found in the standard.

This is all the more true because the very notion of goodness is relative to a measure or norm of some sort. Good means that which is suitable or beneficial to some thing. To what thing? It matters little that goodness is relative provided it be relative to some fixed standard. Just as we need not worry about the position of a freely hanging picture provided a fixed wall supports it, so we need not worry about the relativity of goodness if we have a true stable norm by which moral goodness or evil may be evaluated. One can see that it is a big mistake to confuse the merely useful, the socially correct, the legally right, the pleasurable, or the beautiful with the morally good because the object to which utility, legality, and pleasure are related is highly variable; therefore, it fails to be a constant and general standard.

The quest for such a stable norm and the debates over proposed standards have been a perennial occupation of the major philosophers. We may pass over the tangles of this debate and the complex terminology of its aspects and confine our explanation to the standard accepted by a great many modern scholastics.[4] In this view, the basic and immediate standard which enables us to judge why a human act is good or bad is man himself, the real whole human being. This standard gives the reason why the human act under scrutiny for its moral quality is good or bad: it is good because it suits human nature and is in no way unworthy of man; it is evil because it violates human nature in one or more features.

Which man is the standard? Which part of man is the standard? Which need of man is the standard?

The standard is man as such. He is "the man in all men." He is any man and every man, the universal man, the nature common to all men. Purely incidental differences between men, as of height, weight, or nation of birth, and purely individual needs cannot constitute a norm for judging all men. No principal part or power of men can be a sufficient standard, since it would leave us without a means of measuring moral goods and evils that affect other powers of the complex being, man. No single occupation or vocation in life can measure the needs of all men under all responsibilities.

Moreover, a norm for living men must consider man as he is in the objective universe. Actual man is a person in a huge universe whose members act on him and are acted on by him. In this universe he is cast in many simultaneous parts: as an individual and member of a community; a creature; a worker and consumer; a family man and a citizen. In this universe man is by nature inferior to God, by nature equal in essentials to his fellow men, and by nature superior to mere material things. He needs God, people, and matter, each for different reasons. He is related to each of these in fundamentally different ways and by different bonds. Hence, questions of preference among these relationships arise. Is a man good who treats cattle or monkeys as more sacred than human children; who treats men better than God; who puts the state before the family? The real man is also a historical being in a historical universe. To ignore the effect of history on man's needs, responsibilities, and rights would seem to be setting up a fragment of man as the standard of goodness and as a determinant of the rightness of his choices. Fragments are not the man as man, the man in all men. The major historical facts of religious history that have affected the whole human race and modern political developments which now demand an international society are significant in this understanding of the norm as human nature completely considered.

If we have sufficiently learned who man as such is, this norm is a highly serviceable one in helping us draw the line between genuine good and evil. The norm merely declares that man's own nature measures his conduct and should guide his mind in judging morality. To be good, man must live up to his true, whole humanity; he may violate no part of his humanity either within himself or in his essential objective relationships to other beings. To be morally good, then, is to act knowingly and deliberately according to all the specifications of this standard of human goodness. To be habitually good is to act constantly in conscious accord with this total standard. To be morally evil is to act intentionally against any of its specifications and spoil human nature. Intemperate drinking, for instance, harms the whole for the sake of the pleasure of a part; breaking an oath dishonors God and often harms one's fellow man; treason to country disrupts one's ties to society. In all cases, evaluation is based on conformity of the deed or omission to the total being and total good of the real man in the real universe.

The humanism and sanity of this standard strike us at once. Nothing could be more normal and wholesome than to be fully human and in no way to conflict with human nature. It is a unitary standard for all men, for man and woman, for child and adult, for ancient cliff dweller and modern suburbanite.

The norm calls attention to the fact that man lives not only in a physical universe but in a moral one as well. Man fits in this moral universe to the degree that all his powers are well regulated and all his relationships to other beings well directed. Within himself, the good man must maintain the order of human parts to the whole and regard the proportional importance of the parts. Outside himself, he must consider the hierarchy of values among beings: God before men; men before things; family before state; and so on, for other orders. He must also live in a concrete historical order, for he is a man wounded by sin, helped by grace, specially directed by God, caught in the web of complex international civilization, and perhaps personally committed to some status as husband or wife, as a professional man or a person dedicated by vow to some good work.

The norm is complemented in a very practical way by the law, especially by the natural law which is the basic divine law for our human nature. By itself the norm merely helps man to judge whether an act is humanly good or humanly evil, suitable or unsuitable to human nature. Law is needed to bind the will, to forbid the evil, to command the needed good act, and to grant rights to man that he may do good, avoid evil, and advance in his human perfection. What the norm is to mind and judgment, the law is to will and choice. Both are natural; the norm shows what natural goodness is, the law demands that human acts measure up to this norm. The two are related because the norm, man as such, is the objective evidence for the existence and precepts of the law of nature. Since God is the author of human nature, the natural law is but our Maker's instructions[5] insisting on right use of the nature that He has given us. Our reasoned knowledge of that law is our personal copy of these instructions. The maker of a television set or washing machine supplies instructions for use; and such instructions and warnings against misuse are regarded as wise and honorable; but the maker of the instrument cannot demand moral compliance with his instructions. God's instructions for our humanity are far wiser, for He has perfect knowledge of the natures which He has made. But God not only instructs, He orders us to follow directions. He commands the natural good because He knows it alone is good for us; He forbids the evil because He knows it is bad for the nature which is ours. It is His all-wise rule to treat everything, and man especially, according to its nature. But He will not treat man as less than human or be content with the antihuman in man's conduct.

The natural law which comprises the basic rules of truly human living is then the reasonable will of God for us, wisely directing us and authoritatively insisting that we safeguard, manage, and develop our human nature, and in no way hurt it. God simply wills man to be himself.

3. GOD'S GOODNESS AS THE MEASURE OF GOODNESS

Philosophers since Greek times have suggested a higher, truly ultimate, and more inspiring standard, to follow God, to measure up to a divine standard. This doctrine of the divine standard and man's imitation of the divine pattern brightens many pages of St. Thomas.[6] This standard does not merely mean that we follow the commands of God and bring ourselves into conformity with the divine plan for our living. It means that man, the image of God, should be an imitator of God. Both by the drive of his nature to come near to God and by his deliberate choice man should strive to perfect in himself the image of God, the ultimate good, and to make himself more and more like God by doing good as far as he can just as God does good out of love. The charity of God is the pattern of human perfection. But we should not misread the meaning of this godlike living. As we would think it silly to advise a beautiful woman to become as beautiful as God or a scholar to become as wise as He, so we do not advise a man to become equal to God in holiness. The achievable image can be only an analogical or imperfect likeness to God's being or goodness. It excludes anything contrary to God and being, for evil is nonbeing. Human goodness must remain a goodness proportionate to human nature, yet of a human nature which participates in the nature and goodness of God.

The advice to follow God and be like Him does not underrate the closer, more serviceable standard of man as man. For the truly whole man has an amazing affinity to God; to pursue the ideal of human wholeness is to pursue at the same time the ideal of godlikeness. A good life is a godly life, as the old phrase runs.

4. STAGES OF THE GOOD LIFE

We are not born morally good or morally evil, but must grow to be good men, and there are antagonistic forces within and without which must be managed for success in reaching the ideal. We can chart the stages of our progress to the goal of human virtue on these four foci: the beginnings of the moral life, growth within, influence on the world without, and perseverance to the end.[7]

Certain assets for leading the good life belong to human nature as a sort of birthright. We have free will with its natural capacity and tendency for the good known by reason. We have reason's natural ability to discover the good and to find the main precepts of the divine law for human living. We have some seeds of virtue or inchoate virtues which give us an initial desire and natural bent toward good. We want to be humanly normal and to live up to our nature. We all have some good will to start with. We can see much of this good will and un-spoiled judgment about virtue in children. They love the "good guys" and hate the "bad guys" in their television melodramas; they all love Snow White and hate the Witch. They are docile to good example; they take to training in acts of virtue; they welcome suggestions for good deeds. Without this natural good will toward virtue there would be no start and no recovery of the good life. Perhaps all unwarped human beings have some sense of shame, fear of evil, and desire to deserve honor.

The whole matter of our motivations or intentions reveals the paramount importance of this basic orientation toward the good proper to our nature. Intention is one's deliberate purpose in choosing or re-fusing. Intention is the very core of the moral life. Why do I do it? Why do I choose? For what reason? For whose sake? Is my act merely externally conformed to the usual rules of morality or did I mean interiorly to embrace the moral standard and unite my will with the will of God? Did I direct that act toward God or some good con-nected with Him or relatable to Him? Sincerity here is the beginning of moral conduct.

There are a number of valid moral motives, not all of equal worth. But no truly moral motive is opposed to man's supreme end. The supreme motive in action is to choose and perform good deeds for the love of God in Himself, because of His infinite goodness and right to glory from us. Other motives are gratitude to God, honorable respect for His majestic will, desire for divine rewards and the eager quest for beatitude as a fruit of our actions, and filial reverence for and fear of the justice of God. Even the motive of measuring up to one's humanity and dignity, of not hurting and disgracing oneself, though insufficient as a moral motive, is not ignoble. In the practical moment-to-moment moral situation we must use that motive or group of motives which effectively empowers us to do good and avoid evil here and now. But the whole tenor of our lives should be dominated more and more by the motive of love of God for Himself.

"That man has a right heart who wills what God wills."[8] In this striking truth St. Augustine points to a primary principle of the good life: the union of the human will with the will of God. Virtue re-quires more than the right act; it demands the right reason for it. This interior moral finality is far more important than the act itself. It elevates an otherwise unimportant act to the level either of love or of some other virtue inspired by charity. It excuses even misjudgments about the objective moral good, for love covers mistakes with glory. And the seemingly important deed without the right motive is deprived of its genuine moral value. Sincerity and clarity and purity of motive make the big difference.

To will the good and never do it is not enough. If we admired virtue without practicing it, we would show ourselves spiritually lazy. Nevertheless, he who wills a good deed in the sincerity of his heart has already accomplished it even though external circumstances should prevent him from executing his purpose. Rightness of intention, diligence in preparation for moral deeds, and readiness to perform are demanded of us, but success is not always ours to give or receive.

After hearing people talk of moral strength and moral weakness, we may wonder what these mean in terms of developing the good life? Moral strength scarcely refers in any verifiable sense to some growing firmness of the mind and will itself. It refers rather to a strengthening of the character by improving motivation and by constancy in action through better habits. This improvement of our intention implies not merely living for better motives and more consciously and vividly grasping those motives; it also implies a unification of motives that will in turn unify personality and make all life flow in one channel to the high objective of the love of God or of our beatitude or of some other motive focusing on the will of God for us.

In Chapter Ten, some psychological aspects of the growth of moral habits were noted, among others that (1) habit is characterized by firmness and constancy in performance of some definite type of action, by ease and even pleasure in such action, and by efficiency or correctness in operation; (2) like acts produce like habits; (3) moral habits or the virtues of the good life require the right motive; and (4) habits tend to cluster in related groups. Here we shall look at some of the moral aspects.

A habit of living according to the standard of reason is called a good habit or a moral virtue. There are four big families of these, named after the cardinal or key virtues of prudence, justice, temperance, and courage. Each of these families has a number of branches and relatives. Justice, for instance, has three distinct species: justice among equals, known as commutative justice; justice of the state or society to its members, known as distributive justice; justice of the members to the social whole, commonly called legal justice. Justice also has a number of relatives including religion, filial piety, patriotism, penance. Temperance has a family of its own, made up of such virtues as abstinence, sobriety, modesty, chastity, friendliness, and others. We need not here discuss all these virtues; but to understand the good life we must realize that they are numerous.

Each virtue is good for us. No virtue excludes another or competes with another. Yet one virtue does not necessarily imply another and especially not every other. This we can see from experience. A man who is very just in business affairs may be harsh in his dealings with his family or not too careful about moderation in drinking. A very pure woman may have a biting tongue. These gaps in the spectrum of virtues are found not merely in children whose characters have not been fully formed; they are often found in adults.

Many virtues are needed for the good life; one virtue does not make a good man any more than one feature makes a lovely face. There are several reasons for this need of a plurality of moral habits. First, man has a number of distinct powers each of which needs habituation to control by the human intellect and will to perform acts in accordance with the standards of right living. Second, the virtues are as many as their distinct formal objects. Thus, gratitude to benefactors is something different from loyalty to one's country or obedience to one's parents or reverence for the aged. One may have cultivated acts bearing on a few of these distinct formal objects and have neglected attention to others. Third, the plurality of virtues is due to the great variety of situations and circumstances under which different people live or even the same people live at different times in their lives.[9] The rich face moral problems which the poor do not encounter. The ill may suddenly discover need for patience with themselves and others; they never had practiced this in their healthy days. The child knows little of the adolescent's temptations in regard to sex. The laborer may know nothing of the scholar's battle for faith. Different ways of life, different situations, different needs demand their specific virtues and newer depths in the old virtues.

In our experience of men or in our study of character portraits in biographies and good novels we can discover an interplay of groups of virtues. One strong virtue tends to spread its influence, activate the seeds of related virtues, and so fill up gaps in character. We find, for instance, men who wish to be brave in all respects. Their bravery does not consist merely in facing physical dangers and hardships. Courage animates them to self-denial, to generous forgiveness of offenders, to persevering devotedness to their families, and to a magnanimous disregard for the sophisticated mockery of those who count them as queer or saintly but not as willing sinners and jolly companions. Again, humility helps obedience; and obedience helps humility by demanding its practice when one must obey. Penance helps chastity; and love of chastity embraces penance as a help. Chastity in its white love of God reinforces charity for fellow men; charity by occupying the mind selflessly makes chastity easier in practice.

As every tone and line in a richly colored painting enforces and beautifies the other, so every virtue builds and enriches every other. The instances could be almost endless. In their perfect state each virtue not only does not exclude any other, but it begets or improves all the others.

A true and perfect moral virtue or habit of right choice follows the famous Aristotelian rule of the mean.[10] This implies the influence of prudence in all virtuous living. A virtue is not an extreme; vices are. The virtuous man chooses the right thing, does it in the right way, to the right person, at the right time and place, in the right degree. This attention to rectitude requires insight into moral situations, good judgment, a certain tact in doing good, a self-restraint that will not do too little or too much. It demands that the virtuous man will not act prematurely or too late; it requires a precarious poise that will not be wasteful or stingy, that will not be rash or overcautious, that will not be boisterous or gloomy, that will neither exaggerate nor underplay the truth. As one's virtue more and more approaches this perfect mid-point or balance, the virtue itself is more perfect, more deeply rooted, more human, more rightly motivated. The concrete situation is ever shifting; our judgment and response in virtuous action must be ever true to the line. Good men are like good batters in baseball who must be set to vary their reactions to different pitchers, to different pitches aimed at different spots, and to different situations that may demand a long or short hit, a fly or a ground ball.

For fullness of character man needs to add an extra floor to the house of natural virtue. He must receive the three specifically Christian virtues of faith in God's truth, hope in God's promises and helps, and love of God and love of others for the sake of God. These are sheer gifts of God, never due to our mere humanity. But with God's help they can be cultivated and grow from the divinely implanted seed.

They must be integrated with the moral virtues of nature. They profoundly affect these virtues, the rapidity of their growth, and the depth of their impress on the soul.

Charity in particular has an organizing or integrating influence on the whole bright band of a person's virtues. It teams with prudence to regulate the moral life; prudence supplies the balance; charity, the impulse and direction. All other good acts can be motivated and dominated by charity. All evils can be expelled by charity. All virtues are children nourished by charity or courtiers serving this queen. Charity fosters an eagerness for opportunities to practice all the virtues and especially for those of daily occurrence.[11] More than any other habit, it roots into the soul a certain affinity for good motives and good deeds; it gives man a certain fresh connaturality with the good, a spiritual blood relationship with all that is noble; it gives a relish, interest, firmness, and pleasure in doing good that is one of the best signs of maturity in leading the good life. Stronger than death, love never gives up. More powerful than all the dividing influences affecting the powers of man, it binds all virtues into one personality, with one high aim, which is the love of God above all things and the love of all other things for God.

As the principal form of goodness, charity spreads far when God or His love controls the whole of man. Charity is highly fruitful in moral goodness, more good deeds and fewer faults, more habits, more consistency, better motives, higher rewards, and greater help to other men.

The rays of goodness burst in many directions. From the kind mind and loving will flow encouraging and kind words, praise for others' successes, compliments on their gifts of mind and character, sympathy in their troubles, courtesy in all speech to others and silence about their faults. The heart looking for good appreciates whatever is good in human life and tends to make others better just by approval of the good that is in them. Earnest in his own pursuit of personal improvement, the good man notes, emulates, and imitates, as he can, the good that others show him. He himself without ever knowing it is giving good example, that most important of all forms of instruction, to his children, his fellow workers, his clients. When he has money, he spends some of it in good works for the needy and in great causes. He is active in projects for racial, economic, and political justice; he is willing to join with others in organizations that bring fairness and peace among men. He more and more dedicates himself to others. All year round he lives like a Santa Claus, or better, as a follower of God, with a perpetual Christmas spirit, a man who goes about doing good and never evil, a man for whom joyous giving is the secret of joyous living.

Finally, it is only from good men in the good society that sound human leadership can be drawn and effective reforms, if ever required, be initiated and executed. All the traditions of the ages, all the techniques in the world, all checks and balances, the wisest laws and wizard inventions do not suffice without good men with good hearts and good judgment. It is the saints and near-saints who are the greatest visible blessings of our world.

5. VICTORY IN THE GOOD LIFE

The last stage in the good life is almost as critical as the tender years of growth. Human nature is fickle; the passions are tamed, but do not die; the struggle for goodness becomes wearisome; perseverance remains a problem. Self within is ever competing against God. Opponents without our nature are numerous enough, too, to overpower any one's virtues. The battle storms on with its risks and high costs of vigilance and unselfishness.

But we have great helps and allies to bring us victory. God is on our side in the battle. He is aiding us to perfect our natures according to His plan, to match our wills with His will for us, and to shape our motives to His own intentions. His special providence reaches to each of our acts and, not least of all, to the decisive acts of our last days on earth. The dangers of a late surrender to evil are much diminished by a steadfast good life; good motives find good holding ground in the soul; good habits, long exercised, endure; prayer keeps vivid the appeal of good and peels off the false cosmetic masking of evil that would pull us away from God. Mental prayer in particular is a school of character and of perseverance. It keeps vivid the great motives that, like a mighty magnet, grip us fast to the lessons learned in that school. With a well-grounded conscience, an awareness of duty, a love of God, the wise counsel of prudence, and the help of God, we are in a strong position for waging the struggle for virtue until the end.

This very peril of a late surrender to evil contributes one more to life's splendors. It keeps adventure in life. It keeps the aged growing in virtue. It prepares the good man for a conqueror's glory and the crown of fidelity as he ascends into eternity.

Chapter 13

Man's Place in Nature

1. The Value of Nature in Itself

THE FIFTH main problem proposed for a philosophical study of life concerns man's rightful place in that total order which connects him with God, men, and physical nature. The man who voluntarily puts himself in his true relationships to these other beings is leading a morally good life. We may begin with man's status in regard to physical nature.

Nature is a word of many hues. A natural thing is a complete individual which acts and responds to the action of other things in a regular or necessary way. Nature is the sum total of all natural things, either in the whole universe, the solar system, or at least on earth. Often nature refers to material things only, excluding all spiritual realities such as man's soul, intelligence, will, his purely spiritual activities, God's presence in his soul, and special gifts of grace of the supernatural order. It is this last meaning of nature as including all active material substances, even the human body and the modifications of physical objects introduced by free human action, that we ordinarily use in this chapter.

About the goodness of nature in itself, the history of human ideas presents us with much doubt and misgiving on one hand and exaggerated esteem on the other. Matter has been looked upon as evil, infected, and corrupting other things; it has been seen as a source of evil, a product of chance, an illusion of erring imagination, or the empire of devils. These distrusts and dislikes have specially centered on the human body because of its organic needs, desires and pains, its interference with the flights of the spirit toward the good, and its final repulsive decay in death. Some hold the pleasures of the organism as especially suspect, and they transfer their condemnation to all the external stimuli that strongly excite bodily pleasure, notably to alcoholic beverages and sexual contacts. To what serious distress of spirit and moral weakness this can lead is recorded in the Manichaean youth of St. Augustine and in the medieval Albigensians, who attempted to build a whole culture on such a misunderstanding of nature and the deluded duty of withdrawing from it.[1] Less serious, but sufficiently unwholesome, are Puritan attitudes to the body and spiritualist views of its unreality.

The sane view of nature is rooted in the shimmering old metaphysical truth that every being, in so far as it is real, is good and that evil is only the lack of a right measure of perfection in some good things. To each thing its own existence and constitution are fitted. Each is derived from the supreme Good who created it and whom it in some little way imitates. A given individual object in nature may not have all the good that its nature could or should have; it may be imperfect; but what it has is good. Moreover, as its goodness is controlled by the providence of a good God and as it is an active part of a good universe, it has some sphere of good influence on other things and may well be the recipient of good action by other things. It has some suitable function in God's world, though we may have to search hard to find this in the case of some famous foes of goodness as the rat, anopheles mosquito, and vestigial organs. It is much easier to see the total order, beauty, and helpfulness of nature than to see the goodness of every bit of it.

Nature is normally connected with goodness, yet it is wounded and spotted. Not every deficiency is a physical evil. Snow, for instance, lacks the structure, properties, and usefulness of sand; but it is not for that reason evil. Things causing pain are not evil because they do not cause agreeable responses in us. Pain itself is not evil, however much we dislike it, but is a suitable response to certain stimuli. Each kind of being must be measured according to what is proper to its own constitution, activity, and purpose.

Matter is impersonal, lacking intelligence and volition. Hence, it can have no moral good in itself and no moral badness. No mere thing such as whiskey, sexual organs, cards, or the figures of the dance can be immoral. They may often be occasions of immorality, but that is because some moral being chooses to use them evilly. Nor can nature take moral attitudes toward man. Because of their moral neutrality, things do not specially favor the saint or sinner.

The sun shines on just and unjust; the winter chills innocent and guilty. Nature is for everyone, but not everyone should deal with nature in the same way. Being impersonal, nature never teaches or moralizes. There are traces of God everywhere, but nature never speaks His name or urges us to adore Him. There may be sermons written in stones and exhortations to diligence in the life of ants, but they do not preach to man any more than do books in unknown languages.

It is particularly important that man honor the goodness of that part of material nature which belongs so intimately to him, his own human body. He must not depreciate it for its miseries and decay; he must not rate its sensuous joys and material beauty as superior to his own soul. The body is neither Satan nor Pan nor Venus. Reason dictates that we recognize it as God's greatest gift to us after our soul and supernatural grace. It is precious as part of our single human nature and as transformed by the spirit that gives it life. It is the instrument through which we learn and the medium through which we carry out into the external world many of our best interior purposes. The body is the vesture in which we pray to God, express our personality, love our fellow men, beautify the world, and exert our human mastery over things. Moreover, in itself, in its anatomical organization and physiological marvels, in its origin, laws, mysteries, and many beauties it is one of the clearest evidences of the wisdom, power, and care of God for us. Through the body, finally, man shares in God's creative work, for its toil and sweat produce the goods needed for life, and its generative action brings into the world new human beings through whom God may be glorified on earth and in eternity.[2]

2. The Value of Nature to Man

Nature, besides being good in itself, is very good to man. In the drama of human life it plays many supporting roles.

Seated on a lower grade of being than man, with no destiny to personal union with God, material nature must be a means to man's temporal life and a help to man's arrival at beatitude. Its very real goodness is relative to man's soul, spiritual activities, and immortal gains. It is the human intelligence and conquering will that put it to improved human service.

As man's natural slave, nature automatically obeys many of his demands. It works hard for man. It gives its very being for man. It supplies food and drink to nourish, refresh, and heal its master. It supplies air for his breath and speech. Its fuel warms him and drives his machinery. It provides the stuff for his clothing, bedding, and lodging. It gives part of itself to be his home, that most acute of human needs. In the end it affords a grave for his bones. In addition, nature furnishes the chemicals and the energies out of which man makes his tools, his books, his light, his works of art, his sporting goods, and his means of travel and communication. In their cleverest inventions, scientists, engineers, and craftsmen are merely exploiting the basic materials and capturing the forces which nature puts at man's disposal.

Because nature has being, it is intelligible. Being intelligible, it is open to the prying intellect of man. And the human intellect, since it is united with a sentient being, is particularly apt to grasp sensible things in knowledge. Hence, nature has often been called a dependable teacher of man. In it lies the evidence which our minds must ferret out to gain an understanding of nature. "Nature is a lovely university," man's basic library from which and in which to learn by attention of senses and intellect. Nature's ontological truth is something like a letter written to man by its Maker, mirroring His creative ideas, full of indications of truths about its being, structure, operations, interrelationships with things, and possibilities of improvement for human living. These truths are secrets, we say; but this merely means that we do not yet know them and have not fully mastered the natural symbols which nature displays before us. Little by little we learn to read better in this wonderful book of facts. By observation, special instruments, and mathematics we learn to decode many natural truths and, at long last, catch the meaning of the heaven-made signals which God transmits to man's intelligence through these material creatures. The being of nature measures the truth of man's knowledge of it, whereas man measures the human utility of nature.[3]

This dual role of serving and teaching has led us to regard nature as a friendly ally to our bodily, economic, intellectual, social, and spiritual life. But the benevolent sentiments are not in nature; the friendliness to man is in nature's Author. He has arranged that nature provide us not merely with just enough food, raiment, and shelter, and just enough air, light, and energy for our bodily needs. He has made abundant resources and charged them with their strange plasticity to human change. They are available for our inventions, travel, sports, decorations, and luxurious amenities of life, and not for mere subsistence. The plenty in sky, earth, and ocean makes possible an ever expanding human population; and the submission of raw materials to human inventiveness in industry makes possible leisure for devoting time to the pursuit of the things of the spirit.

Even more wonderful than being man's tool shed and his art studio, the universe is his first stairway sweeping upward to God. Here are the facts and wonders which challenge the mind to think of them and ask who made them. In this sense, the divine name of the Author is stamped on all His creatures for any mind to read; and each creature is a voice chanting His name for any spirit to hear.

Nature has another face besides this pleasant one. At times, it seems to be a threatening opponent, a blindly indifferent avenger of foolhardy human misuse of nature. Nature resists man. Even those who sing that the best things in life are free also see that many other things come to man at a high price of physical toil and pain, long study, immense planning, much waiting and saving. Just as marble does not easily yield to the sculptor's design or iron to the founder's wishes or illness to the physician's care, so nature generally demands an expenditure of much human effort, endurance, and intelligence before it submits to man's control.

In its role as enemy, nature brings physical and moral dangers to man. The most optimistic must regard nature's ways as sometimes resembling a balking servant snarling at the master. Nature has power to hurt, crush, and kill. Its storms, earthquakes, icebergs, floods, droughts, fire, and pests bring sorrow, damage man's works, and cause death to his body. The moral dangers that accompany nature are the more weighty. The human body, so intimate a participant in nature and so close to matter, often swamps the soul with its tempting needs, desires, and aches. Pleasure solicits irresponsibility; property evokes ambition, greed, and injustice to men; the needful yet difficult things so often rebuff courage and invite indolence. Nature too easily can be misused to harm ourselves, as by means of personal and racial suicide, or to harm others, as by the sword, the gun, and the bomb. It can even be our Iago in our futile effort to dishonor God by idolatry or to hurt God by using His gifts against the Giver. In all these ways nature is testing our moral caliber. Without nature as object of our choices, abstinences, and control, how many of our moral achievements would vanish! The virtues of temperance, moderation, courage, patience, prudence, justice, and generosity all come into daily play in our regular dealings with physical nature. The moral danger here is due to our own sickness; nature is good, but it challenges us to prove our health and our right to be its master.

The biggest temptation of all in our times is to be too easily and too well satisfied with mere nature, to stop at its beauty and goodness and not go beyond it to the uncreated Good, and to make the controlled use of nature the be-all and end-all of human existence. Scientific and technological progress presents this moral risk to the man intent on material improvement for the merely material betterment of man. This form of materialism, called by Pope Pius XII the technological concept of life,[4] makes the mastery of nature for temporal welfare the supreme value of life. Like any exaggerated first principle, this view can have devastasting effects on spiritual and religious values both in the life of the individual and in that of the family and the state. It regards man as but one more animal, although the most successful one, in the realm of nature. It seeks to apply the techniques of controlling nature and domesticating animals to the control of man: social engineering, remaking the human race. Perhaps worst of all, this materialism sets up the methods of gaining knowledge of nature and of production as the sole avenues to any truth. When this is done, all the lamps of humane education and broad human interests are blown out; the smoke of technological truth plunges us into moral darkness and religious blindness.

There is one more stern line in nature's unfriendly visage which we must look at. As God's creature, nature at times becomes an instrument of His punishment for man's wrongdoing as well as a healing painful remedy. God judges man and heals him, but He uses His creatures in this admonitory, judicial, and remedial work. Disease in the body is nature's frequent answer to misuse of the body. Addiction to alcohol and other drugs, various infections, injuries from auto accidents are some ways in which the body, as part of nature, rebels against the misuse of nature. Lazy improvidence leads to spoilage of food, destructive fires, and waste of resources with which man's life would have been much better. Nature thus keeps insisting that disregard of our true welfare turns our very subjects into rebels against our mismanagement.[5] An old adage sums up some of these sanctions:

"God forgives, but nature never forgives." Yet it is also true that God often forgives through nature's healing.

To the perceptive mind that tries to see reality in the whole, all these functions of nature are so many aspects of God's providence over us rational animals. God made nature for man, not man for nature. He made it for every man, not only for some of us. He uses the least and greatest of material things as delicate instruments for man's true and abiding good and for man's recovery of the good.[6] The person who uses nature according to the will of God, for the knowledge and honor and service of God, has found his right place in nature. Such a man is making nature a valuable means to human happiness, for human happiness is always a voluntary accord with the all-good divine plan.

3. Man's Roles in Dealing With Nature

Man stands alone at the center of the divine plan for physical nature. He is the purpose of all that is subhuman; he is the end, they the means. Spirit, being more excellent than matter, must have primacy over it; the imperfect is for the perfect, just as within man the body is for the soul. The normal relationship between material nature and rational man is that nature has capacities to help man and man with his sentient-intellectual constitution both needs material things and is able to master them. God has put nature and man into this reciprocal relation. Indeed, it was for man that God created a material universe, for which neither He nor His angels have any special use. The dual nature of man, having matter and spirit, body and mind, gives an adequate reason for the existence of a world of matter. A being with senses as his avenues of knowing can make valuable use of a material world for his bodily needs as well as for the help of his mind and the exaltation of his spirit. Such a being begins by sensory contact with the world and rises by his intellect to a knowledge and praise of the Maker above the world. The whole world, then, seems to be intrinsically oriented toward man; it is anthropocentric.

Englobed by nature as he is, man seems to have three basic functions to exercise in its regard: to know it, to love it, and to use it. Before a natural thing, a flower for instance, man can be the scientist who understands its make-up and parts, its laws of growth, health, and fertility; he can be the child who gazes at it in wonder, the gardener who cultivates it for its beauty, or the painter who represents it on his drawing; he can be the perfume maker or pharmacist who plucks it and crushes it for its fragrance or its medicating particles.

Man using and consuming nature is the role common to everyone, since on our bodily side we are participants in nature. The human body is subject to the physical laws of chemistry, electricity, gravity, levers, optics, and radiation as are other material things. It is subject to laws of nutrition, health, biochemistry, and genetics as are all things with vegetal life. Every breath, every bite of food makes man a sharer in matter. His sentient processes make him resemble many animals. If, moreover, it be true that the human body has evolved by natural processes, then this highest animal body has inherited the whole of nature's progressive change. So close to nature does a man feel that he cherishes for years little material souvenirs of his past life; he cannot give them up, for they seem to be some part of himself even though they are now useless.

Man the microcosm includes nature, sums it up, and yet surpasses all of it. Although on one side of his being he is dependent on and involved in nature, on the spiritual side he is independent of nature and is its king. His is the mind to conquer material bodies and subject them in a considerable degree to his human will and purposes. He imposes many of his own ends and all his moral ends on nature. He wins actual control over nature chiefly by understanding it. It is not human strength, agility, or speed that conquers it, but intelligent re-arrangement and transformation, invention of tools, welding together different natural objects and forces, balancing one force against another, summoning its potencies to meet his ideas and answer his chosen will for it. This manipulation of nature implies a certain limited proprietorship over lands, crops, herds, and machines to which we shall return presently.

Work and tools are the external manifestations of this spiritual interior proprietary power of man over matter. In hundreds of occupations, as inventor, engineer, printer, cook, tailor, gardener, home builder, artist, synthetic chemist and church builder, man converts nature into new forms and beauties and lifts it to noble purposes which it could never realize if left to itself. As long as the purposes are humanly worthy, man is co-operating with God's providence over things, governing them for the sake of man. It is God's will that man turn wood into paper for his writing, timber into chairs for his home, cotton and hides into garments, minerals into tools, apples and fish and many another gift of nature into the bone and blood of his own body. For all these natural ends pertain to human welfare. It is right that man should try to make the world a better place to live in and that he should use his powers to create a better world for his descendants. In these human improvements man is but following the great law of Divine Providence that a free man should give help to himself by using free powers over the resources divinely stocked in the universe.

Knowledge of nature is a nobler human achievement than mere consumption and caretaking management of it. Man, the spectator and student of surrounding nature, is symbolized perhaps best of all by the astronomer studying that most useless natural field, the distant heavens. By his mind man stands above nature, independent of it, aloof, and like a king thinking and wondering about it, measuring it, collating its laws, experimenting with it, asking it what it is, how it operates, what it is for, whether it can be reorganized and redistributed in space and time, whether it has any hidden resources, why it is so changeable yet so constant in its rhythmic changes, and what is its ultimate source and meaning.

Other men cast themselves in the third role of the lovers of nature. A St. Francis of Assisi is a troubadour of nature's beauties. St. Bonaventure sees all things not only as objects but as signs of the divine. A few like the American Thoreau wish to live alone with nature and hold complete faith in its wisdom and freedom from the artificialities of machines and civilization. Travelers and camera fans as well as naturalists never grow weary in roaming over land and sea in search of new wonders. Nature beckons others to love it in the outdoor life, to study its flora and fauna, to sail the lakes, hunt in the woods, mount hills, probe glaciers, and come to know nature's infinitely varied appeals to man's curiosity and pleasure. But the man whose love of nature initiates and deepens his love of the glory of the face of God is the student and lover who has learned the biggest lesson that nature has to offer.

Man has, in fact, the native opportunity to become the priest of this natural creation wherein God has set him. By this function is meant more than man's ability to utilize wood, marble, glass, paint, stone, incense, water, bread, wine, and oil as materials for his places of prayer and acts of divine worship. Nor do we here refer to an anointed priesthood or to persons specially called to represent the human community in its rites before God. In calling man the priest of nature, one means the analogous natural function of the thinking animal as representing the community of the physical universe before God. Uniting in himself the material and spiritual, the temporal and the eternal, man is like a mediator between earth and heaven. He sacramentalizes the universe, as Newman and Sheen have said, by turning material things into means of spiritual sanctification. He consecrates the world and its parts to the glory of God. Matter alone can never be united with God; by thought and love man unites created matter to the uncreated God. Through man's spirit the realm of matter returns to God, its Alpha. Man has the spiritual voice to give praise and appreciation to the Maker of all both for himself and for all irrational things. Sun and moon praise the Lord when man praises the Lord for making sun and moon.[7]

Without man the universe is a palatial home with nobody in it, where no word of thanks or loving compliment is ever heard. Without him it is a great garden of endless glories in which only midges, unconscious of beauty, fly about. Without man it is a temple in which God is present, but no one knows that He is there or what He has done; no one thrills to it, no one cares, no one offers adoring love to the great Benefactor who has made this material universe for His favorites, human beings.

4. Human Rights Over Nature

Man's treatment of the physical world differs from that of other beings, not only in its scope and methods, but also in two other respects. He has not only some material power over things but also has a moral right over them. He is able to turn nature into a help or a hindrance to his true well-being, into a means to material and spiritual life or to material and spiritual death. Accordingly, part of the problem of determining man's place in the universe requires an inspection of any duties and rights by which divine law regulates man's dealings.

Man has no duties to nature for it is nonpersonal and a pure utility for human life. There can be no mutual moral relations between man and nature as there are between men and men. Man must abstain from worship of nature because of his duty to adore only the true God. Man must refrain from cruelty to animals, not for their sake, but for his own sake, since cruelty is unreasonable. He must avoid waste of natural resources, again not for nature's sake, but for the sake of his fellow men and the future of the human race. He may not use nature for any evil, not because this is unworthy of nature, but because no one may deliberately cause evil to himself or others. While there is no barrier to his pursuit of knowledge, yet the knowledge that he gains must be put to good use. It is laudable to discover all the secrets of the fission and fusion of atoms; it would be morally unspeakable to use atomic energy to ignite the earth's atmosphere or to melt the polar glaciers, thereby creating tremendous dangers for countless people and for coming ages. In all our use of nature, there must be a moderation and prudent restraint. Not everything is for everybody. Allergies and toxic effects of drugs that help one person but poison another indicate that mastery over some things demands that we use them with the greatest caution.

Man's rights over nature issue primarily from the wisdom and grant of God. His lordship over nature and his need to use and consume it for his welfare entitle him to acquire ownership over some physical things for his own and his family's exclusive use and disposition. Limited proprietorship over some lands, crops, herds, homes, and machines seems to be the way in which nature and man can best get along with each other, and in which men themselves can best live together. Millions of proprietors make nature efficaciously serve man. Whatever man does with property must be related to the divine purpose in providing man with material goods and giving him a nature that has material necessities. God means to care for every man and provides nature for everyone, not merely for those in present possession of it or with power over it today. God means that each man's needs be supplied and that property be owned, controlled, used, changed, bought, and sold under conditions which respect the dignity of personality and the duties of a free person to care for himself and his family in a decent human way. Physical nature must, then, be owned and used in a system that provides plenty amid peace for as many people as possible. This seems to be the big asset of the system of widely distributed property ownership. This form of control provides an economy of abundance that simultaneously respects human liberty, preserves peace in human relationships, maintains order in ownership and justice to owners by protecting what is duly theirs, and prevents undue concentration and power that is actually or potentially harmful to other men. Wise human contentment desires enough material goods, desires what is one's own, but also desires that others, too, have opportunities to own and be content to have enough and securely possess their own.

Man, then, is a caretaker under God of the things of this world. The divine Donor has set moral terms and moral limits under which He made His gift of earth to man. This managerial talent must be returned to God with accrued interest. Nature is a gift or estate over which man has but a temporary lease; for he is but a tenant on earth and a pilgrim walking the land to a goal beyond the earth. He may never forget that he is better than nature; hence, he may not follow physical nature as his guide. He must never forget that he is born to rise far above nature; and so he may not live for earth or try to find his fullness in the things of earth. He must be mindful that soon he must give up earth; consequently, he must never let his affections and loyalties be completely captured by the things that he has and enjoys now. Attachments to earth will deprive him of that freedom of his spirit to do the right, no matter what material loss this may incur; bound to earth, he will bend toward evil. If earth is his paradise, he will be low-minded and live in dread of that thief, death, who will plunder all his material wealth.

CHAPTER 14

Living Under God and for God

1. REMINDERS OF GOD

NATURE Is man's servant. Man, in turn, ought to be God's servant.
Although we can ignore or neglect God for a while, the bond between
a living man and the living God is so strong that reminders of His
reality keep returning to our lives.

The world about man draws his attention to the fact of God's existence and influence on human life. Things and places, customs and
acts, books and art works, feasts and laws bear witness to man's awareness of God. Crucifixes, cribs, and paintings of religious personages
and events; ceremonial religious articles such as rosaries, vestments,
and sacrificial vessels; churches, temples, synagogues, and consecrated
cemeteries manifest man's acknowledgment of God. The custom of
churchgoing and lighter work on the Lord's day, religious festivals,
conversation about religious matters, the instruction of children
in prayer and religious beliefs, the celebration of marriages and
funerals with religious rites are instances of repeated human concern with the fact of God. The literature of all lands is full of
the theme of God. The best sellers of many centuries are the Bible,
the *Imitation of Christ*, and the Koran. Fiction, drama, epics, philosophy, histories, the biographies of many persons, and even the
writings of some of God's enemies are continually referring to Him.

Because of man's knowledge of God we have many religious societies
and parishes as well as religious institutions such as the priesthood,
seminaries, church-related schools, and religious governing bodies. The
laws of the land often take cognizance of God and of earthly things
related to God. His name may occur in their constitutions, be stamped
on their coins, be heard at the daily opening of their legislative meet-
ings. Oaths of allegiance, oaths of officials, of witnesses, of registrants

for voting, and of citizens paying taxes are asked in His name. The laws must deal with the purchase and management of property for religious uses. In many ways civic action sponsors, helps, respects, tolerates, or opposes man's religious interests.

The world about us continually stirs the mind to think of its meaning, its order, its beauty, its vast magnitude, its origin, and continuance. Nature puts the question; man must answer. He cannot avoid such an insistent questioner. All roads lead to a knowledge of God.

The inner world of man's life also keeps sending out reminders of God. There is the realm of conscience, the personal struggle for the good, the reproaches of guilt, the hunger for happiness, the realization of dependence on something greater than ourselves, the desire for immortal life. Man cannot escape from the world and from himself; he cannot, therefore, successfully flee from God. Religion is as plain a fact as the existence of children or the existence of schools. Our purpose here is not to repeat the proofs of natural theology about the existence of God and His government, but to add to our earlier notice of God's lordship over human life and of His status as the personal object of beatitude, whereby we are committed to know and love Him. The point of inquiry now is whether our relationship to God is the most important of all the contacts of our lives and how that relationship should be expressed in order to make God the actual center of human life.

2. The Importance of God in a Philosophy of Life

Three facts dramatize the importance of God in human life. The first is the plight and unhappiness of people in Soviet Russia where God is officially dead and officially the enemy. The second is the Christmas happiness of those lands which believe that God exists and sent His Son as Saviour. Nothing more vividly shows the change produced in human living by acknowledgment of God than does this feast. The third is an incident which I observed in a midwestern city bus a few summers ago. Two ladies, each with two children of school age, were conversing near the front of the bus. They passed a church, asked each other its name, and mentioned to each other the names of their own parishes elsewhere in the city. After a few remarks, one of the mothers let out a gentle sigh and remarked to her friend, "What would life be worth without our religion?" That haunting remark is a lesson in the human heart and a lesson in life from a wise woman.

Even the most thoroughgoing materialistic atheists recognize that it is a basic and capital decision to live under God and for Him or to live without Him and for someone else. Acceptance of dependence on God or a declaration of independence from Him is a watershed dividing human lives. Most of life's other bigger decisions hang on our commitment to please God or to satisfy ourselves or to serve some human master, the devil, or our fate. If a man shall have decided to live for God and to make Him the first goal and the main love and the incessant occupation of his life, then all other objectives and decisions will fall into order, and sooner or later the place of self, family, government, and employers will be found and adjusted to the primary place of God in life. The kind of God that a person knows or believes in also makes a deep distinction in his fundamental character, interests, ideals, and activities. This is to be expected; since ideas and realities do influence us, the greatest reality should have the most influence.

We may first look at the importance of knowing God and His attributes. For the immediate purpose of weighing the impact of this idea of God, it does not matter whether we gained this knowledge by way of family culture, common reason, philosophical discovery, or divine revelation. Surely, knowledge of the supreme Being constitutes knowledge of the most important kind and knowledge that penetrates and colors all other knowledge. The purer, the more elevated this knowledge of God, the better. The more it represents the true God and not our own ideas and preferences, the more He should be loved.[1] Since knowledge of God is important, education in knowledge of Him is important. There is no room for compromise between theism and atheism on this point, for it would be tragedy to know all else and not know the best, God, to try to explain all else and be ignorant or doubtful about the ultimate, though not always the proximate, explanation of all else. The main function of organized education must be to give youth an acquaintance with God, His outlook, His ways, and His purposes in regard to human beings. Unless one sees the world as God sees it, as a small likeness of God, he does not really know it. Unless one sees God above the world, present in it, distinct from it, and operative in it, one does not know the world or the human soul. Cardinal Newman's famous discourses on theology as a branch of knowledge and its relations to other branches, given in *The Idea of a University*,[2] have said nearly all that can be said on this topic, as far as natural theology goes.

The influence of the fact of God may be seen in the construction of a theory of morality. Ethical systems without God, as attempted by deists and atheists, have a dusty resemblance to vast irrigation systems in a desert, which have nearly everything but the one essential, water. On every major topic in ethics God has a main influence. He is the end of life, the one perfect object who can beatify us. His being is the ultimate model of all being, and therefore the ultimate measure of all moral goodness. He is the eternal lawgiver, the immediate author of the natural law, and, historically, also of certain divine positive laws. He is the giver and protector of natural rights. He is the object of special virtues, of knowledge of Him, love, worship, and fidelity. His love is the chief motive for doing good. His rewards are our great hope. The fear of His majesty and justice is the great deterrent from evil. He is the master of human life whose dominion over human beings may not be invaded. Because His love and imaged goodness is in men, we must love them as ourselves. He is the author of the natural societies of the home and the civic community. He is the original power who delegates some authority to human rulers. He is the maker and watchman of human marriages. Searcher of the human heart, He reads its secret motives and demands not merely outward compliance with His decrees, but sincere inner conformity to His sovereign will. God is omnipresent in an ethical system.

A man with such ethical foundations sees that he ought to be leading a theocentric life oriented to God as its first principle.

The impact of the acceptance of God in shaping a man's personal conduct, and not merely his understanding of reality and of moral issues, is even more notable. The inner life of a man who is striving to love God has hundreds of facets in which it is totally unlike the godless, indifferent, or worldly life.[3] It is almost a truism that in whatever our ideal of God fails our own character fails. It is supremely critical to character formation to have a grand conception of God's goodness in Himself and of His goodness to us, with a consequent perception of our total dependence on Him. God, the most real, the most existent, the most living of all beings, in Himself is infinitely excellent, in every way wonderful, unlimited in His dazzling splendor of being. This Being of eminent perfection has deigned to think of man and love him.

From Him, the Creator, comes every gift of being and every power of life. He is our first and perpetual benefactor. He continues His creative gift by conserving us in being; He concurs with us in every natural as well as supernatural act; He provides for each individual person and governs each act of each man. He is the donor of rights. He is the aim of life, our plenty who will fill our powers to capacity. He is closer to us than we are to ourselves. He is everywhere, working in nature about us, active within us, knowing us, blessing us, empowering us, moving us. As an ant is immersed in a world of crumbling soil and leaf mold, as our bodies are immersed in a sea of air and radiation, so our whole humanity lives and moves in God, while being other than God. From Him is the gift of life, in Him is its goal. Few truths could be more needful than to see human life as issuing from God, dependent on Him, responsible to Him, imitating Him, and panting for union with Him.

Since He is our Creator, we are His creatures who have come into being out of blank nothingness by the wand of His loving power ordering us to be and to live. All in us is created; every new act performed by us in life's course is created. As totally caused by Him, we are dependent on Him, ever dependent on Him, totally dependent on Him, intrinsically dependent on Him. Dependence is in our very bones; dependence is the very brand of our being.

Hence we need Him. We have a physical need of His powerful help to be, to go on, and to act. We have a psychological need for Him, for without Him our minds and wills are incomplete, unaware of the greatest truth, separated from the greatest love, joyless without the greatest beauty. We have a moral need of His guidance in law, His protecting help in rights, His promises, helps, rewards, and His judgment of our deeds and motives. The very roots of our life in every way need His nourishment.

As intelligent creatures, as rational animals, ours is a dependence proportionate to our natures. It is not the dependence of monkeys or of pure spirits, but of our unitary nature of body and soul. Our dependence on God must then be expressed willingly by honor, thanks, submission, request for help, hope, love, repentance, heeding His instruction, giving Him the fair glory which He has a right to gain from us. Humility and worship are, therefore, essential traits of the life of a rational creature. Moreover, our nature made of flesh and spirit makes us religious animals who must express our dependence in both body and soul, exteriorly and interiorly. This dependence is not sincerely and completely acknowledged until we habitually give God the first place in our lives. That means that recourse to prayer is fundamental to a good life.

Of course, we have free wills. It is easy to run away from the reality of God for a while. It is quite a thrill to live for a while as men freed from God and full masters of our lives. It is not rare that men alienate themselves from God by refusing to pray, by compromising with God's claims over them, by trying to set themselves up in place of the one true God. Perhaps this is the supreme modern temptation, to attempt to prove that we do not need God in order to be good and happy. But devotion to self, to the state, to any master other than God turns out, like Faust's service to the devil, to be bitter slavery whose discontent cuts up the very heart. Biography and history surely prove that atheism is no fun, for the devil has a cross of his own for all who are without God and against God, and he never lets them off it, gives no helps to bear it, and rewards no one for torments borne on it.

The character of the man who voluntarily serves God is also different because of his motives. His main objective in life is to please God and to aid his fellow men for the sake of pleasing God. He has an awe and reverence for God's will, a fear of God's justice, a hope of His kind rewards, a confidence in His care, and an intense personal affection for Him. Constantly searching for God, he constantly ascends closer to Him. His vision sees a divine order in the laws of nature, in the laws of morality, and in the laws of the State and Church. His conscience is sensitively alive to the need of meeting his Lord's demands upon his conduct. Ordinarily he follows his principles and his conscience; and then he knows the peace of God's approval. Having a first principle by which to make decisions, it is easier for him to resolve his problems of daily choice and struggle. It is easier, also, to be fearless and confident in suffering and in facing human opposition. Knowing that God has a purpose in every event that He allows to befall us, he can, like St. René Goupil when captured and tortured by the Iroquois, thank God for letting misfortune happen. The God-seeking man may do wrong, but he quickly recovers, for he is sure of God's mercy to the sincerely contrite and has had many past proofs of God's goodness to those who return to His will. Such a man's time, even his leisure, is apt to be occupied in a way different from that of other people. He will devote some of it to prayer and spiritual reading;

even on vacation he remembers that God is deserving of his attention. His deepest ambition is to be a loving servant of God in all things and to become one with God, as far as he can, in the spiritual powers of his being. By this central direction of all life to God, his personality achieves integration and mirrors something of the unity of God.

God is not outdone in generosity to His servants. Though religion is principally a matter of serving God and not of receiving service from Him, still it must be admitted that good people are happier people. The consciousness of God's friendship is a pure, high joy. "The thought of God is the stay of the soul," especially in troubled days. The hope of God's welcome when we face His court is a pure, high hope. Many divine comforts strengthen the devoted spirit, and many earthly blessings of contentment, domestic happiness, and civic goods come to the religious person.

3. Religion as a Social Force

The social influence of religious and irreligious living just mentioned has often been remarked by students of man, by physicians, biographers, and political scientists.

A man who sees the image of God, whom he honors and loves, stamped on his fellow men is strongly inclined to treat men well in the presence of God. He wants to treat them as God would treat them and as God wishes them to be treated. They are not mere things to whom he can be indifferent, not tools for his own pleasure or advantage, not total enemies since God's love rests on them and His radiance shines over them, and not totally strangers for they are members of God's destined band of immortals. The result in honorable treatment, in fairness, courtesy, kindness, helpfulness in needs, forgiveness of another's faults, overlooking the superficial blemishes, and willingness to try to get along with others is very considerable. The heroic charity of religious-minded nurses and the glowing courage of missionaries testify to the social momentum of religion. Would they do, dare, and bear so much except for the love of God?

Religion reaches into the home as one of the main assets of domestic happiness. It encourages control of the passions of anger, faultfinding, irreverence, sexual irresponsibility, and laziness which disturb the companionship, co-operation, and peace of the family's members. Religion teaches and instills gentleness in the use of authority, gladness in domestic obedience, loyalty in marital obligations, mutual charity, common prayer, reciprocal moral example, and loving encouragement to each other in fulfilling life's main task of reaching beatitude. "The family that prays together stays together."

The same holds for public society. Wise statesmen have always fostered religion as a help to civic peace and general prosperity.[4] It is only in recent times that godless and antigod states have appeared; and their careers to date do not give us much ground to judge them as successful in promoting man's happiness on earth. Our American political documents, in spite of their hands-off policy in respect to particular religious bodies, eloquently proclaim the role of religion in our civic life. Our Declaration of Independence, Northwest Ordinance, Washington's Farewell Address, Lincoln's statements, Thanksgiving Day proclamations, and some statements by the Supreme Court manifest this American, this altogether right human attitude. Government knows that evil-doing and crime is one of the main obstacles to order and prosperity; and government well knows that religious motives and moral instruction given by religious-minded people help far more than police forces and jail sentences to prevent vice. Government is concerned with obedience to law. When human law is looked upon as one expression of God's will for us, it is better observed by right-thinking men. Government is concerned with the sanctity of the oath, with man's respect for justice in dealing with his fellow men, with common ideals and common cultural pursuits among its citizens. The citizens on their side have the deepest investment in the religious attitudes of their rulers: that they will not violate their subjects' moral convictions, that they will rule mindful of the majestic authority of God, that they will leave their people free, that they will treat each member of the state as a creature and image of God, divinely protected and cherished. Thank God for rulers who pray, for a government that asks its people to pray in times of crisis and sorrow. Prayer is a great teacher of the art of living; and government personnel no less than private persons must acquire God's sense of values, a bit of God's prudence, and the skill of uniting God and man, heaven and earth, in working harmoniously for the good of man. What does it profit to gain the glory of the nation if the government forfeits the glory of God?

4. THE PHILOSOPHY OF RELIGION

The gaining of knowledge about this important body of truths will require some study of religion or, at least, of God and of our relations to Him. In our culture we commonly associate the study of religion with the study of some particular historical religion, as Judaism, Mohammedanism, Catholicism, Methodism. But there is also a purely philosophical consideration of religion in which reason alone investigates those truths which it can naturally discover about God and about man's status in reference to God. These truths belong to human nature in any historical condition in which it is and should belong in any religion, because they are essential to man. These truths, common to all members of the human race and accessible to every rational creature, may also be regarded as the basis on which supernatural religion builds. They certainly are a basis of human unity in regard to the divine existence and government of men and are a basis of common agreement prior to the fruitful discussion and acceptance of any supernatural religion. But the philosophy of religion is not a revealed theology, nor is it a study of the claims and doctrines of any particular religion purporting to be supernatural.

A philosophy of religion may be described as the reasoned study of the origin, nature, object, and purpose of both religious knowledge and religious practice. It is not a distinct branch of philosophy but it picks up certain points of natural theology, ethics, epistemology, and the philosophy of man. A part of it that discusses the possibility of divine revelation and the miraculous and prophetic proofs of revealed doctrines and duties is often called apologetics. The history of religions and liturgies and the psychology of religious experiences and phenomena may contribute some of the facts which a philosophy of religion investigates.

The student of religion finds three components in any developed religion. These are a creed, a code, and a cult. The creed is the body of truths or doctrines, however known, which concern God and His dealings with man and man's relations to Him. The code is the body of moral duties which that religion teaches to be prescribed by its God. The cult is the form of divine worship practiced by followers of that creed. These three constitute a doctrinal, ethical, and liturgical element, but all center on man's dependence on God. Of the three, the doctrinal or dogmatic element is the basic one; for the code is expected to be consistent with the creed, and the cult consistent with both the creed and the code. Viewed broadly and popularly, religion in itself may be described as the sum of truths and duties binding man to God; viewed in practice, it is personal religion, namely, one's personal knowledge or beliefs, personal service, and personal worship of the Supreme Being upon whom one knows himself to be dependent.

A few comments are here needed on the cultus as known in natural religion.

5. THE VIRTUE OF RELIGION

In the scholastic scheme of the virtues, the name religion[5] is given to the virtue of due worship of God. This is a narrower sense of the word religion than that used above. This virtue is the constant will to give to God the honor and reverence that are due to Him. Because religion is concerned with rendering God the honor and reverence due to Him, this virtue is cognate to justice, which demands that we respect the rights of others.

The acts whereby we pay this honor may be interior or exterior, for the law of right worship holds that the honor and reverence given be both proportionate to God and consonant with the nature of man. To make the worship proportionate to God, we perform certain acts to and for God alone and reserve certain gifts exclusively for God. Hence, worship known as latria or adoration is for God alone. The act of sacrificing, that is, of offering some sensible gift to God as a sign of our dependence on Him and of our interior submission to Him and of our gift of ourselves to Him, is such a reserved act of adoration. The honor paid must also be worthy of and suitable to human nature. Therefore, we worship God not only by interior acts of mind and will but also by various exterior acts as vocal prayer, respectful use of the name of God, bending the knee and bowing the head, religious music, and external rites. One of the most natural positions for erect man is to be on his knees. Furthermore, since man is naturally social and since society naturally depends on God, it is proper to man to worship God in company with other men, particularly to do so in some family or civic group.

Four principal intentions or attitudes of man toward God are expressed in his prayer and worship. These are adoration or honor of Him in Himself and in His works, thanksgiving for His blessings, petitions for helps and favors for ourselves and others, contrition or atonement for evils done to God by ourselves or others. Other specifically religious acts are promises to perform some specific act or series of acts for God, oaths and vows, donations to religious causes, and observance of holydays. In all worshiping the external act requires the right interior disposition; the mask without the actor's heart is meaningless; the gift without the giver is bare.

Finally, worship, when supernaturally decreed, is parallel to faith in revealed religious knowledge and obedience to God's positive law. Since worship must be proportionate to God and please Him, if God prescribes some special form of worship and proscribes some other form, men can please God only by honoring Him in the way in which He orders and by refraining from those practices and sacrifices which He forbids. This is the thought behind the Christian's exclusive use of the sacrifice of the Mass and the seven Christian sacraments in his worship.

6. Religious Rights

Men have also felt strongly about their religious rights and privileges. The deeply personal character of our relations with God and the bitter sufferings undergone in religious persecutions cause us serious concern over religious rights. Because of our various duties to God, we have a whole chain of such rights; for it is a constant ethical principle that when God imposes an end, He grants the required means to that end; when He imposes duties, He grants the moral powers to fulfill those duties; when He fixes full responsibility for some action or omission, He confers proportionate authority to act or not to act as He commands. Accordingly, man has the right of conscience or the inviolable freedom from external compulsion in following the reasoned dictates of his conscience; he has the right to obtain religious knowledge, to receive religious education, to speak and write about religion, and to develop religious culture; he has the right to worship God according to the dictates of conscience, to assemble with others for public worship of God, to own places of public divine worship of God, and to have property that is devoted solely to religious uses exempt from taxation; he has the right to set up institutions for religious education and religious charities, to believe any supernatural doctrines given by God, to the opportunity for sincere repentance or contrition, and generally, the right of access to means for divine help. Furthermore, it stands to reason that since right is a moral power, there can never be a true right to anything contrary to religion. Thus there is no right to blaspheme or to spread atheistic literature.

7. THE RELIGIOUS PERSON AND THE RELIGIOUS LIFE

One of the compliments that we pay in our culture is to praise someone as a religious person. This expression has many shades of meaning. It may refer to a minister or priest who is consecrated or officially designated to worship God publicly for the sake of a human community, as its mediator before God. It may refer to a member of a religious order or congregation. It may designate a member of a particular church. It usually refers to someone whose life has a religious tone or spirit. Such a person does not merely conform externally to some religious practices, while he lives by some other worldly or selfish standard. Rather, his mind considers God the most important of all beings and his own relations with God the most important circle of his activities. He has religious convictions; he believes, and he acts according to his beliefs. He worships according to his conscience; he is reverent to God in private and in public; he prays regularly. He regards the religious upbringing of his children as one of the greatest privileges that he can give them. He tries consistently and daily to serve under the authority of God and to live for the love of God. God dominates his daily life.

In a philosophy that is truly suited to man's nature, capacities, and needs there must be a big view of God and large room for cultivating our connections with God. Since God exists and has such majestic and profound rights over us, no one of us can be thoroughly good without religion. People are not fond of the Sunday saint and weekday sinner. But it is just as bad to seem to be a weekday saint and be a Sunday sinner, to be a man who seems to be inculpable in his dealings with his fellow men, and yet is very blameworthy for his neglect of or opposition to God. The good man must love both God and man.

One of the more encouraging characteristics of human nature shines in the many human beings, non-Christians as well as Christians, who have united in groups to lead a religious life, apart from secular interests as far as possible. We find Essenes among the ancient Hebrews, monasteries of monks in India, Tibet, Burma, China, and Japan, and many groups or orders and congregations for men and women in the

Catholic Church, as well as in a few of the Protestant sects.

The religious life is, of course, a way of life, one based on a clear theory of the high importance of religion to life and on preferred means to reach religious ideals. Out of love for God and trust in Him people band together in a community of like-minded persons to dedicate their total lives to God's glory and service and to use their best united efforts to fulfill the will of God on earth. In fact, canon law defines the religious state as that permanent manner of living together in which the faithful undertake to observe both the precepts binding on all and the gospel counsels by means of the vows of obedience, chastity, and poverty.[6] A religious, then, is a man or woman who has taken vows in such a group. Because the vows are promises to God or religious acts controlling his life, that life is called the religious life.

Other forms of saintly living are not technically a religious life. Thus, the Virgin Mary and St. Joseph led a family life. A holy person continuing to lead a personal life of great virtue, but not in an organized community under authority — as the famous Irishman Matt Talbot — is not leading a religious life in the canonical sense of the term. Nor is the life of a theologian devoted to speculation about God and religious doctrines a formally religious way of living. It must be a common life, under recognized authority, religious rather than scholarly in motivation, pledged to the evangelical counsels, devoted, at least in part, to prayer, and striving for the perfection of Christian charity.

There are various types of religious life consecrated to God. Each religious founder, approved by the Church in his or her organization, seems to have been raised up by God to meet some fairly permanent need of the Church and to meet this need in a particular way, through a particular type of spiritual training. First, we see distinctive particular ends in view in different religious bodies. Some are devoted chiefly to prayer; others combine prayer and active service to their fellow men. Some are designed mainly to take care of orphans or the sick or the aged or vagrants. Others are concerned with preaching or education or converts or foreign missions or with particular classes as the Negroes, the incurables, or prisoners. The variety of such objectives is as wide as the Spirit of God who expresses Himself in these various good works undertaken for the love of Him. Second, the spirit of different groups may differ widely, even when they have the same objectives. Thus, the Carmelite, Carthusian, and Trappist types of contemplative order have each a distinctive spirit, training, traditions, points of emphasis, and special means of carrying out their own religious ideal. Continually, new forms of religious life develop to fit new needs and new conditions in the Church and in society generally.

That a religious way of life offers singular advantages to a person who is free of other obligations to devote himself principally or solely to God seems to be very clear. There are all the advantages of a common pursuit of high moral goodness, with the bonds of tradition, noble example, encouragement, similarity of spiritual formation, and organization. The golden knots of the vows maintain separation from worldly interests and demand constant practice of more than ordinary virtue. One can know from religious authority what is the will of God for all particulars of one's life, with little risk of selfishness. A good portion of each day is reserved for prayer or personal contact with God. A certain element of kindly surveillance protects the members against error and decline of fervor. There is a great treasure of mutual kindliness and helpfulness and loyalty within the group. Above all, religious life confers the deep joy of knowing that each day one is doing one's practical best to please God and that an immense reward awaits in heaven, in God's company. Hence, life for God at its best is often to be found in such a dedicated life.

Chapter 15

Life in Society

1. The Fact of Human Sociality

EACH HUMAN being is a distinct person who is himself and no one else. He has his own private life, his own body and soul, and especially his own interior life of thought and desire. Yet this separate individual whole being usually likes to be in the company of other human beings. Men like to talk together, to work together, to dine together, to worship together. They find that it is more fun to play together than to amuse themselves alone. They wish to have friends and to be well thought of by others. They seek the help of others. They are often restless and discontented when alone or left out of the group. Most significant of all, persons of diverse sexes are intensely attracted to each other's companionship and usually share wealth, habitation, rights, time, and life with each other.

Philosophers inquire into the reasons for this fact of human sociality. Is life together an essential and permanent feature of human living, or is it but an acquired trait which might be absent from human life and some day disappear? Is human group action the result merely of certain historical, evolutionary, and cultural circumstances? Is it like the herd instinct of such "social" animals as graze, migrate, and hunt in groups? Or is man naturally made to live, work, and variously share human happiness and perfection with other persons?

2. The Concept of Society

A society is something peculiar to human nature. It is not the product of a nonrational physical law driving people to unite as sheep gather in flocks and ants in colonies. A society is created by human intelligence and will; it is a work of reason. The mere physical nearness of people crowded in the same place, as in a bus or restaurant, is not a society. Society unites the minds and wills of two or more persons or groups of persons who agree to pursue some common aim together. This unity of objectives known and willed is the special human feature in society. Many men become in some way one. They form a moral union with a bond on the moral faculties of the component members.

Even a moral union of people is not usually regarded as a society unless the union is intended to be rather long-lasting. One date does not make a marriage. One meeting is not an organization. People who come together in one place to view a movie or attend a dance do perform a social activity, but they remain individuals somewhat casually united for a short period, and they do not form a permanent group with an enduring common purpose. When they unite together for a more permanent common enterprise, as for domestic happiness, operating a railroad, marketing wheat, or maintaining national security, then they are properly said to constitute a society.

In this permanent mutual association men's minds and wills must be seeking the same good. If they are at cross-purposes to each other, they are not a society. Moreover, they must not merely mean to share certain benefits together; they must intend to set up some ways of seeking that good together. Whatever the goal, whether wealth, recreation, or learning, they must arrange for the use of common means as determined by the group or its authorities. The common good is to be not only a true good for all the members and belong proportionately to each of them; it is also to be a good which the members achieve in concert and willingly share with their fellows.

This entire concept of society is summed up in the customary scholastic definition that a society is a permanent moral union of two or more persons seeking a common good that is to be attained by their co-operative activity.

3. MAN NATURALLY A SOCIAL BEING

To the question whether his very nature as a free human being destines man to live in society, the scholastic philosophers answer that the facts clearly prove that man is naturally a social being in the sense explained. Society is natural, for men generally have the abilities, interests, and needs for living in fairly permanent association with other persons.

The prerogative of speech, a mark of man's spirituality, is also a main mark of his aptitude for social relations with other men. Speech is a two-way external signal system between human minds and wills. It is mainly a power of conveying one's meaning, one's thoughts, plans, desires, and purposes to someone who can understand thought and aspiration. Through speech men can share their knowledge with each other, ask and learn, instruct each other, inform others of their needs, add to each other's stock of information, tell of their affections and love for each other, and give the signals required to get group action by many following the same purpose and method. Imagine, for instance, how men could cope with a flood if they could not communicate to each other the definite efforts all should make to save lives and property. Concord of action becomes possible through speech.

Human nature has also a natural battery of social emotions and sentiments for other people. Love, hatred, rivalry, sympathy are some of these. The ways of expressing these affections may be learned; the emotions themselves may be more developed in some, more restrained in others; but all men seem to have them as part of their native endowment. They are emotions socially oriented. The native human capacity for friendship with our equals is another one of these inherent trends to social living.

The natural gift of sexual diversity and mutual complement of man and woman in living together is one of the most obvious facts in the world. Neither man nor woman alone is biologically complete as a member of the race.[1]

The powers of leadership and its corresponding powers of discipleship are also naturally found in man. Human beings are born to rule and to be ruled.[2] Some have the talent for planning, organizing, counseling, and commanding; others have the gift of obeying, imitating, and executing others' plans. The ability to copy and to emulate his elders is one of the child's best assets for learning.

These many aptitudes are not inactive, for men commonly find much satisfaction in the mutual give-and-receive of social living. They strongly show their social powers day by day in companionship, in the home circle, in working together, in sympathizing with each other, in commanding and obeying, and in keeping up with the Joneses by imitative rivalry. Most songs and novels are full of the attraction of lovers to each other.

Beyond this constant tendency to associate together, the constant and general need for a shared life clinches the argument for the natural sociality of man. No man can even begin to live without the gift of life from others; and as babies, all once were in hourly need of help from the members of the family. Youth needs parental care in many particulars for a good many years. The ignorant need the learned; the poor need the pooled resources of their class or the help of the wealthy; the ill need the healthy; the grieving need comforters; the very aged need aid from young strength; experts need trained helpers; all need good example and fair treatment; man and woman need each other for the fulfillment of sexual life; the race needs families and communities for its continuance. For thousands of economic achievements, for an abundance and fair distribution of goods, men must plan together, work together, and share in building, training, planting, harvesting, sailing, and many other projects that only the mutual effort of many people can bring about. Labor unions understand the need and strength of union of persons, objectives, and programs. Without human association in works of education and of charity, ignorance and barbarism prevail while culture, progressive science, and the benefits of civilization wither away. Disorder and anarchy, perils from physical dangers of infections, fires, and contamination of water supplies, immense difficulties from lack of roads and other communications, immense risks due to the uncontrolled passion and plundering by the stronger and less conscientious, in short, a semihuman life would characterize most men if they did not live within the strong circle of society. This weakness of man without society is very intelligible, since his nature is no more built to do without people than to live without air.

4. Social Unity and Social Strength

Men can, then, enter into enduring unions with other men; they wish to do so; and they need lasting unions in pursuing common goals by common means. By the very fact of being human, they are in some way one with their fellows. In this context the famous words of the British writer, John Donne, merit repetition. As an Englishman, he is contrasting the tight island of Britain, then so well protected by its sea barriers, with the big European continent.

No man is an island, intire of itselfe; every man is a peece of the Continent, a part of the Maine; if a Clod bee washed by the Sea,

Europe is the lesse, as well as if a Promontorie were, as well as if a Mannor of thy friends or of thy owne were: any man's death diminishes me, because I am involved in Mankinde. And therefore never send to know for whom the bell tolls; it tolls for thee.[3]

I am a part of mankind, I am a member of the human race. All the joys, griefs, experiences, needs, and injustices of any man in some measure concern me who am a man as others are. In the fundamentals of nature we are all equal and are all involved in each other's weal or woe. Our sympathies, our prayers, our honor go out to every man. Our protest against violation of the rights of the innocent anywhere is a mode of protection of our own rights; for if others suffer today, we may be the victims tomorrow. This conviction that men are our brothers and that we are their keepers has inspired many pieces of noble writing, among them the Charter of the United Nations. Pius XII penned memorable words on the unity of the human race and the consequent duty of charity to all men in the first of his encyclicals, written early in World War II.

> It is the marvelous vision, which makes us see the human race in the unity of one common origin in God . . . ; in the unity of nature which in every man is composed of material body and spiritual, immortal soul; in the unity of the immediate end and mission in the world; in the unity of dwelling place, the earth of whose resources all men can by natural right avail themselves to sustain and develop life; in the unity of the supernatural end, God Himself, to whom all should tend; in the unity of the means to secure that end.[4]

The Pope continues on our supernatural unity. This includes our common lot as victims of original sin, our common union with the Son of God as our ransom, and our common sharing in the social body, Christ's Church.

Since all men have the same basic goods of nature and destiny, since all are our equals as images of God, all deserve the kind of love that we give to ourselves because of the real goodness in our own nature. Each deserves good will, appreciation, good treatment, justice, and help when he is in need and I am able to help. Whether it is pleasant or difficult for us to refrain from harm to others and to meet their needs is morally irrelevant. Whether we are prejudiced against others or unduly fond of ourselves is of no concern. I need not love all equally well. But I must equally refrain from harming anyone. All must be precious to me, and I precious to them, because we are creatures precious to God who made us like His goodness and for His goodness.

In union there is strength. Yes, and life, too, and joy. The root of helpful living among men is deep and loyal regard for people. But it is only one of many bonds that hold men together for their common betterment. Friendship is an even stronger bond. This lovely and mysterious human characteristic consists in a mutual esteem and love between two or more persons, resulting in a desire to share one's goods, whatever they be, with the one who is loved. In its selflessness it also strives to share the burden of another's sorrows. Friendship surpasses mere acquaintanceship. Genuine friendship makes the beloved one's other self, identifies self with his good, loves him for his sake and not for one's own advantage or for the friend's presents and tokens of affection.[5] One of its most beautiful forms is found in the love of husband and wife in a lifetime of fidelity to each other. No human association equals friendship in its measure of delight, its expansion of character, and its constructive results. Friendship puts a crowning halo on the reverence which man has for man.

Leadership by the proper social authority is another strong bond for keeping men together in active community living. In the civic community, its instrument for directing the members and enforcing order is law; in a private community, its instrument is precept. In any enterprise that is complex, difficult, or extended over a long time, authority must guide and control the activities of several people so that their minds may unite in a common plan and their work be organized to a common end by the use of common and agreed means. The need of competent authority can be seen in domestic, industrial, military, and civic affairs. A mass of people without a head is a mob doing harm, not a society achieving a common good. In the relatively simple society of the home, husband and wife may easily have quite different ideas about a new house for their family. They may discuss their ideas on its size, style, materials, location, space arrangement, garage, garden, and cost. But after discussion someone must decide just what plan is to be followed, what the details of the building are to be, where to buy, how to finance the purchase or construction, when to move into the new place. Some authority must bring unity of mind, purpose, and action into the family.

In civic matters the urgency of a bond of authority to unite the community is far greater. Society means people agreeing to common goals through common use of suitable means. Frequently, however, it is not obvious what means are to be used; it is not necessary that any one set of laws and means accomplish the national or communal good. If it be a strip of road that is to be built by the community, some agency must decide on the course of the road, its width, its type of paving, the method of paying for it, the employment of surveyors and workers, and the time for beginning the job. Where there is no single way, no one necessary way, someone must decide on a good practical way among various good ways and carry through until the task has been finished.

Stability of social institutions, respect for social customs, and prudent moderation in legal and social changes help much to hold society together. Change, even for the better, may break old bonds and fracture the social cement. This is one lesson which the ideologists and some social reformers find impossible to learn.

Contentment in social living and provision for gradual progress are aided immeasurably if affairs are so managed that the members realize that the good of the community is their own good and that their sacrifices for the common good redound to their own benefit. Where there is conflict between the personal good and the supposed social good, where there is suppression of private rights in the supposed communal interest, where any injustice or excessive and unnecessary burden or exploitation of members appears, there is disorder which breeds discontent and divides rather than unites men. In a contented community people experience that society is an instrument supplementing personality, not a weapon to diminish personality and destroy personal goods.

The man who would live fully must live socially. He will find that unselfish and faithful work for the members of the communities to which he belongs enriches his life and affords wonderful opportunities for maturing many virtues. Life in the family is the basic training ground for this flowering of the social virtues. The demands of thoughtfulness for others, respect for their claims, sharing in common chores, rejoicing and sympathizing and working together, adapting oneself to other people, patience with the peculiarities of others, practice in persuading them to see one's views, tolerant compromises in action, leading and obeying in the domestic circle, these and other virtues learned in the family prepare men for their analogous practice in other communities to which they belong.

"Happiness was born a twin." Man will be happier with persons than with things, happier in society than out of it, happier by generously participating in society, and very happy if he dedicates his life to the service of others, whether in the family, in his profession, or in civic tasks. Without dedicated social leaders life would be less human.

5. DIFFERENCES OF SOCIAL GOODS

Societies differ from each other in many ways. The fundamental difference consists in the good for which the society exists and which it pursues. The family seeks the welfare of its children. A scientific team seeks victory over some disease. A yacht club seeks anchorage and sport for its members. A corporation seeks profit from manufacturing machines. The Church seeks the salvation and perfection of souls. The state seeks general security and temporal prosperity for its subjects. In each case the end or common good pursued specifies a society or puts it in its proper class.

When this common good of the group is determined, the proper means can be settled and steps can be taken to achieve this good. The rights, duties, suitable activities, and the duration of societies depend principally on their respective ends. In the case of the marital society, even the proper membership is determined by the good in view.

It is also true that many societies gradually shape certain institutional means or permanent structures, policies, and customary methods by which they work steadily for the social good. States, for instance, have constitutions and other fairly constant laws, judicial rules, stable organs of governing, and habitual forms of administration which people come to understand, to expect, and to use effectively. Such institutions must be judged by their apt relation to the specific good of the society.

6. THE FIRST SOCIETY, THE FAMILY

The most important societies are the family, the state, and the Church. The most basic is the family. It most clearly manifests the social nature of man, his social interdependence, and his social well-being.

The family as a social structure need not for most purposes be distinguished into the society of husband and wife and into the fuller society of father, mother, and children. The familial group is distinguished from all other societies in the first place by its special common good — the welfare of its members in all daily necessities of life on earth and particularly, the welfare of the children of the home. This welfare of the children has two aspects: (1) their procreation under conditions suitable to human dignity and human need and (2) the long years of their education and development in body and mind until they are ready to go forth and found homes of their own or take up independent vocations in the world. Asylums, orphanages, and foster homes are but substitutes for the family when death, accident, poverty, or parental neglect have deprived the child of its normal environment and normal protection.

This association of father, mother, and children grows out of the very nature of man. It is a society for which human beings have the natural aptitudes, the constant and universal tendencies, and, most especially, the constant and common need.

Man and woman, biologically and psychologically different as they are, certainly have the ability to complement each other in sexual union and sexual affection. They have the power of language with which to share each other's thoughts and to learn how to work together for their common benefit in their home. They have a natural gift to care for, love, and help the children born of their union. Children, in turn, have the natural aptitude to receive care from their father and mother, to obey and copy them, and to grow under the sympathetic guidance of their parents.

Moreover, men and women have a strong desire for each other's companionship, for finding sexual comfort together, for living together in all the intimacies of family life, for having a dwelling of their own, a life of their own apart from other people, and for lavishing their tender providence on their own children. People expect from marriage the largest practicable measure of human happiness here on earth. It is not surprising that wedding bells keep ringing daily all over the world.

Most telling of all is the natural need for just this permanent union of man and woman together with their children. There is a natural need of propagating or continuing the human race. To continue the human race and not a mere animal species, children must be born under conditions that give them fair opportunity to become truly human. For their dependence is total in body and in mind. They need food, shelter, clothing, health care, affection, encouragement, instruction in many human arts, help in walking, speaking, praying, choice, self-management, and every manner of pursuing happiness. Long years of care, patience, devotion, and understanding from persons who love them dearly is needed to accomplish this task of bringing children to human adult perfection. Only the family can do this well. The parents need this society, too, for the control of their passions. They need it as a school in virtue. The children ordinarily need each other's company for their best mental and social development. These many needs are all normally and readily met in the family's mutual helpfulness.

The unique purpose of marriage gives it a prominent religious aspect, since the use of marital rights is the usual occasion for God to produce new human souls destined to give Him glory by union with Himself. Wedlock is unique in its contractual terms and conditions. It starts with two free human acts of the spouses who freely choose each other and grant to each other the exclusive and lifelong right to life-giving acts. Although people may become members of some other societies without their choice, as by birth, draft, election, enrollment, or economic compulsion, man and woman become marital partners only by personal use of their liberty. They choose their partners and choose the married state with its opportunities and responsibilities. Hence, marrying is one of the deepest acts of love that people perform. The usual joyousness of this occasion does not conceal its greatness as an act with profound personal and social values.

At the same time, human experience testifies that fruitful and peaceful marriage is needed for achieving the specific domestic good of the children's welfare and the related goods of mutual happiness of the partners, regulation of passion within the purpose of the sex function, and development of good character in the spouses. For such fruitfulness, peace, order, and human perfection in marriage anything less than a perpetual and exclusive union would be generally insufficient. Temporary or multiple marriages would in various ways defeat or hinder the very purposes of this society. Accordingly, polygamy and divorce are intolerable foes to family life. They offer no relief to family ills, but rather set a trend that destroys family status, creates new hardships, and robs children of normal opportunities for physical, emotional, and moral health and happiness.

7. PRIORITY OF THE FAMILY

The family is said to be the first of societies. One of the confusions of socialism is that it puts society before the person in all or most matters and that among societies it puts the state before and over the family in value, purpose, and rights. In this view, the family and its members belong to the state. The state at most legally permits the association of its members in their own families and tolerates some degree of independence in family matters. This is a serious misreading of the social nature of man.

Scholastic philosophers join with all other Christians and some non-Christians in defending the primacy of the family over the state. It has precedence in several respects.

The family is complete in time before the existence of the state. It has its complete being as a social body before civil society is formed. Heads of families get together for their common protection and betterment and form a state or public body consisting of many families. Historically, the state is their creation. When the state is dissolved by war, corruption, or other disaster, it is family heads who again reorganize the state.

It is clear, too, that human beings must receive the gift of life and its basic advantages through their families; with life come the rights to all things needed for their suitable human development. People must be members of families before they can qualify for civic membership or any auxiliary civic advantages.

Families, also, have juridical or legal priority over states, since their heads consent to create states, decide on political union, plan forms of government, impose limitations on powers, and determine the headship of states. The family does not surrender itself to the state, but forms the state to help families in matters economic, cultural, and political where co-operation of many families under common authority is needed or desirable for human well-being.

Hence the family has a moral priority and superior excellence. It has its own purposes in the welfare of its children and members, in the intellectual, physical, and moral education of the young, and in the general happiness of the whole family group. This purpose is loftier than the protection of justice and the provisions for welfare by the civic unit. The family, furthermore, has its own complete social authority, vested in its parents, granted to it immediately by God, and in no way merely delegated or tolerated by the state. Finally, the family has its own rights and duties, its own sacredness, its own high loyalties to its own members. The rights here come to the members of the family as members of that family, directly from God, and not primarily from state legislation.

The family duties in the same domestic matters are personal responsibilities of the members to God via His natural law. The state can in no way legislate these duties out of existence.

The consequences of this priority and superiority of the family are profound and socially most important. One consequence is known as the principle of subsidiarity, which declares that states are secondary and supplementary to families. Civic communities exist for the sake of families, to protect their rights and to foster their welfare. They dare not destroy or interfere with sound family life.

Consistent with this subsidiary role, the state is not the primary or exclusive educator of the child. Its role is to assist the parents in exercising their inviolable rights to care for and educate their own children. Seizure of the right, destruction or impairment of its reasonable exercise is practically to take the child from the authority and affection of his parents. Children do not belong to the state. Even civic claims on the services of the young may not destroy the antecedent natural claims of parents for help from their children in times of need. Nonsocialist countries, as our own, recognize this fact by exempting sons of needy parents from military service or by supporting parents of sons who must be drafted in exceptional circumstances.

So basic is domestic society that its fundamental moral law is also independent of the state. Human lawmakers may ratify and protect the natural law for families. But human law cannot morally modify or intrude upon that higher law. As it cannot create marriages, it cannot dissolve these unions. It may not arbitrarily separate the members of families. It may not impair the rights of spouses to each other's loyalty, fidelity, care, and companionship. It may not intrude on family privacy. It must recognize the domain of family secrets as privileged testimony. It must guard family property and uphold the right of family inheritance. It must give legal protection for the economic needs of families by fair-wage laws, health assistance, educational helps, and related measures. By the gift of God, not by the gift of the state, parents and children may say: "My home is my castle." My home is my own fort, my own realm, my final stronghold on earth in which we members of the family are sovereigns pursuing our own happiness.

CHAPTER 16

The Life of the Citizen

1. THE STATE'S SPECIAL PLACE IN HUMAN LIFE

To COMPLETE our vision of the basic order in the planes of human life, philosophy must also help us understand the public order of human life. The political wisdom of the philosopher, although only one of many sources of our knowledge of man in civic society, supplies some guidance, especially when it clings close to the facts of universal human needs.

Besides their social lives within their own homes, men lead various forms of public life. In large economic enterprises scores, hundreds, even thousands of men and women combine their abilities and work together to produce machines such as automobiles or provide some public services such as telephone facilities and supermarkets. By united efforts they succeed in supporting themselves and in achieving truly impressive results. Various small associations of persons and families aim at cultural, recreational, and economic advantages by private agreements, contracts, partnerships, and club memberships. In big universities and big hospitals people share some part of their lives and activities for some particular nonfamilial purpose. On a more spectacular and national scale, we see public life in the political parties, labor congresses, and manufacturers' associations.

The modern community to which every man, even the celibate and virgin, belongs is the state. Our intent is not a full analysis of the philosophy of the state but an insight into the ways in which the state can help or hurt human life and affect personal development and family well-being.

The political social group must not be dreamily pictured as a bigger family, more loosely knit than a family in its daily contacts, less intense in its bonds of friendship, severer in authority, and stronger in power. Its purpose differs much from that of the family; and since purpose specifies a society, its different purpose leads to many divergent characteristics between the domestic group and the political community. The state is a life-supporting institution or group of institutions; it is not a life-giving society. It is not the basic society, but a supplementary natural aid to man. It looks immediately to the temporal and external goods of man. It does not bestow on the individual those many tokens of affection, instruction, minute care, encouragement, and forgiving love which the family provides for the nearly total formation of its members. To expect such family-style treatment of individuals in the operations of some government office or army post would be foolishly unrealistic. Instead, the state rather impersonally attends to masses of people and to general needs. A good state will be touched with a spirit of justice and of efficiency, but it does not pretend to that personal consideration of the individual's needs, desires, tastes, and opportunities which the home circle affectionately gives to each of its members. Yet for all its impersonal, corporative nature the state can evoke from its members a remarkable social spirit and a whole gamut of special emotions and virtues: enthusiasm, loyalty, patriotism, honor to the nation and its authorities, obedience to law, generosity in serving the common good, military ardor, reverent memories of its heroes, fierce love of national liberty, and a common sense of united adventure in living.

2. CAUSES AND CHARACTERISTICS OF A STATE

The scholastic philosophers regard the state as a moral union of families occupying a definite territory who permanently unite together for realizing their complete or self-sufficient temporal life. This definition derives from human history and usage rather than from doctrinaire dreams of a state. The causes and essential properties of the state summed up in this definition deserve some unraveling.

The state plainly wears the markings that belong to a true society, for it is a union of the minds and wills of people for a common purpose and it is meant to be a lasting union. The people united are primarily families or small associations of families such as comprise a village or clan. These band together for a fuller temporal life than they can realize by remaining isolated domestic units. It is not precisely individuals as individuals, but family heads as representatives of already existing social units who propose to work together in a distinct and larger social body, the state. They agree upon some plan of organization and of co-operation in their activity for the intended public benefits. The drafting of this plan or constitution is the first step in the formation of a government for the conduct of public affairs. The founders give their consent to some form of rule; they designate a ruler; they set up procedures for making the public laws and provide some means for defraying public expenses. The more politically trained and astute these pioneers are, the clearer they will be in framing the political program by which the public good is to be obtained, the lasting existence of their state assured, the main organs of governing started, and the dangers of misrule and imbalance avoided. Sage leaders will know that life is often changing; and so they will provide for a certain flexibility of political arrangements to meet new needs, emergencies, expansion, recruitment of government personnel, contacts with other states, and other potential developments. The union thus established must be kept alive by various bonds: public authority, good will in the members of the state, agreement on essentials of the constitution, political consciousness, and the social virtues of legal justice, obedience to law, and patriotism.

Families make the state and always remain its principal part. Other social groups and individuals without families of their own are admitted. Government, on the other hand, is a group of official organs or institutions and is only an official legal part of the state. There is no proper contrast between government and people, but rather between rulers and subjects. For the government officers of every type are also members of the state, subjects of its laws, and subordinate in some points to other officers within the state and to the people as a whole. Only despotisms and mechanically contrived states regard the government as the state and the nongoverning masses as chattels, happy slaves, or raw materials to be processed by the managers of the machine.

Since the end specifies a society and determines the main features of its being and operations, it is important to discover the reason that brings family heads together into this larger formal community. What do they want and expect from it? What arguments do they advance to induce others to join with them? Why do they need such an organization? What is the common good that they find themselves unable to achieve by their individual family efforts or by private arrangements with other relatives, friends, and neighbors, but hope to gain from this broader association? Clearly, this larger federation is sought for some temporal and external good, for some needed or much desired aspect of their temporal happiness. This is a common good, to be obtained for all participating members in due measure and to be gained and kept by their common efforts. The objective is something suitable to man, not something which will harm or impair rights, safety, dignity, humanity, and happiness. Through a united community they mean to provide advantages that will make life self-sufficient for all temporal needs. Because of this ultimacy or self-sufficiency of its end, the state is the highest, the most complete, and the most powerful social body which men set up to realize their temporal well-being effectively and permanently.

The nature of this social good by which a big public organization will supplement the family's efforts for its human welfare has been wisely voiced in the preamble to the *Constitution of the United States:*

> We, the people of the United States, in order to form a more perfect union, establish justice, insure domestic tranquillity, provide for the common defense, promote the general welfare, and secure the blessings of liberty to ourselves and to our posterity, do ordain and establish this *Constitution* for the United States of America.

Our *Declaration of Independence* struck the same note, claiming that the British government of the time had shown itself for a long while unwilling and incompetent to protect the rights and see to the public prosperity of the colonists. Both documents have won the common consent of mankind as expressing basic political aims.

The twin political objectives, then, are temporal peace and temporal prosperity, security and abundance, justice and welfare, protection and development of human goods, public order and public progress. Both categories of goods are in the temporal order. Furthermore, though in practical statecraft these goods often overlap, they are consistent with each other; peace and prosperity involve but do not preclude each other. Temporal goods, we should note, mean not only material goods but also the material means to human spiritual goods of education, family stability, culture, virtue, and religion.

These goods are sought for the people, for their children that will be, and their children's children. Thereby the founders build for the permanent interest of their families as beneficiaries of this civic union. The government and its institutions and laws exist for all the people, not for the rulers or nobles alone, not just for the rich or a political majority or any favored racial or religious enclave. All living within the state are to be benefited proportionally from the co-operative functioning of people and rulers.

To succeed in its long-range purposes, a state requires certain moral powers and physical assets. From the viewpoint of justice, the first of these essential characteristics is the consent of the people to the existence of the state, its constitution and political type, and its actual rulers. From the viewpoint of its temporal sufficiency, the state requires supreme political authority in its conduct of its affairs. As the state has the highest or ultimate temporal end, it must have the highest and ultimate type of temporal authority, able to bind its members by moral bonds and to enforce fair laws by which the common good can be effectively realized. This sovereign authority must also have the moral power to treat with other sovereign states on an equal basis. From the viewpoint of its permanence, the state usually will need stable political institutions, some continuity in its ruling body, a constant legal and fiscal program, a steady foreign policy, and sufficient economic resources to maintain its independence and supremacy as a political unit. Accordingly, physical as well as moral assets seem to be a civic necessity; especially in a time like ours when almost the whole earth is occupied, permanent sovereignty requires independent territory, subject to only one political authority, definitely known and controlled by legally recognized owners, and on the whole economically able to subsist. When, then, families bring their members into the state, they at the same time bring their lands and properties into the state (unless they also own properties under the jurisdiction of some other existing state). Thereby they submit their property to regulation for the common good of all other members in the state, though this does not mean the surrender of what they own to public ownership.

Apart from these basic and universal features, civic institutions may vary widely in different periods, in different nations, and in different opportunities. No one political system, no one type of governmental distribution or concentration of powers, no type of political alliance is at all times needed for the common good. Perhaps, however, there is a practical necessity today for some form of representative democracy and some international league of states lest separate peoples or the human race perish.

3. A NATURAL, SOVEREIGN, AND LIMITED SOCIETY

Living in a state is so normal to man because the state is a natural society. Reason recognizes it as natural to man's abilities, desires, and needs. Men generally have the aptitudes for political union in which they use their powers of speech to find agreement on means; they have natural capacity to rule and be ruled, to command and obey; they can serve each other in temporal needs. Men have through history shown a constant trend to form states or to form them anew when any public disasters, revolutions, or defeats in war have sent states crashing. Men, finally, have regular and universal need for certain human goods of justice and welfare that can be attained only in such a society. Since these aptitudes, tendencies, and needs are natural in all men, they come from the Author of man's nature. From this we infer that in natural societies the essential end and means, the essential rights and duties of leaders and subjects, and the primary measure of authority come directly from God and are regulated by the natural law, not by human opinion, social compact, or mere public law. Though other matters in the state depend chiefly on variable human choice, these fundamental natural matters are chosen under a divine moral obligation laid on all men.

Those natural human necessities for which the state alone can provide with sufficient promptness and efficiency make an almost endless list. Only a people united under authority and law enjoys the substance of justice. Public protection of one's rights must be firmly maintained against the foolish and the criminally disposed. A higher visible authority alone can effectively settle many disputes over private rights and make the settlement stand among the rival claimants. Very often the system of rights and duties among men needs clarification, defense, restoration, and even enrichment by the use of objective public power. This goal of security or peace includes the broad areas of natural, civic, and supernatural rights. Some effectual institutions must safeguard these rights by making all comply with their duties to commutative, distributive, and legal justice.

The welfare of the people also needs public care. Such problems as a water supply for a large population, flood control, protection against fire, housing safety, sanitation, road-making and traffic regulation, keeping of public records on property, marriages, and related matters involving rights, assistance to the large groups of poor, ill, unemployed, and orphaned in our society are a few typical needs that must be met by some power with considerable resources and powers of action. The functions in regard to relief and welfare become ever more numerous; and with increasing wealth states enlarge these benefits, especially where private initiative cannot do what is necessary or cannot do it swiftly enough or at practicable cost or without undue interference with other private interests and rights.

When it functions within its proper ends, the state has that sovereign power which consists in the moral right to command *all* the temporal resources of wealth, services, and restraints which may be necessary to protect justice and open up to all the opportunities for temporal prosperity. The family head can tap only the membership and the usually limited property resources and abilities of his family. Corporate economic enterprises may often have less ability to secure co-operation than has the family head. The state, however, can pool the physical, financial, and personal resources of the whole nation. It can punish injustice, invasion of its members' rights, neglect of public duty, and interference with the common good by fines, imprisonment, and, on occasion, even by death. In defense of justice it may at times go to war. It has the full measure of temporal power to use the necessary means to secure its double temporal purpose, as long as those means are morally licit.

Because of this vast concentration and scope of public power and because of the undoubted success of great states in doing much that private business and private charity cannot do adequately, the tendency has arisen in recent times to look to the state to provide for all human needs and to demand that states enormously expand their services to their people. But expansion of services leads to expansion of powers. Powerful states seldom keep within due limits. Even the grant of extraordinary powers for emergencies commonly runs the risk of making temporary situations permanent, at least in the opinion of the ruling groups, with the result of a socialist, welfare, totalitarian, or even a deified state which vexatiously limits the liberties of the people and saddles upon them the colossus of bureaucracy.

4. The Principle of Subsidiarity

For the sake of human living, therefore, political philosophy must sharply define the boundaries of civic action. The family has a priority over the state and an independence of it. It has created the state to be a helper, not its master or its substitute. The state is only a supplementary or subsidiary society. It both exceeds its purpose and defeats its own role as a helper if it takes over too many functions or assumes too much authority. Even if it does this as a kind Caesar, it is attacking human personality and the family. Under the mask of social benefits, it is doing an evil work.

The principle that primarily measures the legitimate and connatural activities of the state or its government is not its own laws or assumed abilities; the principle is precisely that double temporal public end for which the state has been formed. This principle on ends leads to the consequent principle of subsidiarity,[1] as it has come to be called, which limits the state to a proper secondary role in human activities. According to it, the state has only subsidiary functions. It may act only to supply those goods and opportunities which persons alone or private societies such as families, schools, businesses, and unions by themselves cannot provide, but which are necessary or at least notably useful for public order, human welfare, and human perfection.

This principle does not coincide with the old-style integral liberal view that restricted the state to the performance of only the minimum essentials of protecting rights and contracts of its members. As though justice and prosperity are opposed! It does prohibit the state from assuming unnecessary and useless tasks and from interfering with the rights of persons and societies within its territory. The role of government is added to the roles of persons, families, churches, cultural groups, and other societies; it does not supplant them. The state must not become a huge mushrooming supersociety that absorbs and annihilates all other societies and all other rights. This principle on limited state action is most important in regard to all matters pertaining to the spiritual welfare of men and the freedom of the Church; all these are outside the competence of the state, since the state has only a temporal and external immediate objective for its existence.

In harmony with this principle of subsidiarity is the conception of the state as a pluralist and organic society. As a pluralist society, it contains and preserves many societies, each with its own end, its own autonomy in its sphere, its own rights, its own duties to its members, and its limited duties to the general civic good. Within the state, though only partially under its jurisdiction, thrive many families, religious societies, schools and universities, hospitals and charitable agencies, businesses, labor unions, cultural associations, and other free human groups and corporations. As an organic society, the state has diverse component parts, each with its proper functions. The whole state is healthy if the component parts are retained, if their proper structures are conserved, and their natural functions allowed to operate. The organic view does not reduce all to the same level of ability, merit, and need. It does not demand that all members do the same thing. It gives equal protection of rights to all, confers proportionate benefits, and imposes duties proportionate to the members' ability, office, health, financial capacity, and special experience. The organic state is not a herd of people, but a living spiritual unity; not a mass, not a machine, but a land of men, a unity of persons, a spiritual organism of minds and wills.

5. The State's Contribution to Human Living

Men, having set up states, maintain and control them as powerful helps to living well. A roll call of the institutions and agencies by which governments operate today would give some glimpse of the practical ways in which states contribute to human living. Any good civics book, any superior newspaper often mentions them and their services. What concerns us is the relation of the state to the opportunities to live better now and in the future.

We may begin by noticing the part played by law in the lives of the people. Whatever the state does for its members, it must do in virtue of human legislation and by procedures legally approved; it must act by authorized reasonable and just measures. The benefits of law come to the people both by government action and by popular obedience to the laws.

The juridical recognition of liberties and the administration of justice gives that security under law which is necessary for contentment, peace, and the sense of safety which precedes investment and work for growth.

Laws have an educational value, also, for they guide the minds of men in social standards of human relationships and even in popular moral ideals. For it is commonly assumed that what the law commands is good and what it forbids is evil or a source of evil. The discussion of laws, promotion of their observance, and general reflection on their meaning and worth decidedly contribute to forming our thinking on many issues. Traffic laws, for instance, stimulate thought about care for the lives, health, and convenience of our fellow citizens. Tax laws encourage thinking about the causes for which government revenue is needed: roads, schools, hospitals, relief, and foreign aid. Civil-rights legislation awakens consciences to the needs of minorities and improves our outlook on the plenitude of justice for all groups and races.

The laws also set up a milieu which demands the practice of some civic virtues and provides many excellent opportunities for several social virtues. In this way law habituates us to do at least the civic good, enriches personality by breaking down our limiting selfishness, opens the fields in which people work with and for each other, and encourages obedience, prudence, loyalty, patriotism, honesty, moderation, courage, and charity. Law thus helps create the moral climate that most of us need. It not only fences us from dangers by its restrictions and censorship, but positively promotes the many virtues that good citizenship requires. These precious advantages for human values can, however, be expected only in the free society, in which the largest pursuit of human values, of Christian virtue, of intellectual and moral perfection, and, therefore, of the greatest human happiness becomes possible.

6. THE STATE, A SOURCE OF DANGER

History and experience, however, warn us not to glorify the state as an angel that can do no wrong. There has ever been the problem of the conflict between the individual and authority, between private liberty and public law. The problem of harmonizing private and public good is never perfectly settled. In our days of huge governmental staffs, the dangers to liberty and private good are immeasurably heightened. One of the most recent instances was the tragic spectacle of the government of Hungary and Russia versus the people, not *for* the people.

Governments become sources of danger in many ways. Sometimes they practice injustice to their own people or to other nations. The violation of justice sometimes is caused by imprudence, imperfect laws, legislative compromises and partisan spirit, or mere official bungling. The misconduct of some officials, as in cases of bribery and connivance in vice, which may hurt individual citizens, is usually discountenanced by law and government policy. Sometimes, however, injustice is deliberate policy for the aggrandizement of the state or for the prestige and enrichment of some officials or bureaus or for promotion of a doctrinaire public philosophy. Sometimes the weight of public power stands behind favoritism; partisanship deliberately discriminates against the rights of political, national, racial, and religious minorities and weak neighbors; government distributes its benefits and burdens on unfair bases, providing unequal protection of laws, interfering in and crippling family and cultural life, heaping on needless tax burdens, thwarting religious life and progress, and serving only special interests in a way that deprives or imperils legitimate competing interests. The evils can become so fearsome that, like the unhappily married lover who cannot live without this woman and who cannot live with her, the citizen cannot live outside the state because he is human and has a bad time living in the state because it will not treat him as human.

Another danger to the people lies in weak governments that do too little, that have no clear consistent policy, that are unstable in tenure, or that have been weakened by bad fiscal and diplomatic failures. Governments operating under the theory that the best government is the least government, by *laissez-faire* and *laissez-aller* policies, by multiple small parties, by continual pressure of the electorate on the legislature and cabinet (as in the French parliamentary system) fall very short of fulfilling their duties to their people. Weak governments are peculiarly prone to tolerate or even to manipulate great injustices to their subjects. Because weakness breeds injustice, then disgust, and ultimately violent opposition, crises develop in which such governments fall easy victims to vigorous rebels who seek totalitarian control. Totalitarian states at least manage to get things done, though they often do the wrong things and achieve even right goals in a way that least accords with humanity and justice.

A third and greatest danger comes from the modern Big State, which wields too much power and tries to do too much. One of the great needs of today is the security of the people against their own government and its excessive use as well as its abuse of power. Autocratic systems do not govern by reason and by natural justice, but by the will and desires of the ruler and for his advantage or that of his party. Totalitarian systems more or less completely take over the lives, rights, properties, and careers of their people. The Spartan mirage of uniformity, efficiency, and universal militarism becomes the ideal of government. Subjects are no longer regarded and treated as persons with all the manifold interests and needs of men; they are held to be primarily subjects, followers, prisoners, faceless ciphers wearing dog tags. Everything becomes a state monopoly, not only police, armed forces and courts, but business enterprises and labor unions, banking, farming, transportation, marketing, schools and churches, science and entertainment, housing and care of the needy. If anything is left under private initiative and control, it is by tolerance as long as the ruling body lacks the time, energy, ambition, and opportunity to assume full control or to bend private ownership and personally chosen action to the naked power and arbitrary purpose of the state. In such systems the government or the ruling party is both owner and paymaster, Santa Claus and Bluebeard, the one god and omnipresent devil of its people.

We see all this today in Russia, China, and elsewhere. We saw approximations to it in governments devoted to military imperialism as well as in those states which adopted an unnecessary system of nationalization of major industries, banks, and heavy transportation even when private ownership and management was doing its task well and consistently with the common good. Caesar may be very fatherly and very kind; how long will he remain so? He may be trying to protect his children from every danger; but he becomes a greater danger than any others. Caesar may be a father who allows no responsibility, no choice, no initiative, no privacy to the members of his family. Such a Caesar is governing not men, but animals, robots, disgraced prisoners, doomed slaves. Such a Caesar may find that some of his sons' and daughters' stomachs are full and their little flats warm, but he will not find them free, human, spiritually strong, self-reliant, or happy. No one can ignore human nature and treat men contrary to their spiritual, free reality without destroying human happiness.

In America we are used to the idea of limited authority of the government under God, under the will of the people, and under the law. We have learned well history's lessons of unlimited power in cruel Caesars. But we seem to be slow at learning the lessons about the paternal Caesar and that the same ruin of society follows whether rulers illegally assume unlimited powers or the people so heavily trust the bureaucracy that step by step they give it such powers. Banking, industry, labor leadership, and many educators show signs of being infected with this civic disease of trusting or demanding that the state do too much and settle every one of our problems for us. What is worse is the naïve tendency to transform the government's supplementary powers into original and exclusive powers in regard to education, social charities, health care, marriage legislation, marital morality, and population control. The state's function of assisting, stimulating, watching, and regulating becomes exclusive power to do all things and refusal to allow any person or group to decide upon or accomplish anything. The creature of the people has become a devouring monster. Excessive governmental activity usually costs more and wastes more than private efforts. Governments have no more resources than they can take from their people: the land, the wealth, the personnel, the thinking are all drawn from the people. All that government does, it must do by people and with their property. It can organize and distribute better in some matters. It can invent no wealth nor mystically multiply it just by writing a law. Usually, when it tries too much, it will bungle because it attempts something for which it is natively unfit. Worse, it always weakens liberty; it degrades the human dignity of its subjects; it mistrusts private right and leadership. Its monopoly in educational and moral matters is sure, sooner or later, to sink to very low quality, as its experiments in monopolizing marital legislation have already shown. There is a big place for the operations of government in life; but it must not try to fill the place which only God, the free spirit, and human love can occupy.

A fourth peril lies in the poison of materialism or secularism that is endemic to the political community for at least two reasons: its immediate end is temporal and external advantage, and its popular support requires visible, material results. This focusing on material goods and on the successes that go with wealth makes ruling powers forget that these things are only part of the lives and needs of men, and a subordinate part at that. The duty of the state to guard and promote the spiritual interests of its members by temporal means of protection, encouragement, and even some financing, if needed, is completely neglected. Indeed, the Church comes to be regarded as a rival of the proud, all-powerful state. The state engrossed in the affairs of earth insists that God has nothing to do with public life, political morality, civic ideals, and governmental procedures. It becomes a godless state. It is then hurrying to the graveyard where wicked states lie buried, for it has forgotten its origins, charter, and secondary place in the divine plan for human living.

7. OFFICIAL PHILOSOPHIES OF LIFE

The foregoing principles of the civic community are principles of natural law, valid for all men. They constitute the "public philosophy," the natural political wisdom which reason discovers as universally true and necessary wherever men gather into states. But a most alarming peril exists in those modern states in which the government or the dominant party adopts an official philosophy of life, often containing irrational and antihuman elements. Every engine of propaganda, censorship, and education then inculcates it and it alone into subjects. Every state, of course, must have some body of ultimate principles on man and human society which stand behind its political system.[2] There is no constitution, no political structure, no code of laws without some aims and some conception of justice and success. Such public documents in a free state are made known to all; they are subjects of reasonable discussion and criticism, and are open to amendment, adjustment, and improvement.[3]

But a government which adopts an official philosophy as its own is often very conscious that this is not the people's philosophy. It extends this partisan view of life far beyond the political realm and into nearly all phases of human activity. Seeking conformity of all minds with its official political doctrines, it puts its full power behind the teaching of this dogma. It uses its monopoly of schools and of means of communication to promote the official line of thought. The party line fills the press, the air waves, the books used by unsuspecting children in the schools. Orthodox adherence to this line becomes a condition for government and military service, for teaching positions, for executive promotions, and even for obtaining ration cards and employment. Such a government forbids all reasoned examination of its position. It threatens doubters and terrorizes dissidents. It censors all news reports or even historical accounts that do not agree with the government's official policy. Thought control, brainwashing, mind-closing, conditioning minds to react instantly as the government desires are the aims of all this indoctrination; truth and ability to find truth are by no means sought. The government becomes a teacher, whereas it really has nothing to teach. The state becomes a philosopher, whereas it must borrow its principles. The politicians become the judges of culture. The bureaucrats set up a false religion with a creed, code, cult, and pantheon of its own. The state seeks to make men good, to form, that is, the official type of mechanical goodness which the rulers believe consists in automatic conformity of thought, emotional enthusiasm, and sacrificial action for whatever good or evil the government wants. There will be no questions, for the will of those in power has all the answers about truth, virtue, beauty, law, life, and happiness.

God, the standard of all things, deliver the peoples in those lands whose rulers' wills are the measures of goodness and truth!

How the citizens will effectively oppose these dangers is more a matter of political science and strategy[4] than of political philosophy and morality. It is political intelligence rather than political vigilance which philosophy teaches. Clarity of ideals does, however, precede prudential action. There is a double need for the personal good and the common good; there is a double danger of too little and too much government for human perfection. Hence, there must be limitations on erratic personality and on overpowering governments. Since the people are the state, their own providence must preserve both liberty and law, cherish persons as well as the community, achieve the good of all to the injury of none.

CHAPTER 17

The Ideal Human Life

1. THE DISCUSSION OF IDEALS

LONG AGO Socrates and Plato opened a path dear to all moralists and religious thinkers when they reflected on the perfect pattern for the individual man and for the society in which man lives. The model, the *eidos*, the supreme type of human life perennially evokes the attention of the "dreamers" — poets and schoolmasters, philosophers and theologians, political theorists and reformers, conservatives and revolutionaries, atheists and believers, Marxists and anti-Marxists. Every one of them has his own version of humanism. Each wishes to be on man's side. All appeal for thought and action in order to make the man of their dreamland come to life.

The theme of the paragon of human excellence has several levels of meaning. The best for man may mean the best in itself or abstractly; in that sense, the pursuit of wisdom in contemplation is said to be the best. It may mean the best in the concrete, the best suited to the temperament, gifts, opportunities, and the historical social situation of the individual person; in this sense, the philosopher-king of Plato or the magnanimous man of Aristotle might have been the best for their days in Greece. It may mean the best for the individual man or the best for human society. It may mean the noblest, the most heroic, the most successful, the most winning, the most cultured, or the most permanent ideal man. It may mean the highest ideal that is open to every human being who will do his part to achieve it, or it may merely mean some aristocratic ideal accessible to only a favored few. It may mean a type of life marked by great fullness and unity as presented in the arbitrary portrait drawn by a philosopher or it may mean some splendid form set before us by a religious sage or biog-

208

rapher. It may even mean a life resembling a divine model set before us by God Himself.

The question of the ideal man and his ideal life becomes inextricably tangled with discussion of the best society in which to realize the human ideal and with debate over the educational means by which to develop such men. Such considerations assume that the world and social institutions are, like man himself, good and perfectible but not the best. The ideal is not taken for granted but is still to be achieved.

An ideal is usually an idea or concept of something excellent. Less frequently an ideal refers to an actually existing person or institution which is considered to be the best possible of its kind and exactly what one would desire for one's own life or community. Ideals are born in many ways: from experience, history, analysis of character and failures. But however it dawns on the mind, the ideal begins as something known.

In its portrait of perfection the ideal may contain various elements, of which the chief will be the goals or goods which belong to the mental model, the motives for striving to realize that ideal, the principles of its structure and the norms it provides for action, the graded set of values, and the unifying or integrating resultant of all these factors. The ideal must be both high and unified. It must, too, be possible; otherwise, it will be elusive, purely visionary, misleading rather than energizing. As a sort of absolute, something at the top of the ladder of beings of its kind, the ideal lacks nothing that is proper to the nature of the being of which it is a model; it is simply good, for it has all perfection due to such a thing.

Born in knowledge, the exemplar picks up effectiveness by becoming an object of aspiration, a criterion of choice, a spring of action, and a guide to development. The ideal excites admiration in the intelligent agent. Its goodness, conceived as a practicable goal, stimulates desire. The more it is thought about, the more it is desired; the more definite it becomes, the stronger tug it exerts on the agent's will. The ideal, conceived and appealing, becomes an end. As an end, it motivates the agent. He chooses to work to make it come true. Guided by it in his efforts, he deliberately seeks and uses the means which will actualize the ideal. The ideal itself stands as the polar star by which men set their course through all the variable seas of circumstances, means, mistakes, and partial successes until the dream comes true, until the thought and hope become an accomplished fact. The process demands vividness of conception, enthusiastic appreciation, and practical effort.

We can trace this process from ideal through finality through agency to success in many human aspirations and discoveries. The flight of birds inspired the Greek effort at a flying man and the modern efforts at airplane construction. The floating of tree trunks on water suggested boatbuilding. The sounds of birds, rustling leaves, and moving waters in spring woods have suggested tone poems to musicians. The gentleness of a mother guides a son to courteous manners. Some unbelievably perfect vision guided Michelangelo in his presentation of the figure of God the Father in his *Creation* and of the figure of the Virgin in his *Pietá*.

All this is possible because our rational nature gives us capacity to think of the best, admire the best, love it, desire to share in the noblest, begin to live for it, and carry on until the nearest approach to the best is achieved.

2. Modes of Imitation of the Ideal

The agent striving for his ideal deliberately imitates it in his actions. When the model is a real person, its power to evoke the imagination and love of the imitator tends to yield superior results. For living near a perfect man makes a deeper impression; the enlarged imagination acts more spontaneously; the emotions, purposes, and methods are centered in one well-loved being to whom the soul aspires to be united. Hence, a highly personalized ideal is most desirable from the viewpoint of effectiveness.

There are four styles of deliberate imitation. The first consists in copying such external features as appearance, manners, clothes, and deportment. At best this is a start toward imitation of something better; usually, it is trivial; at its literal worst, it lies open to insincerity, rigidity, and mere aping without adaptation to the new medium and circumstances in which the copyist must fit his own likeness to the ideal.

The second style requires more use of the intellect. It consists in following directions given either by the model person or by someone who guides us to the imitation of the model. Such, for instance, are the directions of a rule book, setting the pattern for the education of a prince or for the daily life of a perfect nun. But all rules and routines need living adaption to personalities and circumstances; rules have not the constancy of principles. Followed inappropriately or imprudently, they lead to discourtesy, comedy, inferior results, and even to mere external gloss.

The third mode of imitation goes much deeper. Here the person looks to the ideas and motives of his ideal; he tries to take on his inner spirit and sentiments; he adopts his principles and set of values; he devotes himself to the same cause as his ideal and for the same reason. He merges his own personality with that greater interior personality of the model. Such would seem to be the kind of constant copying which St. Paul recommends as a way of forming Christ's image in ourselves. It is the message of Thomas à Kempis' *Imitation of Christ*. It is that interior knowledge and love of Christ the King which St. Ignatius Loyola is always urging in his *Spiritual Exercises*. This style Christ recommended when He urged men to become like little children, to follow Himself as the way of life, to share His cross-bearing, to love each other as He has loved us. Uniting with the mind and heart of the idealized person, such imitation penetrates the depth of the soul and fashions character within. Where there is such internal matching of copy with model, it matters little whether there is external conformity. This imitation resembles the original in a way proportionate to individual potencies. There will be room for hundreds of external differences between Christ and modern Orientals, Negroes, Eskimos, urban factory workers, and university students; but there is a place for an inner identity of all of them with the same one mind, love, cause, and purpose of Christ.

Dramatic instructors and directors of motion pictures use a fourth type of imitation. They teach by doing the thing before their pupils; they act, and the pupil tries to copy the action. Here the power of example unites with the gift of imitating to bring about improvements. Sometimes the power of rivalry, the ambition to do one's best under competitive conditions, is added. In all cases action to achieve the ideal is initiated; practice under right conditions is begun. The imagination and its image-moving power mold manner, gesture, and tone until one at least acts as if he were like the original or the ideal. Such active imitation, however, may remain a mere stage play and a pastime. It involves the dangers of hypocrisy, of merely seeming to be what one interiorly is not. The sophist is a mere actor; and actors and actresses who are notorious misers, bigots, or adulterers may for a few hours play a glittering role of generosity, tolerance, or virginity. Genuine gold in character requires interior acceptance of the principles, high aims, noble motives, sound ideas, and steadfast values of the exemplar. This belongs to the third style of following the ideal.

3. HISTORICAL PRESENTATIONS OF THE HUMAN IDEAL

A rapid review of some historical presentations of the ideal human being will help us to grasp the complexity of this ideal and to approach the selection of a true ideal.[1] Greece, cradle of so many ideas, gives us the Athenian free citizen, Socrates the unswerving servant of truth, the philosopher-king of Plato who knows, practices, and administers perfect justice in the republic, the Sophists' savant who makes the individual and his success the measure of all things, and Aristotle's contemplative philosopher and his magnanimous man of affairs. The Romans exalted the just administrator and later the universal man — scholar, general, ruler, and reformer — in the persons of Julius Caesar and Julian the Apostate. The sapiential books of the Old Testament describe the God-fearing wise ruler, the God-fearing sage, and the God-fearing woman in the home. Tobias portrays the model husband. With Christ comes the ideal of the total loving service of God.

The Christian man who follows Christ's principles and example is lauded by St. Paul as the new man recreated in Christ, endowed with Christ's grace, devoted completely to Christ's cause, having the mind, the heart, the very spiritual figure of Christ in his being. As Western society became Christianized, particular forms of the ideal Christian man appeared. The monk withdrawn from the world is one variant of the ideal; the monk helping to save the world by participating in its life is another ideal; the knight devoted to the Church and to the needy is another type; the prud'homme and the honnête homme of France and Burgundy is yet another variant. Throughout this period the Christian contemplative seems to dominate all other ideals.

During the Renaissance new views bring out new ideals. The universal man appears in Dante, Da Vinci, and others. The magnificent man, the cultured and wealthy patron, glows in Lorenzo the Magnificent and some pre-Reformation popes. Pagan humanism by reviving pagan interests splits the human ideal from the religious and ascetic ideal. A counter Christian humanism for the cultured elite of the sixteenth century captivates such personalities as Erasmus, St. Thomas More, Estaples, and Vivés.

As the Counter Reformation progresses, the very attractive humanism of St. Francis de Sales and his many followers, including Capuchins and Jesuits, flourishes in France. To this group of writers, scholars, and mystics Brémond has given the title *devout humanists*. The main charter of their humanism of holiness for the populace is in De Sales' *Introduction to the Devout Life*. The decay of religion in other circles brings to the fore the diluted ideal of the civilized man, the so-called gentleman, the ideal aristocrat. This ideal, sketched by Shaftesbury, received literary immortality from Newman in his *Idea of a University*.[2] It persists in our times in naturalist, humanitarian, and rationalist ideals of refinement and respectability.

Of the newer ideals today we may mention the superman, the man of power and moral independence proposed by Nietzsche, G. B. Shaw, Hitler, and others; the scientist, the arbiter of modern civilization; the Marxist socialized man and dedicated worker and insolent atheist who despises the saint as inhuman. We have the integral humanist spoken of by Maritain. Pope Pius XI seems to have best proposed the current statement of Christian humanism. His ideal we may identify as the Catholic humanist, the all-round ideal, or, simply, as the supernatural man.

It would be rewarding, were it possible, to evaluate the merits and drawbacks in each of these proposed ideals, and especially to examine Aristotle's great-souled man who comes so near to, yet stands so far from the Christian man. We can, however, examine only the portrait drawn by Pope Pius XI. But first, a word on humanism in general.

4. HUMANISM

Humanism[3] is the somewhat indefinite label under which various patterns of human perfection in thought, motivation, character, occupation, sociality, and leadership are grouped. Beneath the many different forms of humanism proposed in Western thought there is a neutral core of common aspirations, though not of common doctrines. Humanist interests center mainly on problems touching man's nature, destiny, and dignity within the universe. In that sense, this whole book could be considered a study of humanism. All humanists look to the

best possible life for man. Therefore, they also discuss the improvement and organization of both nature and society for the sake of
man's best life. Humanists always oppose views which they regard as
antihumanistic; they often challenge each other's doctrines because
of such alleged antihumanism. Christian and atheist, especially the
Marxist atheist, regard each other as antihumanist. Some prefer Socrates
to Christ as the paragon of human excellence. Classicist opposes the
scientific humanist in many a modern university. The peace-loving man
regards the cult of military heroes as antihuman. These divergences
involve more than merely different educational and social backgrounds
for developing humanists; they are rooted in opposing philosophies of
human life. We may not lump all humanisms together as though they
constituted one corpus of thought.

Every humanism, it would seem, must declare itself on the following
issues and be rated on its declarations. (1) What is a human being?
What is his total nature? (2) Is man naturally good and worth while?
Is he capable of greater perfection? What can we expect of his efforts
at progress? This is the issue of optimism versus pessimism and
cynicism in regard to man. (3) What is the destiny of man, the direction of human life, and the term of human progress? (4) Upon
what principle can we base our view of man's dignity? (5) What is the
relation of the individual human being to all men, to the human race,
and to human institutions? (6) What is the place of man in time?
What is his present duty? What temporal ends should he prefer?
(7) Are men and their works partially or totally sufficient for achieving
man's perfection and destiny? How much does man need help and in
what respects? (8) Is the individual or society or God the measure,
the source, and the limit of achievement?

5. THE SUPERNATURAL MAN

All these issues receive their best answer in the ideal of the supernatural man; and all the ideal men proposed throughout history are
in a way summed up in this Christian ideal, for it includes the good
points of all others and surpasses them. The basic text for any future
humanism is given by Pope Pius XI in his encyclical, The Christian
Education of Youth.[4]

> The proper and immediate end of Christian education is to cooperate
> with divine grace in forming the true and perfect Christian, that is, to

form Christ Himself in those regenerated by baptism. . . . For the true
Christian must live a supernatural life in Christ . . . and display it in
all his actions. . . . For precisely this reason, Christian education takes
in the whole aggregate of human life, physical and spiritual, intellectual
and moral, individual, domestic and social, not with a view of reducing
it in any way, but in order to elevate, regulate, and perfect it, in accordance with the example and teaching of Christ.

Hence the true Christian, product of Christian education, is the
supernatural man who thinks, judges, and acts constantly and consistently in accordance with right reason illumined by the supernatural
light of the example and teaching of Christ; in other words, . . . the
true and finished man of character. . . .

The true Christian does not renounce the activities of this life, he
does not stunt his natural faculties; but he develops and perfects them
by co-ordinating them with the supernatural. He thus ennobles what is
merely natural in life and secures for it new strength in the material and
temporal order, no less than in the spiritual and eternal.

This is the supreme and proper ideal because its union of nature's
perfections with the riches of grace gives the only complete ideal that
provides the best for all sides of man and recognizes his full perfectibility in the natural and supernatural planes of his living. Humanism and Christianity together form the perfect man, the man like
Christ. We may rapidly look at the two components of the ideal,
human nature and grace, and then at the union of the two.

The ideal of natural perfection accepts the whole nature of man and
all the valid principles, standards, and motives known to human reason.
Accepting all nature as a good gift of God, it seeks the completion of
human personality in all its powers: healthy body, accurate senses,
lively imagination, sensory appetites rightly directed to their objects,
sound intellectual habits, clear and steadfast conscience, taste for the
beautiful in all forms, communion with God, the social sharing of life
under law with one's fellow men, and all the virtues needed for one's
legal duties as well as the full round of the habits of the gentleman.
Personality thus developed enthrones man over nature, unites him with
his fellows, and urges him closer to God. He has the largest measure
of human happiness obtainable by personal and social effort in this
world. Such self-perfection is not selfishly pursued for one's own advantage and complacency, but for the sake of honoring God in His
image. "The glory of God is a living man."

These various excellences of human nature must be sought in a way
proportionate to man. Man may not pursue beauty without regard to

conscience, nor mastery over nature without attention to the human service and dangers of science. Man does not achieve the humanist ideal by attending to only one or two aspects of human perfection. The scientist who loses his sense of beauty, the artist who lacks a sense of responsibility, the philosopher with little imagination and humor, the miserly, unsocial recluse full of learning about rare coins, even the saint with a minimum respect for amenities and learning are not humanists. A genuine humanism has not only a high and radiant sense of human dignity but also a proportionate respect for the worth of each power and interest of man. This multiple fullness of appreciation constitutes one of the big sources of human energy that prompts man to master nature and organize society as well as to rule himself. Tools and techniques do not make the best man; men who believe in human worth make tools and enrich their lives by creating homes, gardens, universities, and other means of better living.

The human standard further demands that man measure up to his humanity consistently and constantly, especially in the areas of right thinking, practical judgment, personal conduct, prudent guidance of others, and social activity.

But the Christian humanist may not stop at these gifts of nature, either in his thought, ambition, or achievement. His very fervor for human perfection moves him to seek any further perfection that life may proffer; the very love of life invites him to a higher life and a higher love. He is gladly sympathetic to the dictum of Plato that man must meet a divine standard and to the maxim of Aristotle that we must live according to the most godlike element within us.

That God calls man to transcend his natural perfection and his mere natural likeness to God is a matter of historical fact. Since the Son of God became incarnate, we are called to an incarnational humanism as graced sons of God. Let it be noted that the son of man did not become the Son of God; but the Son of God took the initiative and became a perfect man. So, too, our human nature does not lift itself up to grace. God alone lifts human nature. Grace, then, is a force coming from beyond this world and into human nature. It is a sheer gift, which at the start is beyond our earning. The best natural acts cannot start it, merit it, recover it; at most, human nature can prepare to receive it at God's inner prompting.

Of the varied aspects of this gift to human nature, one is famously stated by the principle of St. Thomas: "Grace does not destroy but perfects nature."⁵ In this adding and elevating, it supplies the mind with a new body of truth through revealed doctrines about God and man. It gives a richer dimension to life, adding to the soul both new life and its associated living powers known as the theological virtues and gifts of the Spirit. Graced man is an adopted child of God, a friend of God, the heir to an eternal Father's estates and perfection. In the form of actual graces, the supernatural life supplies light for the mind, love for the will, strength to rule the passions, pardon and healing for the various wounds left by sin. The incarnational gifts also destine man to a new and infinitely higher end, the vision of God. Human gifts of reason, virtue, and bodily perfection are directed and made submissive to that superior ultimate aim of living. The new destiny also brings the promise of a permanent sharing of the human body in the perfection of the graced man when God will have resurrected his flesh and introduced it to the perfect land of heaven. The supernatural order contains a new ideal of human conduct, conformity to the principles and example of Jesus Christ, Son of God and Son of Man. The perfect Model of living is given us. Finally, a new divinely founded society with a divinely guided authority is provided to help man imitate the Son of God and find the divine Father's love in heaven.

God, then, has opened up a new world to human personality, raising human nature to an entirely new order, a supernatural order of being, destiny, and activity. Nature still has an essential place in human perfection, but a lower place than grace. In the standard of incarnational humanism, nature and grace both play a role; neither is optional, neither is compromised, neither is belittled. It is not a question of either nature or grace or of rivalry between the two. The two meet together and operate together, as sentient and rational life or eye and intellect smoothly function together in the union of body and soul. Likewise, as the union of body and soul does not leave man an animal, but something different and better, a human being, so the union of human nature and grace does not leave man a merely human being, but a human child of God. Being different, the graced man should act somewhat differently. As a thing is, so it should act. The supernatural man should think, judge, and act by and for this new supernatural manhood which is his.

Perhaps if the non-Christian understood better the maxims about the relations of nature and grace he would be less suspicious or jealous of what grace might do to him. For grace does not enter one's life like a conquering destroyer or as an avenging kill-joy. Three aspects of the interaction of nature and grace may help our understanding of their connections: how nature aids the supernatural, how grace aids the natural, and how grace must have primacy without suppressing the gifts of nature.

Nature aids grace in a number of ways besides the initial one of supplying the base in which grace may dwell and function. Health, a natural endowment, assists in giving that contentment, energy, and delight in doing difficult good which high virtue so often demands. Natural practical ability in managing affairs of daily business keeps us from that economic, domestic, and social decay and that loss of dignity and hope which often occasion overpowering evil temptations. Intelligence aids good judgment in spiritual choices. People who lack health, practical ability, or good judgment may still be blessed with God's grace, since God loves the poor and needy better than anyone else does. Yet His reason for gracing anyone is not bad health, stupid judgment, life in a slum, ignorant practice of false religions, rude manners, or civic inabilities. God has mercy in spite of, rather than because of, these natural deficiencies. And these deficiencies, like other material subjects or causes, tend to limit the full play of grace in souls.

The natural traits and virtues of the gentleman give excellent preparatory training for the virtues of the Christian life; self-respect, courtesy, gentleness, thoughtfulness of others, ambition to succeed in one's duty, devotion to family, profession, and job dispose the soul for the higher Christian attention to the divine will. Good natural motives, too, reinforce exclusively supernatural ones and make them more effective. Natural motives may be sub-Christian and alone are insufficient; but at the same time they are pro-Christian and are not unworthy and inhuman. Evil motives, not natural ones, are inhuman and opposed to the supernatural. Hence, the good humanist is naturally oriented to Christianity: as Tertullian phrases it, *anima naturaliter Christiana*.

Grace, in turn, wonderfully aids nature. United with grace, human nature is better off. Grace cleanses, heals, strengthens, stimulates, soothes, and orders it in many respects: in regard to the darkness of the natural mind in front of natural truths, the weakness of the will in pursuing natural virtues, the crookedness of motives in natural activity, the slowness of interior spiritual development, the anxiety of the human spirit about our falls and our future, the feeling about God's great distance from us, the paralyzing fears that cripple interest in the better things. The difficulty of the imagination in finding an ideal is remedied by the historical example of Christ. The deep need for inspiration is met by the gift of dynamic love for the all-lovable personality of Christ. Grace helps natural powers by raising natural gifts to the plane of godlike being and by consecrating man to a divinely given goal of life. Thus, it spreads its gracious influence over the mind and will in particular and, through these powers, over the faculties that are subject to man's command.

Such consequences are to be expected since nature is made in view of grace and nature's finality is not purely for itself but for something beyond itself. To damage or destroy nature would be a big mistake, for grace would thereby prevent its own success in human souls. Grace treats nature much as a builder treats the site and materials for a perfect home. He selects and adapts all to the needs of a family, to the demands of climate and exposure, to the requirements of accessibility and of protection, to the possibilities for scenic views, gardens, and play area, and to the other tastes of those for whom the house will be built. So, grace works, adapting itself individually to each soul, making the best use of the aptitudes of each man, exploiting his good tendencies, filling in his low spots, meeting him in his own inherited tradition and society. This individual congruence and variety of grace shines in the lives of highly different personalities of the same age, as in King St. Louis of France, St. Thomas Aquinas, and St. Bonaventure in the mid-thirteenth century. Grace does violence only to the corruptions and vices of nature.

Although nature comes first to man, grace is better. Grace is essential for the chief end, heavenly union with God. It is a greater gift than nature. Hence, it has primacy over the natural; and the natural must willingly yield to the supernatural. As we may not neglect the supernatural in pursuit of the natural, nor underplay the natural in pursuit of the supernatural, so neither may we let ourselves so interpret the dominance of the supernatural that it means a dwarfing of natural being or any sacrifice of the natural in its proper sphere of action. This would militate against the stated ideal of the whole man, the unit of nature and grace. It is true that the loss of some natural gift is not irreparable, whereas final loss of the supernatural is tragic. Ordinarily, however, the cherishing of the supernatural also requires great care and noble use of all natural powers and gifts and all man's natural co-operation with the plans of God. Hence, nature or reason, the servant of grace, may not play as the equal, rival, or judge of its superior. It must heed the demands of grace for time, cultivation, and room in one's life. The natural interests and occupations of man must not merely refuse to crowd out the supernatural, but must let the supernatural rule him and tranfuse his viewpoints, his standards of the good, noble, and beautiful, his sense of order, his motivation, and his pattern of action. This supernaturalization of human traits may perhaps be best exemplified in the complete Christian gentleman; he keeps all the traits of the gentleman but transforms them with his motive of love of men for God's sake; he is principally a Christian, secondarily, yet completely, a gentleman.

6. Christ, the Ideal

For the supernatural humanist, the ideal of human personal perfection is Christ. The pagan philosophers' ideal of godlikeness becomes specifically the ideal of likeness to the Son of God made man; human perfection means Christlikeness. In personal knowledge of Christ, we have that highly personalized, real, vivid, lovable ideal that human nature needs to spur it to imitation of God. The old natural riddle of becoming like to God can now be answered because God has appeared in human form as the historical model of men.

Christ is man's model in a triple way.[6] First, in His being as Son of God, He is the model of the state of divine sonship, the possession of sanctifying grace by the gift of the Father. Second, in His role as Teacher, as the Light or Word, He states clearly all the right principles concerning human nature, human destiny, and human conduct. Here we have such striking principles as the eight beatitudes and the doctrines of forgiveness, of love of God, of right order in pursuing first the kingdom of God, of the filial approach to God in prayer and in need, and the mysteries of the relation of the cross to the resurrection.

Third, in His own human living He shows us the supreme example of the perfect life. In this model the humanist's gifts shine splendidly: concern for God and for men, sensitivity to beauty, passion for truth, pursuit of goodness, awareness of God's importance, amazing powers of friendship and leadership, alertness to the issues of the times that touched His life. Here is the serene penetrating mind. Here is perfect unity of character where no virtue excludes any other, where all is in fullness and yet all in perfect balance, where each trait fits and each is at its highest pitch. Here is the great giving Heart of one who loves God and loves men for the sake of God. Here is the faithful, heroic Man who lives and works, who teaches and travels, who heals and at last dies for others. Yet for all His elevation of mind and character, He is so near to men, so fond of them, and so approachable; He is indeed the God and Model of the common man.

In Christ's teaching and example, charity is certainly the highest virtue, the form and spirit and end of all other virtuous deeds, the motive above all other motives, and the unifying factor in character. "I do always the things that please Him," said the Model. Love the Lord your God with your whole heart, soul, mind, and strength. This is my new commandment that you love another as I have loved you. The life of perfection for everyone who copies Christ must be the life of charity, positive, constructive, and total. This charity means a total dedication to the will of the Father, sincere love of God for Himself, for His own inner goodness and His goodness to us, and the love of fellow men in due order for the sake of God because God loves them, made them like Himself, and wishes us to love them well. All acts fall under the reign of the one motive, love of God. All ways of life — contemplative scholarship, teaching, devotion, healing, domestic and industrial production — are to be led for this motive of love of God, and not merely for insufficient humanitarian, patriotic, or self-interested reasons. Where life has one aim and plan, one mind and one love, one motive controlling all decision and action, there the organic unity of nature and grace binds together all facets of human personality.

Christ's attitude to a Christian humanist's participation in the work of this world is best viewed in this context of charity. His social awareness is one mark of the perfect poise of His mind. He recommends that man seek first the kingdom of Christ, but He also recommends paying taxes. He recommends moderate solicitude for the necessities of this life, joined with great trust in the Father's providence. He mercifully heals diseases of body, though His chief concern is spiritual ignorance and moral diseases. He attends the marriage ceremony of His friends, He shares in the fishing trips of His followers, He visits homes, He provides food for the multitudes. He is all aglow in praise of every good word and kind deed done for our fellow man, particularly if done in His name. He invites men to bear and welcome the cross of His pain, but He is severe to those whose wealth or power fastens human nature to the cross.

So social is His view that He organizes His own society to give men spiritual benefits first and, indirectly, earthly blessings that come from widespread virtuous living. His plan for men is a social one, a living union between Himself and all His followers in that Mystical Body which we know as His Church. Here a new supernatural society with a unity of authority, mind, obedience, worship, and love contributes to man's social perfection. This Body, lasting through the centuries, will share in His life. In it each Christian, as a living cell, will receive the potent helps of the whole Christ, learn its guiding principles, rejoice in its vital love, enjoy a fuller measure of Christian manhood, and contribute his personal bit to the perfection of the whole Body. The Church will keep him human by confronting him with the fact of God and with the fact of his own human nature; it will keep him a man of grace by giving him every opportunity and assistance to rise to Christlikeness.[7] The Church will stimulate and temper all sides of his human nature, for she is Christ helping man. She will tell him of his dependence and weakness, move him to humility and reverence, and at the same time exalt his confidence in Christ and stress his near omnipotence in union with Christ and His members. The Church will mother him and mature him until he becomes the graced man, the supernatural man. But man must yield himself to the formation offered by Christ and His society. If he would think, judge, and act consistently and steadily by the bright standards of graced nature, he must very humbly pray for the gift, like that great humanist, St. Thomas: "Lead us along Your way . . . to that light in which You dwell."[8]

Some say that this is too high an ideal for man, and some say that it is too harsh. In one chapter we cannot face all these misunderstandings. But history justifies this induction from the miseries of man and the causes of human woes: Where there is no God, there is no man; where there is little grace, there is too little nature. Without Christ, the God-Man, we have neither enough of God nor of man in human life. The Christian philosopher may claim that if man could have invented a religion to assist humanism in the best way and contribute most to human perfection, man would have done just what God has done. Man would have brought the Son of God into the world, invented the Christian religion and the Church of Christ, and lifted man to his proper status by the example and teachings of Christ.

CHAPTER 18

The Place of Suffering

1. SUFFERING AS A PROBLEM OF LIFE

THE SUFFERINGS and tragedies of life and the menace of death may seem to cry defiance to the optimism of the views so far proposed about the worth of life. Pain of body and sorrow of spirit, memories of misery and worry over the future, the anguish of the innocent and the success of aggressors announce the many tragedies that mark the roads of life. One wise man in weary sadness at this picture of humanity remarked on the vanity of all things.[1] Albert Camus,[2] a French existentialist, comments that suicide is the main philosophical problem as it involves the decision whether life is worth living or not.

The present discussion will not strike a Leibnizian pose and defend God's reputation against doubters and mockers of His existence, goodness, and power. The doctrines of God's providence and of redemption by the Cross constitute the apologia for troubled human existence. It is our task here to appreciate how this truth of divine providence gives meaning and comfort in face of the living experience of suffering. It seems relevant to our subject to limit ourselves to suffering in the present life of man, for any who suffer in purgatory or in hell do not ask philosophers for answers to questions that they have.[3]

The philosophical task seems to be twofold: (1) to help us see how suffering can fit into the divine plan for man and into the probationary character of our present life; and (2) to find right attitudes that will shape right action toward suffering. Beyond this philosophy has no consolation to offer. It can never give an emotional solace, as a kiss from a friend in time of bereavement or a glimpse of the Mother of Sorrows can do. But though powerless to take away the sharp sting, philosophy can remove our misjudgments about suffering, show us that pain and grief are not irrational, purposeless, and meaningless, and that evil is not the end of things or a twilight ushering in a night of irremediable despair. By finding that suffering is a valuable aid in human living, a helpful means to high divine aims, and a sane part of the temporal order of things, the mind can gain quiet even if the feelings continue their protest.

2. THE CLASSIC TYPES: JOB AND BOETHIUS

The foremost discussions of the problem of evil are the Book of Job and Boethius' *Consolation of Philosophy*. Christ's treatment of the problem is more by example than by discussion.

The Book of Job is a religious poem of the early half of the fifth century before Christ, presenting both popular and profound views on the themes of temporal misfortune, disease, death, divine punishment, and divine purposes. Job is presented to us as a very wealthy Oriental rancher with a large family. He has been a simple, good-living, God-fearing man. Job has a hidden enemy, Satan, who sneers that Job's goodness is due to the fact that God has shielded him from trouble. Permitted by God to test Job, Satan arranges that all in a day two bands of marauders capture Job's flocks and kill his servants, lightning kills his sheep and their shepherds, a windstorm sends his home crashing down upon his children. Job's patient comment is that the Lord gave and the Lord took away: blessed be the name of the Lord.

Satan then goes further and afflicts Job with a disease from head to foot. Rudely challenged by his wife for his fidelity to God, Job replies "if we have received good things at the hand of God, why should we not receive evil?" But as his disease lingers on, three old friends trouble his soul with their gloomy arguments. The general tenor of their remarks flows from the common Hebrew persuasion of that period that the good man is blessed by God with temporal abundance and that, therefore, human miseries are a sign of God's justice visited on the wicked. Later in the poem, a younger friend, philosophical in temperament, Eliu, begins to refute both Job's deficient viewpoint and that of his friends. Finally, God Himself comes to ask Job questions to which he cannot reply. Since Job knows so little of the world of nature about him, of its causes and secrets, how can he know and judge God? God and His ways must be even greater mysteries.

The poem ends with the sufferer's adoring submission to God, his confession of his ignorance of the divine plans, his repentance for his daring complaints as though he were God's equal with whom he can quarrel. He prays, too, for his erring friends. A Hollywood ending is added with Job's recovery of his vast temporal wealth, the gathering of his friends, and his many long years with a large new family.

Numerous lessons are stated and implied by Job, Eliu, and God. The mystery of man's contest with evil is not solved. It remains a divine secret, yet the attitude of the Hebraic mind to the mystery is rectified in the new recognition that temporal evil may befall both good and bad men and may strike at the good even more fiercely than at the wicked. The poem bursts the illusion that temporal goods are the signs and reward of virtue and protests against the supposition that temporal losses are proofs of vice and divine punishment. God's bounty to men, His arrangements for men, His permission given to Satan to try men depend on His exclusive sovereignty and incomprehensible government. They are beyond our doubting, above our present understanding, and not within our right to challenge. The whole problem of suffering is pitched in a higher perspective which sees every vicissitude of life as part of some great whole. In that greater whole the afflicted human body shall rise again to see its redeemer; and only in that afterlife is the proper court of divine justice set up.

The poem also highlights the preventive values of suffering and not its merely remedial and punitive aspects. Immediate experience of evils is a condition for learning great lessons and for obtaining higher, less immediate, and spiritual goods. Job proves himself faithful to God not only for His gifts but for Himself. He continues to pray, he continues to hope, he adoringly accepts God's secret will. From his great trials Job has gained heightened spiritual stature and wisdom and even regained the equivalent of his domestic happiness and economic position. He is in every way better off for his loyalty to God.

Boethius' sixth-century work of prose and verse, *The Consolation of Philosophy*,[4] lacks the poetic and dramatic qualities of the Book of Job and has no happy ending. Its procedure is strictly philosophical, with a dialogue between the majestic woman visitor, Philosophy, and the complaining prisoner, Boethius. The book, though written by a Christian, lacks the religious quality expected of such a mind and does not refer to Christ's passion and resurrection. Yet in some points it reaches a profounder insight into the providence of God than does the Book of Job. The peak of the work for our purposes is the sixth prose passage of the fourth book.

Boethius, a Roman patrician, happily married, a wealthy senator, successful consul and diplomat, and an intimate of King Theodoric, finds himself imprisoned without a hearing, with his property confiscated, his family and friends removed, a victim of political intrigue and perhaps also of religious persecution from the Arians. Toppled from his previous good fortune, he naturally wonders what it is all about, what happiness really is, what order there may be in the world, what reason has to offer for his problem.

The central insights seem to be these three: the uses of misfortune, the true happiness of man, and the total order of the universe under God's government.[5] This last point is the main consolation which Boethius has to offer.

God's sovereign goodness orders and governs all for the sake of the good and in a good way. The mystery is due to our incapacity to see that all is governed by God, that all is for the good, and that all God's ways of accomplishing His ends are good. The riddles that trouble our minds when they measure evil come from our limited vision that does not see the entire order, the total control, and the final climax. We are interested in immediate fortune and the happiness of the present hour. At any moment of suffering we are involved in only a portion of the whole order of things and glance at only a small segment of the full stretch of time and eternity. We cannot see how present misfortunes work toward a future good. The success of the wicked, their escape from punishment, the fate or necessity in things, chance and mischance, coincidence, inequalities in men's lives, injustices, the uncontrollable free wills of men all seem to contradict any divine integral order and divine management of human affairs. So we think because we cannot see.

But to God nothing of evil or good, of present and future is hidden. Nothing escapes the powerful control of the divine will at the immovable center of all changing things. The intersecting lines of necessity are from God, giving to things their natures and their laws; coincidence is not outside His foreknowledge and planning; for Him there is no chance; it is He who lets the wheel of fortune spin. Surely evil is not unpunished. In some ways vice is its own punishment. In some ways it is an evil that evil does not get immediate punishment, for then the wicked take advantage of their momentary escape in order to perpetrate more evil; and there is always eternity awaiting them in which justice will be balanced and come forth victorious. Yes, God treats men unequally; but he treats all according to their natures and according to His total knowledge of them. He spares trials to certain good men lest they become evil. He permits trials to others who, He knows, can bear them, and, by bearing them, exercise virtue and earn rewards. Sometimes the wicked become agents of good even to the wicked, for by doing evil to the evil they draw their victims to repent and reject their former evil ways. The great power of God turns evil toward the good.

The great order of the universe under God also embraces all the activities and consequences of free will. Human free will especially tries to break the bounds of the divine order. But its activities are foreknown and, as known, can be controlled by divine power. Though free will escapes some particular order within the whole, yet divine power, love, and justice bring it back again within the laws of another order within that whole. In this integral order of God, infallibly foreseen and perfectly controlled, confusion disappears, fortune favors the divine plan, inexorable law bends down before divine love, evil moves to the divine good for its eventual outcome, and our prayer, submission, and virtue are co-workers with God.

The cluster of ideas given by Boethius resembles all philosophical treatments of the problem of suffering by giving some satisfactory reasons why evil is an intelligible part of life; nevertheless, it fails to remove all obscurity, and is unable to explain the mystery of evil. Mystery, however, means lack of full comprehension and not contradiction with the evidence of the facts or with other truths. Reason provides us with at least four lighted lanes which we may follow toward some better understanding of this problem.

3. GOD'S PERMISSION OF EVIL

If the mind misconceives the problem by regarding God as the cause of evil, it will never arrive at any solution. Evil is not being. It is a lack of some being or order that properly belongs to a being according to its own nature. It is a shadow of an absent good, a wound in that integral perfection that naturally belongs to a good thing, a hole in being, a minus quantity. But it is not something hideous, putrid, diabolical in itself. Since in itself it is nothing, it cannot be a cause of anything, neither evil nor good. Nothing causes nothing. Therefore, if good follows evil, it is not because of the operation of the evil, but because some good agent uses evil as the opportune occasion for doing some good.

Since evil is nothing, God does not cause it. Only being needs God's causality. But since God knows of it and could by absolute or abstract power prevent it, He must be said to permit evil and its possibility. This permission must be based on reasons consonant with His wisdom, goodness, justice, and power. Being infinitely good, He permits evil only for the sake of good — either to preserve some good, as free will, or to enhance the value of the good that remains in spite of evil, as the glory of the Church in spite of its sinful members, or to draw even greater good out of evil, as the heightened heroism of the martyrs and the innocent.

Our minds will ask, then, what goods are preserved or increased by the divine permission of evil. The answer to this question involves an understanding of the economy of suffering. An economy in material goods signifies an order, apportionment, purposiveness, and management of lands, resources, supplies, finances, and employment in the direction of human welfare. In a cognate sense, the economy of suffering refers to the divine order, distribution, direction, and management of all things that cause suffering so that the supreme welfare of man is helped by the evils that he undergoes in this world. What are some of these compensations or goods that follow upon the presence of evil?

It is commonplace that evils act like nettles to sting us to exercise many virtues and amass much merit. Many opportunities for patience, courage, and perseverance spring from pains and troubles. Hope must be practiced to counteract the discouragement and despair which evil tends to instill. Human injustice calls forth glorious adventures for the recovery of rights and liberty, inspires charity for our fellows, and evokes the shining witness to faith in God and conscientious loyalty to higher things. An important moral virtue, penance, requires man to bear sacrifices and prefer God's will to his own personal preferences. The steadfast pursuit of good in spite of evil helps test the sincerity of our motives. The need to struggle keeps us from drifting into selfish intentions and into doing good because it gets pleasing immediate results. Evils also remind us that we are not as wonderful as we sus-

pected, that we are needier than we realized, and thus we are helped
to humility.

Others' sufferings lead us to many forms of charity — sympathetic
words, nursing, financial aid, prayer for others, and the social virtue
of penance for others. A child's sickness has often mended a parental
rupture; hard times lead people to rediscover the happiness of their
homes and the depth of their domestic affections. The man attacked
by highwaymen in the parable of the Good Samaritan discovered who
his true neighbor was. Thus, troubles separate our true friends from
mere acquaintances. Great disasters provide the stimulus to build great
organizations for human relief, as the Red Cross.

Another feature of God's management of evil is to use some evils
to preserve us from other evils and to keep certain goods in our lives.
The unpleasantness of bodily pain arouses us to take prompt care of
the organism and to discover remedies for people similarly afflicted.
Pain is the piercing signal that we need before we react to the urgency
of the danger. The experience of disgrace helps some people break
bad emotional, moral, and social habits. Trouble has a way of stopping
worse troubles; trouble teaches some people to stop trouble not only
in its consequences but at its source. That is gain. Some saints, indeed,
have spoken of pain and illness as God's gifts, no less than pleasure
and health. If they are gifts, the one as well as the other deserves
our thanksgiving, though it is understandable that we might give
heartier thanks for the more desirable gift.

At the same time, the divine tolerance of evil preserves some very
precious goods in the universe. It is extremely important to preserve
free will and the possibility of human progress. A total prevention of
evil may imply prevention of all existence other than infinite existence
or prevention of all freedom except in a few most perfect beings.
If freedom goes, human perfectibility goes; and dignity and virtue
and merit and adventure and humor and love and the glory of God
go with it. If freedom remains, the possibility of evil, of human conflict,
of dangerous decisions, of personality disintegration remains. This is
a high price, but an understandable and not excessive price. The
presence of evil also seems to be involved in our highly complex universe containing immense forces and an astounding number of members.
The lower is often the food of the higher; the local damage is permitted that the operation of the general laws of nature may continue;
variety rather than monotony is maintained; progress rather than static

completeness is the rule. But all this seems to involve some physical dangers and human exposure to such evils as floods, droughts, storms, fires, and other local disorders in nature.

4. THE TOTAL ORDER OF PROVIDENCE

A return to the conception of the total order of Divine Providence will add some light to the discussion. The total plan of God embraces the end of the universe, all its members and especially men, and all means to the end; it embraces all parts in their mutual relations to each other and in their subordination to the whole universe and the complete purpose; it includes all time, from its beginning to ending; it envelops all partial purposes in the total one for all creatures. The total plan, finally, actually includes both the natural and supernatural orders.

If, then, we would see evil in life in its proper place, we must see it as God sees it. For it is not isolated. It has a relation to the good, a place in the whole scheme, a subordinate and temporary role. It is not running amuck, but is under control for the main purpose and the total order of the universe. The constant danger of the limited human mind is to see evil only as a fragment in the whole network of being. Man concentrates on it and overlooks the good that accompanies or follows it. Because man cannot check and rule evil fully, he comes to suspect that its disorder is also outside the strong grip of God's might. Man attributes some evil to chance, whereas all coincidence and all irregularity fall within a fuller knowledge and planning of the infinite mind. Man attributes it, half blasphemously, to a lack of divine wisdom or a lack of sufficient interest on God's part. But it is human blindness to the total plan and human distrust of the sweet, efficacious, and most gracious government of God that leads us to entertain such foolish views. We must try to stand on God's high tower where we get a bit of the spacious and boundless divine view of all time and all existence. There we will see some of the laws by which divine government acts, adjusting and contriving all to the appointed good.

One principle of divine operation is to treat each thing in the universe according to its nature. Any other treatment would be useless, disorderly, or open to endless miraculous exceptions. God deals thus with physical nature, and He deals the same way with human nature. He gives man a nature; He aids him according to that nature; He expects from him what his nature can do. He lets his sensitive nature bear bodily pain rather than give him a nonsentient organism which could experience neither pleasure nor pain. He lets him know evil rather than deprive him of an intelligence able to know either good or evil. He lets him misuse free will rather than turn man into a puppet deprived of the blessings of liberty.

Moreover, God treats man according to his many individual differences of capacity, opportunity, environment, vocation, and destiny. For God has infinite knowledge of every detail of each man's life and the way each moment and act fits into His total plan for the individual person's ultimate welfare. The ball of life does not bounce by chance, but, by plan, for the good. God has a special place for each man in the scheme of things, since each man is personally destined for union with Him in beatitude. A person is not just a member of the human race, a number in the lottery, but someone individually cherished by God.

As He is interested in us individually, it is not surprising that the divine Governor treats us in a way that not only makes for our generic human goodness but for our personal genuine goodness as well. He parcels out goods and opportunities to different people in different ways. He gives us what we need for our perfection, not what we want for our pleasures or for our destruction. He is interested in higher ends and loftier ideals for us than our individual comfort and self-will. He knows, too, what we can stand and cannot withstand; He will not try us with adversities beyond our strength; He will never leave us alone, without His help. He is continually caring for each of us, continually helping each, continually courting loving service from each. The orders we need He manages to communicate in His own ways. Our immediate spiritual good is always kept in His sight, and other needs are managed in view of the spiritual welfare of each person. He is arranging the future that we cannot foresee. The whole interplay of fortune and misfortune, the milieu in which we live, and the circle of people who influence us for better or worse are fully known to Him and controlled for our eternal spiritual good. Chance and bad luck are words, not realities, to God; for everything is intimately plotted, each item permitted, each movement held taut in the omnipotent hand of the Ruler.

Within that full and ultimate perspective in which God sees things, time is correlated to eternity, moments are fitted into immortality, and parts are shaped according to the whole. This world and life were never meant to be all; hence, the meaning of the present moment must be sought in the whole of life. Its sufferings were never intended to be permanent; like organic life, they disappear while the blessings derived from suffering and living on earth endure. The testing period passes; the glories of beatitude remain forever. The point is not whether labor is pleasant or unpleasant, but whether it is fittingly rewarded. The issue on present suffering is not whether we like or dislike it, understand or misunderstand it, but whether it is an apt means to eternal success. Suffering known as a step toward happiness makes sense. It is like appraising the worth of labor in the pattern of the pay and the products.

In a universe of hierarchical values, with both material and spiritual realities, with grades of being, the temporary presence or absence of physical evils has no necessary connection with the value of the spirit and the supreme end of life. A man's rating before God cannot be judged by the absence or presence of temporal goods. There is no good reason why saints as well as sinners should not catch colds, shiver, and starve and why convents as well as gambling centers should not be hit by lightning and jet planes. Sun and rain fall on both the just and the unjust. Furthermore, there is no good reason why God should interfere with the laws of nature, of psychology, and of business operations in order to confer instant temporal rewards on the good or impose instant temporal penalties on the wicked. The regularity and predictability of nature is itself a great good, worth preserving. The meting out of instant benefits would tempt man to do good and avoid evil for the wrong reasons, to love the gifts and not the Giver, to turn divine service into selfish acquisition. Instantaneous dispensation of punishments in this world might do more harm than good. It might, for instance, bring innocent children into unnecessary sorrow because of a wicked father; it might close to the wicked the chance for spiritual recovery. Also, it would seem to do more harm than good in the long run if the good succeeded on earth in spite of their impracticality and failure to use right natural means in the affairs of this world. The appropriate cause brings its own appropriate effect. A scientist makes discoveries because he is trained, observant, curious, diligent, and not because he is chaste and religious. A lawyer succeeds because he is highly qualified with legal knowledge and intellectual abilities, and not because he is a kind father or a steadfast church member. A good lawyer ought both love God and know the law.

God permits evil in order to save and sanctify souls. Evil will not injure the spiritual welfare of good men who bear it rightly. As for the wicked, it is evident that temporal suffering fits into God's plan of leading them by a roundabout route to supreme union with Him forever. God spares evildoers for a while and at other times afflicts them, in both cases in order to save and sanctify them. Times without number the story of the prodigal son has been re-enacted when bodily suffering and abandonment by friends have driven a soul back into the arms of God and acceptance of His loving will. The mysteries of God's mercies are repeated daily on hospital sickbeds. How many times God has been discovered in shell torn foxholes! Disease and war are terrible; yet it is sheer gain for spiritual values that some men gain God only under such conditions. "God writes straight on crooked lines."

5. MORAL GOVERNMENT BY GOD

The carrying out of the providential plan of God is known as God's government. Divine rule operates within time, effectively guiding the members of the universe to His purpose and their ends by suitable means, and specially leading the members of the human race to their supreme end by proper human acts.

Good government requires good order. Order requires law as the instrument of the ruler's control and as the means of providing for the common good. The larger, the more active, and the more changeable the community, the greater is the need of law to correlate activities and prevent disorder, destruction, and chaos. The absence of law brings evil; its presence develops and preserves good. This need of regulation by law is unusually true when the ruler of the community must deal with so noble and yet so fickle a thing as free will that varies so much in its choices, that swings now to the good and then to moral evil. Such a mysterious gift needs direction both from the man within and from the Ruler of the human community without. Moreover, free man must be governed according to his free nature; and therefore, the law proper to his humanity is moral law which respects liberty; it cannot be physical law which necessitates to action of one kind in one uniform pattern, measure, and direction.

One who governs by moral law will try every way to encourage moral good and discourage moral evil; but he will not tamper with liberty. He will reward the good for suffering endured for the law's sake. He will punish the evil for doing harm, for defeating the purpose of the law as far as they can, and for running away from the hardships that the law requires its subjects to bear in resisting evil and selfishness. The law must be sovereign always; and especially must its sovereignty be shown in the end; the law and the good must win, not the law-breaker. If the ruler should permit final victory for the wicked, he would have abdicated to disorder and would have favored destruction of the good.

Therefore, to prevent moral evil God uses the fullness of His moral authority both to command men to do the morally right and to forbid them to perform the morally evil. If they misuse their freedom and violate the law, then the law applies its penalties — physical sufferings, losses, and other proportionate sanctions which champion and restore the order of justice. But the divine Judge metes out His sanctions at the time He judges wise. There is no reason why He must inflict full punishment immediately or why He should withdraw all blessings of nature from the wicked or why He should risk losses of goods as great as liberty itself by extreme efforts to prevent all evil. It is, in fact, part of the amazing goodness of God that He offers pardon to the wicked who freely change their hearts and give up evil. Mercy is far more mysterious than justice, for mercy heals what seems incurable and pardons the inexcusable. But if in the end mercy is refused, the justice and high purpose of the law and its sovereign order win by excluding the unrepentant wicked from further participation in the blessings of the common order enjoyed by the good men of the divine community.

We must recognize, then, that it is a mark of excellent government to allow evil to have a subordinate and secondary place in the great scheme of things and in the administration of the perfect order of the universe. God, who is the measure of all things, will also be the perfect measure of reward and of penalty, for each one, and according to the works and desserts of each. Under a government of divine love all things in due time work together unto good, and all move ultimately toward His love.

Human preoccupation with the woes of life betrays some people into forgetting the other side of the picture, the sunny truths about

God's efforts to give temporal happiness to men and God's farseeing concern to alleviate suffering. He has provided many curative measures for men and many natural methods of relief for body and mind. Sleep, rest, release of emotional tension through tears, the comic element in life, the catharsis of tragedy in the theater, the bright world of music, dancing, fiction, and sport, the demands of work and of caring for the living which distract us from our own losses, the gift of pity for others, the power to discover drugs and treatments which greatly relieve or prevent pain are all merciful arrangements of God. In that same kindly spirit He has concealed from us most of the details of our own futures. He lets us live one day, one moment at a time. A glance at our whole future with all its difficult spots might plunge too many into discouragement and melancholy. God lifts the curtain of the future either not at all or only inch by inch, for our immediate needs. About that future we can be carefree because He is so careful of us.

6. Progress Through Sacrifice

The constructive providence of God directs things to the better. But progress to the better often seems to involve surrender of the inferior. We must, for instance, choose to bear temporary loss for more permanent gains, endure the painful in order to acquire the noble, give up the lower in order to have the higher, even uproot the smaller and natural good which impedes the birth and growth of the greater and supernatural good.

This same trend can be seen in that law of assimilation in living things when the being of the lower realm becomes the food and instrument of the life of a higher realm, as when animals feast on plant life. By assimilation into a more perfect form of life, the lower life loses itself but also gains a better form of being. The germ of wheat loses its own identity in order to find new being in the ripe sheaf of the next season. The same law of growth appears in human character and society. Parents sacrifice for their children. Almost all have their "growing pains," periods of trouble and adjustment before acquiring the rich maturity of character that marks the leader, hero, and saint. The few die in battle to make their countrymen secure. Love proves its wonderful depth by giving great things, bearing hard things, sharing its best, giving even itself for the beloved. These sacrificial gifts and willing wounds nourish love, deepen friendship, and bring forth bright and permanent fruits in human relationships.

The same law of surrender and of endurance for the sake of love often functions in our human love of God. Love must freely sacrifice nondivine things for God; it must put to death the desires for unneeded temporal goods that spiritual goods may have living room in the soul; it must yield the pleasant for the important; it must bend the body to the soul, fight against nature for the sake of grace, yield its whole being to the sovereignty of God. Man is lifted up to the fuller divine plane of a loving life only at a great price. But this is good order. This is altogether wholesome progress. This is sane co-operation with the wise government of an all-good God. His love is the measure of all living, and our love of Him is the summit of our achievement.

7. RIGHT ATTITUDES AND RIGHT ACTION IN REGARD TO SUFFERING

Besides winning intellectual contentment with the mystery of suffering, we must adjust our way of living and feeling to the truths which we have thought over. Face to face with pain, hardship, sin, waste, and sorrow, we must live through this problem, not merely think our way through it. The adjustment of a loving will is needed together with a sincere desire to get the fullness of benefit out of the sufferings that will come into our lives.

A capital point lies in our right attitudes to God or in our proper spirit of praying in His presence. Since God has designed this universe, put us in it, and assigned a correct place for pain and distress in His complete plan for us, we must win patience by uniting our mind with His plan and uniting our will with His government. "God knows best," and "Thy will be done," are the two perfect popular prayers that state the right attitude. However incompletely we understand God's ways, His wisdom deserves our admiration, adoration, and trust. The order He has devised is very well done. We are sure that it is good for us. Similarly, we owe obedience to that will, co-operation with it, loyalty to it though we do not know its ways, patient surrender to its permissions of evil, acceptance of His disguised blessings, even thanksgiving for the trials that He does not spare us in the course of duty. Some day the faithful soul learns that these troubles were the best days of life in terms of eternal achievement; they marked the big advance; they concealed the great favors from heaven. Eager to work will in will with God, the trusting and grateful man offers up all his disappointments, sorrows, and patience to God for the fulfillment of His will and glory.

The human will aligned with the will of God must take the right stand in regard to evil. This consists, first, in controlling the causes of evil in our own lives and in the lives of others as far as we may, and second, in remedying evil as far as we can. Prevention, relief, forgiveness, and cure constitute a program of effective action that will keep men occupied with something more than their doleful worries. Always the main attack should be the prevention and cure of moral evil or sin. To some comes the vocation to spend their whole lives in assuaging the sufferings of the sick, the mentally disturbed, the impoverished, and the handicapped. Some can prove their love of God and men by that most amazing type of relief, an actual sharing with others in their sorrows and losses and by offering their own sufferings in voluntary reparation for the crimes that others hurl at God.

Lastly, as it was fitting that the Son of God should suffer and die and in that way enter into His glory, so it is fitting that men should imitate the divine Model in facing suffering and waiting for the final sacrifice of life. Here, as in so many other problems, the Christian possesses a fuller answer and a calmer peace. To him the cross as gift of love and symbol of victory is the chief sign of his philosophy of life. Confident in God's goodness, he trusts God in the hour and circumstances of his death: "Father, into Your hands I commend my spirit." Knowing the bittersweet doctrine of participation in Christ's sufferings, he accepts his own death to fill up what is wanting of the sufferings of Christ. Sure of Christ's victory over death and of Christ's call to the soul to join Him in heaven, the Christian welcomes the sundering of the bond between body and soul as the great moment of triumphant union of the soul with the Father in heaven.

This is the true answer of true love between God and man. For those who love God all events, none excepted, but all things, even death, join together to achieve the good.

CHAPTER 19

Christ's Contribution to a Theory of Life

1. THE INSUFFICIENCY OF A REASONED PHILOSOPHY OF LIFE

BESIDES A philosophical wisdom about life there is a theology of life, and in particular, a Christian design of life. The merely philosophical view uses only human reason as its instrument and both physical and human nature as its base of evidence. Its conclusions about human life do not have the fullness and firmness which Christ's teachings on the same subject have. Nor is this surprising. Man was meant to have truth and to live by truth; but he was never meant to live only by philosophical truth. God made special provision for men by revelation, by a wisdom descended from God's own being and mind. The same God who created nature, reason, and philosophy also created grace, revelation, and theology. In His own unity of truth He has so harmonized reason and revelation or philosophy and theology that all the valuable principles, insights, and conclusions of philosophy are absorbed into and are serviceable to a theological view of life. Nature is made in view of grace; natural human life is made in view of its uplifting to the diviner plane of Christian life.

We may say even more. Not only is the philosophical view of life incomplete when compared with the Christian view, but the philosophical view can never be a sufficient view of human life. That it has not been a full view is manifest by the record of the best philosophers when they were left to themselves without revealed help.[1] In fact, the best philosophers have echoed the masses everywhere in praying for light from above, for the coming of God to earth that men might better learn the deep secrets of God and lead more fruitful lives. Many philosophers hungry for truth and life have themselves realized the inadequacy of their own conclusions. They have asked themselves: Is this all? Is this the whole truth? Have we omitted something important? Have we been blind to some of the evidence? Have we interpreted the meaning, causes, and relationships of the evidence rightly? Have we denied something which was true? How sure are we of our teachings? Why is there so little agreement among us philosophers on so many important questions? Have we put a disproportionate emphasis on some truth and thus thrown the whole out of balance?

Philosophers who are aware of the history of their subject will point out some of the particular shortcomings of philosophy in its doctrines concerning the origin, destiny, value, and capacities of human life. There is the never ceasing difficulty of getting a satisfactory knowledge of God through analogical comparison with His creatures. Here is a barrier that the human intellect cannot of itself break through; God must break through the barrier by His special revelation of Himself. Man wants to know with greatest certainty what his future with God is to be like. But he has from himself such slight resources to know that future. He did not even suspect the vision of God until God told him of it. He never had a satisfactory proof of immortality in pagan times when reason stood alone. Reason cannot tell us whether our ethical analysis of our duties, especially in regard to God, is complete. Does God perhaps want something more of us? How does He wish us to treat Him? In religious matters it is important that we honor and please Him. Is the type of religion that we rationally invent or see about us the type of honor and gift that would please Him?[2] When men do wrong, does God forgive them and give them a new start? Or is their situation after sinning hopeless and irremediable? If there is a remedy, what is it, and how can we know of it, and to whom must we go to receive this divine healing? Can we merit a reward from God? Has God any special helps for us in our many desperate needs? Has God any extra truths in the great treasury of His wisdom that He wishes us to know and live by? Is every one of us dear to God? Is the civil state the highest authority under God on earth?

The questions pile up much faster than the answers. What answers are given run a risk of being misleading because of their incompleteness, since one does not well understand the part without the whole.

This chapter is addressed to those who are Christians that they may see the full view of Christ, for they appreciate Browning's phrase: "God may have other words for other worlds; but for this world of ours, His word is Christ." For Christ is the wise Word of His Father.

To those who are not Christians but are philosophers, this chapter may serve as a help to understanding the ideal of the supernatural man and as an interpretation supplementary to the philosophical view of life.

2. CHRIST'S CLAIM AS A TEACHER OF LIFE

Millions called Christians today look to Christ, a historical personage, as Teacher and Model of life, as the Saviour of their souls, and as the God who is the center of their living.

It is a historical fact that somewhat over nineteen hundred years ago in the reign of Tiberius Caesar, a person named Jesus Christ lived and taught in Palestine. He claimed to be the expected Messias whom the sacred books of the Jews had been predicting for centuries and in whose life their minute prophecies were verified. He claimed to be the Son of God, as well as a son of man. He claimed to be the Saviour come to redeem man from the death of sin and to restore the life of grace to the sinner. He claimed to have a doctrine straight from God. He worked mighty miracles to back His claims, and He staked all on the promised miracle of His own resurrection. He founded a teaching and sanctifying organization to keep and promote His ideas after His return to God in heaven.

He supported His divine commission as a Teacher of life by His own life of heroic love of God and of man. He shared man's lot and faced the sorrows and conflicts of human life. By bearing these and in spite of them rising from the grave, He taught the right attitude to human miseries.[3]

Men, then, have been taught by God in person.[4] The mental attitude of the majority of minds influenced by Christianity has been well put by Peter, the Apostle. When many of Christ's disciples abandoned Him because of His teaching on the need to eat His flesh and drink His blood as nourishment for the spirit, He asked the twelve Apostles whether they too wished to go away. Stunned and stung by the question, Peter showed how unthinkable is abandonment of Christ's teaching: "Lord, to whom shall we go? Thou hast the words of everlasting life."[5]

Since Christians are so numerous, Christ's doctrine on life deserves attention. Since He is the Author of life, the Son of the living God, sent into the world to teach life, give life, and lead us to eternal life, a grasp of His main doctrines on the problems raised in this book is indispensable to a thoughtful and reverent mind and to a happy and noble life.

3. AN OUTLINE OF CHRIST'S TEACHINGS ON LIFE

In this presentation we may follow the order of problems given in the second chapter. This directs us first to Christ's teaching on human nature.

The doctrines of Christ on man's living gifts partly coincide with the best philosophical conclusions, partly supplement these, and always add larger perspectives of meaning and deeper certainty to the philosophers' remarks. Christ unequivocally teaches that each man has a soul, which will exist forever and which is much superior to the body. He claims that the human intellect, naturally ordained for truth, is also open at God's touch to new revealed truths. Man is physically free to do good or evil; but at present he is badly wounded by the fall of Adam and by his own personal wrongdoing. Wounded man is much troubled by his adversary, Satan, by his own flesh, and by the world about him. He needs help and healing, which God is willing to give and which God prompts man to beg for and to accept freely. The mercy of God is offered to wounded man, person by person; pardon brings man a new and very special form of life, sanctifying grace. Given by God and not earned by human virtue, this gift elevates man to a godlike plane of being. Man is born again of God, becomes a new creature, an adopted son of God, a friend of God, an heir to heaven. Henceforth, the main point of each man's life will be to retain this grace and grow in it, thereby to save his soul and make himself ready to join God in heaven. It is one of Christ's major doctrines that the one destiny of all men is vision of God and rejoicing in God forever because of their graced status. At the end of the world, the ultimate victory of God over all things, over God's and man's enemies, will be made manifest. Those who have saved their souls will be welcomed into God's blessed kingdom to share in His eternal victory. Part of the victory is to recover the life of their long dead bodies and join the risen Son of God in His glorified flesh.

By this body of teaching Christ has restored to men the knowledge of their dignity and their equality in nature, their need of grace, and their vocation to salvation. No wonder the downtrodden found the new Christian teaching so exhilarating. To learn that God cared for and loved each one, and had died for the sake of each one, and is providing for each the means to divine companionship in heaven! To learn that earth with its misfortunes and indecencies is not all, and that in God's sight there is no respecting of persons, no preferences grounded on power, wealth, sex, or type of labor, but that all are beloved of God!

Christ has a wealth of teaching concerning man's relations to other beings in the universe, to God, to other men, and to nature.

He repeated the doctrine known to the Hebrews but not to the pagan sages that God is the Creator of heaven and earth, and therefore, too, of man and his world. He gave this doctrine world-wide circulation and made it a test question in the conflict with idolatrous Rome. He also made it clear that God is personal, and indeed three Persons in an amazing social life within the unity of the Godhead. This trait of divine personality is emphasized by His constant reverential reference to God and especially to the First Person of God as our Father, by His reference to Himself as the Son of God, and to the Holy Spirit as the Love of God. As a Father, God thinks of us as His dear children, gives us life, preserves us, helps us, cares for us, forgives our wrongdoing, sends His only-begotten Son into the world to redeem us and to teach us to live rightly and happily. To make His divine nearness more evident and appealing to us, the Son of God took a human soul and a human body and dwelt among us as Emmanuel. The Third Person, too, is in the world, sent by the Father and the Son, to continue and perfect the divine work in the souls of men and in the supernatural social organism, the Church.

On man's relationship to God, Christ is very clear. There is the duty of reverence to God as a Father; the duty of trust in one who loves us far more dearly than He cares for the lilies of the field and the soaring birds in the air; the duty of obedience to the will of God in daily decisions and daily conduct; the duty of filial prayer to our Father in heaven; the duty of desiring the Father's glory through fulfillment of the Father's will; the duty to obey men who hold social authority as delegates of the heavenly Power; the duty to resist evil fearlessly and to repent of evil committed; the duty to love God with all one's soul, mind, and strength. This filial spirit between man and God is something very new in human life on earth.

But the unique and central theme in this teaching about the person-to-person relations between God and man lies in the article that Christ living among men is the very Son of God, true God of true God, as well as truly human, born of the Virgin Mary. As God, He has God's own rights over men. A divine Teacher, He demands their full belief. He loves men as God and demands from them total devotion. He leads men and demands that they follow Him to God. He offers them new life; He gives them new orders; He invites them to partnership with Him and service under Him; He asks them to join Him in suffering; He founds for them a new society for spiritual purposes and admits them to it; He prepares their heavenly reward and promises to award it to them after He has judged their lives. He is everything to them. Lest men's minds be stunted, He feeds them on His divine truths; lest their souls be famished, He feeds them on His own flesh and blood; lest their weaknesses part them from God, He forgives them. To preserve their union with Him, He and His Father and the Holy Spirit come to inhabit their souls and to bind them to all His other true friends in His Mystical Body.

This astonishing doctrine of the union of our lives, activities, ideas, virtues, and destiny with that of Christ is taught again and again. It produces a surprising and fruitful simplification of life's issues and ways. For everything has become a matter of union of mind, will, motive, action, and very being with Christ, the Son of God and of Mary. One external expression of this union is a life of growing virtue patterned after the life of Christ and flowering in Christ's favorite virtues of religion, humility, sincerity, chastity, and charity. St. Paul, having all but achieved this perfect union with Christ could sum up his own life as a sparkling identity with Christ's: "I live — now, not I — but Christ lives in me."[6]

The teaching of Christ on man's relations to his fellow men sets higher standards than those ever before known. Like other great teachers, He is interested in the golden rule of conduct among men, but with His own new motive: "As often as you do anything for one of these My brothers, you do it for Me."[7] He proposes an even fairer motive, a new rule of life, a new initiative, universality, measure, mode, and depth to human regard for men: "Love one another" — not as you love yourselves, not because another first loved you, but "as I have loved you."[8] His was a love when men were yet His enemies; His was an all-embracing love, a suffering love, a love faithful to the end.

In His doctrine of religious fellowship Christ enlarged our social relations with our fellow men and gave us spiritual support of many kinds. He made this society a bulwark for all times against the crushing power of an omnipotent state. Now conscience and the rights of the person have their authoritative spokesman and defender in Christ's own Church. In all the basic matters pertaining to salvation, the Church is independent of the power, the weaknesses, and the corruption of any civil state. No matter what the state may do, man's soul can be saved through loyalty to Christ's society. Physical power may from time to time be exercised in almost unlimited degree by mighty tyrants; but spiritual power and all pretense to it has been taken from civic rule forever, to the great peace of men's souls.

Even our relations to the physical world have been modified because of Christ. He, God in the flesh, lived here on our earth, and, as far as we can know, on no other material spot in the universe. In the plan of God this earth is geographically the center of all spiritual things. God dwelt here, and, in fact, still dwells here in the Blessed Sacrament under the forms of bread and wine. God gave Himself a material, sentient body. The human body can never again be considered corrupt, immoral, unworthy. God used the air, water, wine, fruits, and animals of this earth. God loved nature about Him and taught us to see it with new eyes and to glimpse in one poetic sight (what God sees in a glance) the bond between God, man, and natural beauty. He showed us, too, that physical nature is the creature obedient to God's power of working miracles. He used nature to instruct us in His parables and comparisons. He selects several natural objects — water, oil, bread, wine — as both signs and carriers of grace in His sacraments. He even let nature fulfill the mysterious roles of being the battlefield of His struggle for our redemption and of supplying the instruments which caused His pain, shed His blood, and pierced His heart. Not least of all, His own example of poverty insisted on moderation in possessing earthly treasures and peacefulness in meeting our material needs.

On the most crucial question in a philosophy of life, the problem of suffering, this divine Teacher has His own answers and His own encouragement. Truthful, realistic, and sincere, He does not pretend that evils are not present and that sorrow does not spoil the happiness of the lives of even good people. He is anxious to lessen the causes of anguish, especially as they proceed from the ill will and thoughtlessness of men. He uses His great power as God of destinies and Judge of all men to pronounce woes on the wicked and to picture hell to them as the ending of their cruelty to other men. But His efforts at stopping evil on this earth would be somewhat ineffective, He knew. He has consolations of His own for those who suffer for justice' sake, for His sake.

One of these consolations is His assurance of the moment-to-moment loving providence of God over each of us, over each hair of our head, over each experience of life, over each pain endured. He guarantees God's watchful protection and continuing blessing even in the hours when we are the victims of misfortune and of others' wickedness. He encourages us to be fearless in facing evil and in sacrificing even innocent natural goods for the sake of the soul and the supernatural, to regard the price paid in time as immensely worthwhile for the priceless delight of eternity. To prove that this teaching really solves the mystery of suffering, God's Son Himself suffers the most extreme cruelty. But, rising, He is the triumphant answer. God's victory in the resurrection of His Son after terrible disgrace, agony, and death is the ground of an unshakable hope that we are to share in His victory by using His means to conquest. He even invites us to take up His cross, to share His burden and suffering, thus to become more identified with Him, to do more good, and to participate more fully with Him in the victory of God that solves all problems.[9]

4.   THE CHRISTIAN MAN IN A CHRISTIAN CULTURE

This sketch of the contribution of Christ has mentioned only some high lights of His theory of life. No other theory is closer to living reality and better welds together a speculative understanding of life and a way of living. Those who follow this way of Christ mix in the same world with non-Christians, but they are very different in mind, hope, motive, and love. The Christian has a body like other men, made of the same elements of nature, obedient to the same natural laws, having the same natural needs, pains, and repugnances. His intellect and will need training in natural habits as any other man's. He dwells on earth, walking the same streets, using the same autos, patronizing the same stores, playing the same games, studying the same sciences, serving in the same armies, living in families and nations, just as any non-Christian. But the Christian has faced the supreme question, "What think you of Christ?" and has answered, "I believe in Jesus Christ, God's only Son." He has in some way been touched in spirit, intelligence, in will by Jesus Christ. Mingling now with his natural life is that new life of grace, a new life of the mind in spiritual truth and insight, a new life of love of heavenly things. He has not abandoned nature, but has added to nature and gone beyond it. He has accepted Christ as King of Truth, as Prince of Peace, as the Redeemer from sin, as Head of His Church, as the Model of virtue. He lives to give glory to Christ. He shares in the mind which was in Christ Jesus, he loves with a heart beating in union with the Heart of Christ. His world is a fuller world, for it embraces nature and grace and their integral wedding. His gladness is a deeper happiness. For he is freed from sin and spiritual ignorance and degrading superstition; his eyes look to the coming splendor of life eternal; his ears have caught the prelude to heavenly alleluias; and his heart is lifted up to the throne where God waits for his soul. This is a miniature of the man, beloved by Christ and formed by the Church, who follows Christ, "the Way, the Truth, the Life."

It is up to each one of us to lead the full Christian life for himself and to harvest Christ's gifts in this life as well as in the next. But more than a personal wholehearted acceptance of Christ's views and wishes is needed. We also must foster a new Christian culture in which the majority of men can find the optimum social conditions to assist them in forming a truly Christian mind and leading a nobly Christian life.

In an atmosphere favorable to Christian culture, the traditions, organization of society, and laws of the people work together for the good of a man who is specifically Christian. Home and school unite in impressing Christian ideals and in expecting Christian behavior; customs, habits, popular feasts, example, general manners, common interests all have a Christian tone and accent. The conscious ideals of all people, the points of emphasis in thought, teaching, and judgment, public praise and public disapproval go together to give both greatest protection for the Christian in this world and greatest opportunity for the flowering of the ordinary Christian virtues that lead to salvation and sanctification of the soul. Even opportunities for heroic virtue are widespread, though these do not take the form of public suffering for the faith.

We see vigorous efforts to maintain such a Christian atmosphere and build a thoroughly Christian culture in the tradition, spirit, and daily routine of monasteries and nunneries. There everything is organized with the glory of God and the practice of virtue as first in view. Daily concern with the complete mind of Christ and imitation of Him build up a total milieu that gives the members powerful social resources for Christian living.

But today there linger only relics of such a vigorous social milieu in public life and in much domestic life. Thoughts of the soul's welfare and of God's glory, will, and nearness do not dominate public organization, policy, decision, and activity. Religious organization and political units are far apart. Religious education is not the common thing in our country, showing that the interests of the soul and of Christ are not our basic consideration in education; many laws of the land do not favor the Christian concept of marriage; weddings have forgotten Christ and Cana; the customs of the land and many businesses, as entertainment, advertising, publishing, and the fashion trades do much to create a spirit hostile to Christian ideals of modesty, purity, and faith. The saints are no longer the people's heroes. The international viewpoint so congenial to the Christian spirit and to the sentiment of the brotherhood of man under God is having a hard struggle for recognition.

In this home world and public world in which the laity live, much, therefore, remains to be done to create such a Christian culture that encourges the finest supernatural thinking and living. The Church has succeeded in making Christmas and Easter feasts beloved by all. It succeeded in bringing learning into the service of Christ in the high Middle Ages. It reconstructed Europe when it brought the military interests of the nobility into the service of justice and devoted it to the help of the needy, of the unarmed woman, and of the unarmed Church. It taught artists and craftsmen to dedicate themselves to the glory of Christ and His Mother.

What the Church has done before our time with the help of Christ, she can do in our age with the help of Christ's devoted laity. Our times, marked by high organizational and technical ability and dominated by a lawyers' and workers' culture, present unusual opportunities for apostolic creation of a new Christian culture in our United States. The educated laity, the lawyers, and workers, if organized, can do it. There is need of the fundamental decision to give the time to learning the mind of Christ better and to devote our spirits to living the Christ-form of life more splendidly.

CHAPTER 20

The Life of Peace

1. PEACE, A PHILOSOPHICAL THEME

As PEACE is an urgent issue of our days, it seems fitting to close a modern book on life with some reflections on the peaceful life.

Peace, ever dear to men, is intensely longed for by twentieth-century men whose days have been darkened by disorder, discontent, conflict, disintegration, and tragedy in nearly every sphere of life in almost every part of the world. Many men have little peace in their minds, desires, and consciences. The stormy head of an exploding bomb seems to symbolize the pressing anxieties and mental troubles confronting modern man. The crumbling state of many marriages speaks of disunity and quarreling among spouses. Our restless homes, jangling nerves, and feverish mobility find their image in undisciplined school children, in youthful crime, and in noisy exciting music. The rivalry among men in business and the clash of race with race add to the tense unrest. Most spectacular of all in magnitude, bitterness, and consequences are the unceasing contests among nations, whose armed truces, cold wars, and unhonored treaties flare into cannon fire and blood-letting battles. So delicate is the balance of international resources, armaments, and statecraft that we seem to be waiting each morning to hear the wave of war roar over the boundaries of every land in the world.

Our concern here is to consider what philosophy, seconded by theology, can contribute to peaceful living for men. Being a matter of principles and ideas, philosophy must make its specific contribution by implanting right principles, true values, noble ideals, and valid standards within the minds of men. Through ideas philosophy generates right desires and corrects evil inclinations and thus moves into the fields of right action and peaceful living. Its gift to peace is reasoned truth and calm understanding. It cannot competently deal with techniques of peace building and trouble prevention. But philosophy does call attention to the analyses of peace contained in its own and related literary fields. It presents a specific study of peace, its essential features,

248

and its causes. It discusses the various types of peace that affect human life. Being a wisdom, it studies order and, eminently, that order of living which we know as the state of peace. Philosophy studies life and its demands; it studies the goals of life which will give us happiness; it studies norms of orderly living; it studies the nature of society, human fraternity, and the fundamental tasks of government as a peace organization; it studies justice and rights in considerable detail; it teaches many virtues productive of peace and encourages man in their practice. It invites man to peace of conscience in regular service of God and His will. It opens the way to that better peace campaign of theology which we know as the peace of Christ. Perhaps most importantly, philosophy's insistence on truth as the guide to life promotes a fundamental condition for peace.

A theme as precious to man as peace has evoked an enormous literature.[1] The Bible has many notable passages in connection with Christ's peace mission on earth. Plato and Aristotle, Thucydides and Polybius comment on peace and war. The most influential writer has been St. Augustine in his careful study of peace, especially in his *City of God*. To him all later writers owe an immeasurable debt. Pseudo-Dionysius' *Divine Names* has a few points which St. Augustine did not stress. St. Thomas Aquinas has written but a few footnotes to Augustine's treatment. The great treatises on justice and government of the post-Reformation scholastics add more detail. The popes of the twentieth century, Benedict XV, Pius XI, and Pius XII, must be credited with writing the really great modern treatments of peace. From these sources we cull most of the points which follow.

2. ORDER AND TRANQUILLITY

St. Augustine's sentence, "Peace is the tranquillity of order,"[2] has captured for all times the essence of peace. It also suggests what the causes of peace and of disturbance are. For whatever affects good order or whatever bears upon tranquillity influences the presence or absence of human peace. To understand true peace we must grasp these two fundamental features, order and tranquillity.[3]

Order arranges many elements in a whole or a group and puts each in its own place in the total unity formed from these elements. Wherever order is established, there is some sort of unity, whether among the several parts in a physical whole or among the many members of a related set of beings. The unity springs from some connecting or unifying principle that binds the parts or members together. Order then seems to comprise these four constituents — multiple components, relationships between these, some bond or connecting principle, and a resultant unity. Disorder by contrast shows lack of unity, mere unrelated multiplicity, disproportion, unbalance, conflict of forces and purposes, confusion, and resulting waste and damage.

There are many types of order. The types pertinent to peace are the order of parts to the whole, the relation, of means to the end, the order of subjects to superiors, the union of the members of a social whole or community, the juridical order between the parties involved in a system of mutual rights and duties, and the comparison of values among unequal goods.

We see examples of physical order all about us in the natural cycle of seasons, the structure of a plant, the organization of a colony of ants, and the positions, sizes, and movements of the solar system. We find many varieties of order dependent on human action, as orderly automobile traffic, service in a restaurant, and arrangements of furniture in rooms. We also have various social orders. That between parents and children readily shows the elements of multiplicity, unity, interrelations, and the principle of unity in generation and authority.

Peace among men requires good order, an arrangement of beings, values, and rights that is suitable to man's nature, that promotes man's moral and spiritual perfection, and that locates everything pertinent to human life in its truly proper place. Since persons set up good order in their lives by their choices, they are bound by the natural-law first principle to keep order and not disturb it. Since human order concerns a complex being, man, who has many relationships within and without himself, order must meet all these essential needs binding man into interior personal unity and external social unity. Good order is, then, a moral good or an object of moral choice.

The multiple levels of good human order may be listed as the rule of God over man, the rule of soul over body and of conscience over action, the rule of law and just authority over the acts of subjects, the rule of justice and charity among men's free associationships, the rule of man's end over the means of living, the rule of grace over natural goods. If such general rule is observed, each thing is in its own proper place; for good order does not require that everything have the same place or that everything be equal. Good order demands that no thing and no one be neglected, that all be put in their right place, without excess or defect, with impartiality, with consideration of the needs, functions, and rights of each participant in the order.

Before good order can be achieved by men with good intentions, they must know what good order for persons and societies is and requires. Since God and man must work together to bring about the right disposition of things, man must sufficiently know God's truth, God's authority, God's will, and God's plan of order for man's life. Since men must think, will, and work together to achieve order, they must have a common fund of principles, a shared knowledge of basic truths about right order, and a like desire for good order. This may briefly indicate the importance of truth and, by corollary, of education in fundamental truth, as a prerequisite of concord of wills and harmony of action.

Since the disasters of our times are provoked chiefly by disorders in the realm of justice, that is, by actual injuries to man's rights or the threat of such wrongs, it becomes necessary to examine carefully the meaning of juridical order. This order of justice comprises all the rights granted by any legitimate law and the corresponding duties of persons and societies to honor the exercise of these moral powers. Rights comprise a huge system, stemming from the grant and guarantee of lawgivers, binding all persons within the system to allow each person and each society to use, keep, claim, and enjoy what is his own in so far as it is his own. The juridical order both gives liberty for acting to parties that have the right and controls interference by others who would impede their action; the law, that is, grants and defends freedom and self-perfection for the holder of the right, giving him both opportunity and immunity, freedom "for" something just and freedom "from" everything unjust.

The key to juridical order is the maxim: "To each his own." Observance of this principle gives every person or society his rightful place in the juridical system. "To each his own" also means that each without exception, strong and weak, black and white, native and foreigner, ruler and subject, has his privileged rights, to which everyone else has obligations.

In a complete peace the total juridical order must be kept in mind. This corpus of rights and duties includes all man's natural rights, all rights granted by any legitimate form of state law, all supernatural rights granted by God for the life of grace, and all canonical rights granted by the Church. In this total order of justice, the three great circles of commutative justice between equals, distributive justice between communities and their members, and legal justice between members and community must be included. Good order is complete among men only when everyone, singly and socially, has all that is due to him, when no one is deprived of what is his own, when each one can freely exercise his rights within reasonable limits, and when every person or group respects the rights of others.

This mention of the juridical order indicates why modern discussions of public peace so often refer to a new order of justice and to definitions of the rights of states, persons, economic groups, races, and the Church. The discovery, cataloguing, and universal acceptance of a sufficiently complete bill of personal, social, and international rights is a primary step toward world peace. Rights will constitute the main content of honorable treaties and of most other agreements or contracts among men. For the sake of peace, justice must first be established among men. What intellectual and moral qualities may be prerequisite to the universal willingness to be just is another matter.

An alive, functioning juridical order must have juridical security. This leads us to the theme of tranquillity, the second constituent of peace.

The state of peace resembles the lilt of a May breeze and the rhythm of a happy song. There is an ease and naturalness about it, a repose of desires, and a sense that all is well. And this satisfaction is climaxed by fearlessness, confidence, and joy. Peace implies calmness, contentment, and serenity of mind in possession of the truth and of good order. It includes security or safety in the enjoyment of our rights and the many goods of life, the promise of permanence for this set of conditions, willing acceptance of the laws which maintain the order, liberty and energy for fruitful action for the sake of our own and others' well-being, and a glad co-operation with others within the framework of the order. Men at peace are not disturbed by the measures which build order; they do not find these contradicting their desires or denying their needs. They are conscious, instead, of a beneficent joy and a happy unity flowing from their tranquil living together in order. The order pleases them because it seems to them morally right, worthy of human dignity, stable, connatural to man's vital pursuit of his true liberty, and productive of general justice and all-round perfection.

In such a peace, then, there is a harmony of powerful forces even if they be unequal. Its order does not reduce all persons and all rights to deadening equality, but locates all rights and opportunities in their proper places within the whole scheme. It is not built on pacifist compromise which often sacrifices truth and yields to disorder instead of preventing and healing it. Peace is not a cynical name for hidden disorder and mock tranquillity when red terrorism hushes all protests and beats down all efforts to rectify injustice. While the spy and armed guard watch, there may be external conformity and united action, but the inner union of wills, the living bond of unity, the very heart of order is wanting.

Part of the paradox of this imperfect world is that true order must be protected against injustice and disturbance and that right must be guarded by might against the ever recurring forces of selfish desire. Yet many of the instruments devised to protect social order are also threats to that order. Justices of the peace, officers of the law, military forces, and armaments are meant mainly to prevent disorder, but they are easily misdirected into agencies to create and perpetuate disorder to one's own people and to other nations. This ambivalent character of human law in practice proves that military and diplomatic means are never enough to direct power rightly. Peace ultimately is a problem of character, demanding deeper foundations in the human will to be just, fair, kind, and liberty loving. The spirit of peace must prevail and sheath the sword. This spirit of peace within men consists of a complex group of desires, fears, and other feelings, as well as of judgments, beliefs, motives, values, typical dispositions, and habits. Included in this spirit or good will are an intense belief in the worth and nobility of peace and a strong desire to promote effective order.

3. TOTAL PEACE

Complete peace extends to all orders of justice. It also belongs to the three main spheres of human relationships so that total peace requires right order between man and God, within man personally, and between men in society. Good order has been called the foundation of all good things — of liberty, contentment, prosperity, scientific and cultural progress, missionary growth, human perfection, and holiness.

But the foundation of good order itself is the right order of subjection of man to God. This is but to recognize that the moral law, the law of God, is the rock beneath all good things that depend on human effort. Our Lord knew this primary law of peace when He composed the greatest prayer for peace: "Thy will be done on earth as it is in heaven." God wills only what is for man's good and bans what is evil. If the will of God were followed, justice, love, order, and, therefore, peace would fill every corner of human life. If God's will were done, there would be no war.

Peace between man and God would overflow into interior peace of one's spiritual powers and into social peace.

Peace can dwell in many of the powers of man. The imagination possesses a quiet order when a person has command of his attention, checks disturbing and rancorous memories of the past, denies himself useless anxieties over the future, allows no brooding over wounded feelings, and polices those images that would excite anger and lust. The mind has its own peace of conscience and of truth. Conscience is orderly and contented when it is clear and correct on moral issues, when it has succeeded in leading man to conform himself to the will of God, when it is free from consciousness of guilt either because of its innocence or because of pardon bestowed by God, and when it readily masters the other powers, making them comply with the dictates of right moral judgment. The intellect is calm when it is sure that it has the truth and is secured from the seductive disorder of false doctrines. The desires and feelings are at peace when one appreciates the blessings that are his, has learned to keep captive his foolish, wild, extravagant, and even sinful longings, and warms his soul with love of permanently worthwhile, heavenly things. This personal peace reaches a deep perfection or peace of character when all the powers and activities of man are harmonized in pursuit of one central aim in life such as the glory or love of God. At this point of high charity and organization of life the Spirit of God produces His special fruit of spiritual peace in the virtuous soul.

Peace, like charity, begins at home. But it need not stay at home. The man in peace will radiate peace to others in ever widening circles. Total peace for a social being must mean an effort to live in good order with one's associates in the family, at work, in the community, and in the Church. In all our little worlds we must live tranquilly with one another. This good order with our neighbors consists radically in a willingness to unite our wills with those of others. Men have individual preferences, but they also have the talent for harmonious life with one another. If they have mutual respect and a high sense of others' value, they will be able to work toward a consensus of minds, an interior agreement of purposes, a concord of wills seeking the same good, a sufficient compatibility of temperaments to get along together, and a practical collaboration in using the same means or methods for attaining common aims and sharing fairly in common benefits. When, however, mutual respect is lost, unity of wills is lost. Then the divisive forces of passions and dislikes break down social peace, and human interests become contradictory rather than complementary. The collapse of peace in the home turns it into a hotel housing rivals or strangers. The collapse of peace among nations turns the world into an armed inferno.

Good order among men requires not mere agreement but free consent to do the right things and to maintain the good. A pirate crew has not good order since it sails and fights together for the wrong things. Social peace can come only from seeking ends or means that objectively belong to human perfection. It requires mutual agreement and fidelity, for it takes two to make social peace. It is desirable that concord of wills be based as far as possible on agreement of minds between the parties. Their minimum agreement must be to accept the mind of authority and the road of law in matters of practical mutual action.

What may men do to bring peace to their own lives and to that of others? Before answering that question, we must attend to the greatest historical force for peace, the advent and labors of the Prince of Peace.

4. THE PEACE OF CHRIST

Total peace even on earth cannot be achieved until it is a Christian peace. Total peace needs the resources of Christ and must be realized in a Christian order of things where human efforts are lifted to the supernatural plane of living.

The fair title, Prince of Peace,[4] appropriately belongs to Christ. His teachings, example, and work breathe the spirit of peace for men. The prophet Isaias had heralded Him by this name. When He came during the Augustan temporal peace, His angels sang of His peace mission: "Peace on earth to men of good will." He revealed His own peace policy by the sign of unarmed infancy and the soft light of a star, thereby declaring His reliance on love and the spirit, not on physical strength and the sword of authority. He showed Pilate that His armies are fishermen and devoted women, not brawny legionaries. He dies, peaceful in His tragedy. After His resurrection He adopts peace as His special greeting: "Peace be with you." "Peace! It is I; fear not."

His words taught peace to men. His doctrines tend to remove the very causes of disorder, which we know to be spiritual ignorance, error, and all the bad will of sin. Without truth and right values, men are like the children of Jerusalem over whom Christ wept, knowing not wherein their peace lies. Sin tends to rip apart the order within human nature, to rend the union between men's will and God's plan for their lives, and to turn our fellow men into strangers and enemies. Christ urges that we find peace by aligning our wills with God's, concentrating our desires first on spiritual things, and coming to Him to find refreshment of spirit after our labors. He urges men to moderate their cravings for material things and their anxiety for their material future and to substitute for restlessness and discouragement a better trust in God and a fuller use of prayer. He proclaims lofty standards of family affection and conjugal loyalty. All the virtues which He taught would produce glorious peace if practiced. He teaches forgiveness as a start in reuniting men. He opposes meekness of heart to anger, and humility to pride. He proclaims the mandate of brotherly unity based on true love for others. He unites all in one family under one Father in heaven. The peace that He taught wears its own special features of completeness, interior sincerity, loving submission to the will of God, concern with spiritual values. It aspires to a spiritual unity of mankind, is ready to forgive and help, is animated by genuine love of God, and eagerly copies the bright beauty of Christ's peaceful ways.

Christ's example also taught peace. He comes in peaceful guise with a spontaneous offer of pardon to men, a renewal of God's friendship with men, and a foregoing of divine justice. He makes every effort to win men; He is courteous, affable, patient with mistakes, and is boundlessly willing to help. Though He knows men's weakness, He trusts them, even those who will desert Him in need. He obeys authority. He prays for those things that work for human peace. He is meek, calm, and without bitterness in facing opposition and bearing suffering. In every situation He remains unruffled, no matter how deep is His trouble. He tries to gather all men together in one flock so that they may be one in love, grace, and truth as He and the Father are one. He does not meet force with force or guile. His only battles are against the ancient foes of peace: sin, insincerity, greed, pride, unbelief, and inordinate human desires. The tranquil order of human dignity and human kindness still shines in His conduct on the cross.

Because the pattern of His life from birth to death to resurrection so clearly manifests the blessing of peace, Christmas has become the great feast of peace and Eastertide recalls the Victor's peace after the conflict with sin.

He began His peace work in His life on earth and still continues it. Christ is the cause and price of our peace, for by His personal sacrifice He has reconciled God and man, reunited heaven and earth in grace, removed the roots of disorder in hardened self-will, and continues to help men forgive each other, to start anew, to bear with one another, to be fair and kind, to avoid conflict, and to persevere in true brotherhood. To make the work of peace a permanent result of His mission on earth, He pronounced one of His greatest blessings on peacemakers. He works for our peace today through the peace efforts of His Church, of her popes and members. Before His Father in heaven He continues to pray for our peace. He sends the Holy Spirit from whom we receive the sweet peace that surpasses all understanding. The altar of Christian sacrifice finds the continuing Gift offered to God for our peace and the gift of Christ's own charity to each one who receives His Eucharistic Body and Blood. For this love for God and for men is the specific fruit of Eucharistic union with Christ; the charity infused with His flesh is the very cement of Christian order, gathering all together in one body, one purpose, and one living spirit. He heals old wounds of sin in the sacrament of penance. He heeds the prayers of His mother, the Queen of peace, begging mercy for men, and pleading for interior helps to enable men to hold down the headlong passions that burst into disorder. Christ standing at the right hand of His Father is the greatest proof of the triumph of His peace policy. From the throne of heaven He calls all men to share His eternal peace, after serving the cause of peace in this life. When peace triumphs, Christ triumphs. All things become well-ordered and tranquil when they are newly ordered under the leadership of Christ.

5. Peacemakers

The spirit and state of peace are so dear to the Prince of Peace that His platform for living singularly rewards peace work: "Blessed are the peacemakers, for they shall be called the children of God."[5] This seventh beatitude is given to the sincere, stouthearted champions of good order who dare and labor for a peace befitting God's children on earth and preparatory to the eternal peace of the just. The promised reward is one of the best, indicating the high rank of this beatitude: to be a son dear to God, to be of the family of God, the first Peacemaker.[6]

In his vocation, the peacemaker has fascinating models in the example of Christ and in the conduct of the Church to sinners, prospective converts, and enemies. As a spiritual diplomat among men, the peacemaker must have some of the diplomat's endowments. He must, for instance, know the truth, be sure of his principles, really love order and justice, and know what these require and forbid. He must also know human nature, where men are sensitive, how they look at the matter in dispute, what ambitions and fears of theirs block their willingness to act peacefully, how they are won over, and what is feasible step by step. The peacemaker must have something of the career diplomat's gift of waiting, of patient re-education of the disputing parties, of constant effort to show his good will to all so that he is an apt mediator, and of persistence until a workable friendly accord has been established.

Such a high apostolate of making peace in the world is a lifetime work of reason and of grace. Because of the universality of the problems of conflict today, every modern leader must play some role in peacemaking.

Pacification begins within one's own personality by ordering one's life under the will of God, in whose will is our peace, and by subjecting one's sentient nature to its spiritual life. Externally, pacification starts where Christ started, by taking the initiative in forgiving others and thereby showing good will to them.

Reason has much to do with the creation, restoration, and preservation of tranquil order among men. For peace, like most good things, begins in the mind. Reason discovers those two primary rules of peace which St. Augustine[7] mentions: do injury to no one, help everyone whom you can. Reason, then, will find out what thoughts, desires, and misdeeds identify troublemakers, unprincipled patriots, warmongers, and bitter, selfish people who advocate struggle. Prudential reason will speak to the will about avoiding such practices. Reason, too, must actively discover ways of increasing unity among men. It will discover that peace does not flow automatically from one's good will, but that it demands hard thinking, good planning, strong organization, widespread sharing in peace work, apt institutions, constant leadership, and courageous sacrifices. It must find means of lessening the threats to peace in all lines of human interest. It must learn the high arts of impartial arbitration, of judicious compromise in nonessentials, and of friendly manners when disagreement is necessary. Reason will seek out and continually strengthen the bonds that unite men and never overplay the distinctions and inequalities. It is also the work of reason to build firmer connections between the program of modern education and the whole policy of world peace. When intelligence makes permanent peace one of the clearest, most popular, and most cherished ideals of our culture, then we will have made a good beginning toward peace. For our educational programs and culture consist largely of the things that we love and find needful; we do what we love, we educate to what we love, we grow to become what we love.

Another function of reason in the development of peace is its usual role of guiding the will in developing the virtues that belong to the peaceful life. The minimum is justice or honor to the rights of other persons and avoiding of offense in regard to what is actually others' good. Pope Pius XII has adopted a phrase of Isaias as his personal motto: *Opus justitiae pax,* "Peace is the work of justice." Though justice involves very much, still it is not enough for lasting peace; by itself it tends more to remove obstacles to peace rather than positively develop it. Justice needs the good heart of charity.

Even natural charity looks at men and situations with friendly eyes and not with the coolly calculating squint of one measuring exact rights on the scales of justice. Charity has a manifold influence on peacemaking. It better motivates men to give to another what is his due; in its good will to another charity prompts one to give to another more than his own; it is ready to give something of its own. Charity forgives and so heals bitterness. It closes the book of the past; it rubs no old wounds; it soothes prejudices generated by ancient injuries; it is ready to make concessions; it mildly restrains impulses to just reprisals. Charity is daring, constructive, magnanimous.

Being willing to help another's need, charity recognizes that compassion and forgiveness may be one's neighbor's greatest need, though not his right. To seal off the past by forgiveness could heal many family dissensions, business quarrels, political factions, and international troubles. No charitable nation can indulge repeated hateful cries as

"Remember Pearl Harbor." Peace requires a discipline of forgetting that will calm the passions. Charity seeks the viewpoints of others, and desires, wherever it is right, to make its will one with another's will, and to please him by doing what he wants. It welcomes the privilege of marching with former strangers and even with old enemies into a better, happier future. Because of its many ways of promoting union and order among men, St. Thomas emphasizes the role of love rather than of justice in the work of peace. For him, peace is properly the fruit of charity.

The necessity for charity is one of the evidences that peacemaking is a work of grace which reason cannot adequately accomplish. Here we must return to man's need of accepting the divine leadership and divine program of Christ, the Son of God. God is the beginning and the end of all peace. This splendid gift is dependent on His omnipotent and kind action. From Him descend truth, justice, and charity which are so basic to peace. His lawgiving will is the source of all rights among men. His goodness is the exemplar of that good will, charity, and order which we should promote in our relations with men. He has revealed that He wills all men to be united in one faith, in one religion, in one Church, in one peace of charity under His divine Son. From God, moreover, comes the forgiveness of those sins which are the major obstacles to peace. His is the might that softens hard hearts, sweetens bitterness, allays passions, renews respect for rights, and revives hopes.

He has also given to man an instrument for peace, infinitely more powerful than all philosophical reflection and planning for order. This is the power of regular prayer to the God of peace. In some respects prayer remains the most important factor for peace. It is something which everyone can do daily, even before peace is granted to us; it whets our desires for peace; it unites us with God, the fountain of peace. A world-wide union in prayer to the Father of all men may be the first concrete union among men. It is also the means needed for that perseverance on the side of God and for constancy in the efforts to realize peace on earth. It mobilizes the forces of religion and of grace with the forces of reason and human organization in the great project of peacemaking. The liturgical prayer from the Mass for peace[8] both expresses our dependence on God for this favor and names some of the constituents of true peace.

O God, from whom are holy desires, right counsels, and just deeds,
Grant us that peace which the world cannot give,
That our hearts may devotedly keep Your commandments,
The dread of our foes be taken away,
And our times by Your guardianship be tranquil,
Through our Lord Jesus Christ, Your Son.

Just as happiness on earth will always be imperfect, so will peace. Beatitude and perfect peace can be found only in ultimate union with God in eternal life. Meanwhile we can much improve peace on earth.

We so easily forget that Christ died to give us this peace for which we pray and work. We forget our countrymen who have died that we might live in peace. They deserve a great return of thanks shown in our unflagging hopes for right order and our lifelong efforts to create, preserve, and broaden peace among men. The great visions of many philosophers, theologians, popes, and other sages which we have inherited should be our own master visions of the reign of good will, good order, plenary justice, and perfect love among men. Perhaps this vision of peace is the scholastic philosophers' fairest gift to the human spirit and a providential instrument to unite all thinkers in common knowledge and common love of the true good. Yet here, as so often in other matters, philosophy admits its inadequacy to develop a man of peace in a peaceful society; consequently, it turns to Christ for completion of the vision and realization of the daily order of peace.

For so great a good as peace is far more a gift of God than a fruit of the philosophical life. It is a gift which confers superhuman opportunities on human powers and makes superhuman demands of disordered nature. The divine reconciliation of men, the reign of God and His will on earth, an age of universal good will and justice, the quieting of all conflicts, a tranquil order in time that prepares for man's immortal peace in God's peaceful presence is a treasure of happiness far better than man deserves in return for his selfishness, hatred, and inconstant desires for peace. But God gladly proffers it to us. His gift, however, demands our intention to cherish it; His promise of peace is conditional. The condition is our good will, our free desire to receive and practice peace.

This is the last counsel of a sound philosophy of life: that men pray for peace and hope for peace and plan for peace and live in peace and move forward to eternal peace under the leadership of the Prince of Peace.

Notes

Chapter 1. Man Looks at Life, pages 1–9

1. Plato, *Phaedo*. The edition of Plato's works used throughout is *The Dialogues of Plato*, translated into English by B. Jowett, with an introduction by Raphael Demos (New York: Random House, 1937), 2 vols.

2. Interesting comments on philosophies of life will be found in G. K. Chesterton, *Heretics* (London: John Lane, 1905), chap. 1; Father James (O'Mahony), O.F.M.Cap., *Preface to Life* (Milwaukee: Bruce, 1936); Edward Leen, C.S.Sp., *What is Education?* (New York: Sheed and Ward, 1944), chap. 9; Walter Moberley, *Crisis in the University* (London: SCM Press, 1949, third impression), chap. 3 and pp. 107–109; F. Sherwood Taylor, *Two Ways of Life: Christian and Materialist* (Westminster, Md.: Newman, 1949), chap. 1; John Wild, *Introduction to Realistic Philosophy* (New York: Harper and Brothers, 1948), pp. 3–4.

3. T. S. Eliot, *Murder in the Cathedral* (New York: Harcourt, Brace, 1935).

4. *The Official Catholic Directory* (New York: Kenedy, 1957), shows these coats and mottoes at the beginning of each diocesan list.

5. Wisd. 2:1–10. From the *Old Testament*, Vol. II in the translation of Monsignor Ronald Knox, copyright, 1950, Sheed and Ward, Inc., New York.

6. Shakespeare, *Macbeth*, Act V, scene 5. For checking the context, the edition by G. B. Harrison, *Shakespeare: The Complete Works* (New York: Harcourt, Brace, 1952), is recommended.

7. Bertrand Russell, "A Free Man's Worship," from *Mysticism and Logic* (New York: Barnes and Noble, 1954 reprint), with permission. The same view appears in his essay on "Useless Knowledge" in the collection *In Praise of Idleness and Other Essays* (New York: W. W. Norton, 1935).

8. Plato, *Apology of Socrates*.

9. The primary tradition on the four causes is contained in Aristotle, *Physics*, II, chap. 3, 7, and *Metaphysics*, V, chap. 2. The edition used throughout this book is *The Basic Works of Aristotle*, edited with an introduction by Richard McKeon (New York: Random House, 1941).

Chapter 2. The Big Questions, pages 10–24

1. The General Council of Vienne, 1311–1312, defined that the rational or intellectual soul is truly, *per se*, and essentially the form of the human body. The Council did not indicate which concept of form then current among theologians and philosophers it had adopted. Cf. Henricus Denzinger and Carolus Rahner, *Enchiridion Symbolorum, Definitionum, et Declarationum de Rebus Fidei et Morum* (Friburg, Brisgoviae: Herder, 1943), No. 481.

2. See Plato's prayer for the assistance of God in *Timaeus*, 27a.

3. Aristotle, *Nicomachaean Ethics*, 1098b, 11.

4. Aristotle comments on heeding the opinions of the philosophers in his *Physics*, I, chap. 8; *Metaphysics*, I, chap. 3; *On the Soul*, I, chap. 2.

5. Several formulations of the principle of economy will be found in Bernard Wuellner, S.J., *Summary of Scholastic Principles* (Chicago: Loyola University Press, 1956), No. 292.

Chapter 3. What Is Life?, pages 25–37

1. On self-motion confer Aristotle, *On the Soul*, especially I, chap. 2; and St. Thomas Aquinas, *Summa Theologiae*, I, q. 18. The Ottawa edition, 1941–1946, of the *Summa Theologiae* is used throughout, with translations by the author of this book.

2. St. Thomas Aquinas, *Summa Theologiae*, I, q. 18, a. 3; *Summa contra Gentiles*, IV, chap. 11; Fulton J. Sheen, *Life of All Living: the Philosophy of Life* (Garden City: Doubleday, 1929 and 1951), chap. 1. The Editio Leonina Manualis of the *Summa contra Gentiles* (Paris: Desclée, 1934), is used throughout, with translations made by the author.

3. *Summa contra Gentiles*, III, chap. 22, "Cum vero . . ."; IV, chap. 11 on the grades of life. Cf. Edward P. Cronan, *The Dignity of the Human Person* (New York: Philosophical Library, 1955), chap. 3.

4. See George P. Klubertanz, S.J., *The Philosophy of Human Nature* (New York: Appleton-Century-Crofts, 1953), 43–46; 364–367.

5. C. S. Sherrington, *The Integrative Action of the Nervous System* (New Haven: Yale University Press, 1947), foreword to this edition.

6. Alexis Carrel, *Man the Unknown* (New York: Harper and Brothers, 1935), pp. 106–109. Cf. C. S. Sherrington, *Man on His Nature*, p. 106.

7. Aristotle, *On the Soul*, II, chap. 1–2; St. Thomas Aquinas, *On the Unity of the Intellect*, article 1. English text of the latter is given by Sister Rose Emmanuella Brennan, *The Trinity and the Unicity of the Intellect* (St. Louis: Herder, 1946).

Chapter 4. Thought, Desire, and Choice, pages 38–53

1. Aristotle, *On the Soul*, II, chap. 6; St. Thomas Aquinas, *Summa Theologiae*, I, q. 77.

2. St. Thomas Aquinas, *Summa Theologiae*, I, qq. 78–81 on human sensory powers. Cf. George P. Klubertanz, S.J., *The Philosophy of Human Nature* (New York: Appleton-Century-Crofts, 1953), chap. 5–7, 9, 11; Etienne Gilson, *The Christian Philosophy of St. Thomas Aquinas*, translated by L. K. Shook, C.S.B. (New York: Random House, 1956), Part II, chap. 5.

3. Some sources for proofs of the spirituality of the human intellect and for its superiority to sensory knowledge include: Aristotle, *On the Soul*, I, chap. 4, 408b; III, chap. 4–7; St. Thomas Aquinas, *Summa contra Gentiles*, II, chap. 66, 50; Michael Maher, S.J., *Psychology* (London: Longmans, Green, ninth edition, 1940), pp. 230–241, 470–473; Mortimer J. Adler, *What Man Has Made of Man* (New York: Longmans, Green, 1937), 51–57, 179–181; Barbara Ward, *Faith and Freedom* (New York: Norton, 1954), 270–272.

4. Ortega y Gasset, cited in *Theological Studies* 1953 (XIV), 45.

5. Note that acts of opinion, of divine faith, and of erroneous assent are acts of the intellect commanded by the will, for the evidence in these cases is not compelling.

6. Some of the Thomistic passages on priority of intellect over will are *Summa Theologiae*, I, q. 82, a. 3; q. 82, a. 4 ad 1; I–II, q. 3, a. 4 ad 4; II–II, q. 23, a. 6 ad 1; *Truth*, translated by Robert W. Schmidt (Chicago: Regnery, 1954), q. 22, a. 11.

7. Proofs of liberty drawn from the nature of the intellect are in St. Thomas Aquinas, *Summa Theologiae*, I, q. 82, a. 1; q. 83, a. 1; *Summa contra Gentiles*, II, chap. 48; *Truth*, translation cited, q. 22, articles 5–6. Cf. Michael Maher, *op. cit.*, chap. 19 for other proofs.

8. Popularizations on freedom in G. K. Chesterton, *Orthodoxy* (New York: John Lane, 1909), "The Maniac," and *What's Wrong With the World* (London: Cassell, 1910), "The Fear of the Past."

Chapter 5.   *Spirit and Form*, pages 54–69

1. Those who like their philosophy sweetly spiced with literary elegance will enjoy reading M. C. D'Arcy, S.J., *Death and Life* (London: Longmans, Green, fourth impression, 1948), chap. 1–4 on the soul.

2. "The white-hair'd shadow" is Alfred Tennyson, *Tithonus*. Shakespeare's ghosts appear in *Julius Caesar*, *Macbeth*, *Hamlet*, and *Cymbeline*. Lord Dunsany's fantasy "The Kith of the Elf-Folk" has an imaginative construction of a soul.

3. The doctrine of form followed here comes from St. Thomas Aquinas, *Summa Theologiae*, I, q. 76; q. 77, a. 5; q. 84. Excellent exposition is given in Anscar Vonier, O.S.B., *The Human Soul*, reprinted in *The Collected Works of Abbot Vonier* (Westminster, Md.: Newman, 1952), III, chap. 3, 5, 6, 10, 14, 20.

4. The Bukharin quotation appears in Jacques de Bivort de la Saudée, ed., *God, Man, and the Universe*, translated (New York: Kenedy, 1953), p. 329.

5. This is no. 194 of *Pensées*. See also the dialogue on life and death between the captive and the swineherd in Christopher Fry's play, *Thor, With Angels*.

Chapter 6.   *The Source of Human Life*, pages 70–78

1. Popular and scientific descriptions of the origins of atmosphere and organic life in Editorial Staff of *Life* and Lincoln Barnett, *The World We Live In* (New York: Time, Inc., 1955, distributed by Simon and Shuster). A scholarly discussion is given in the essay "The Origin of Life" in Jacques de Bivort de la Saudée ed. *God, Man, and the Universe*, translated (New York: Kenedy, 1953).

2. Essential difference is discussed in chapter 3, *above*.

3. Gen. 1–2; Ecclus. 17.

4. On the evolution of man see George P. Klubertanz, S.J., *The Philosophy of Human Nature* (New York: Appleton-Century-Crofts, 1953), pp. 412–427; Vittorio Marcozzi, S.J., "The Origin of Man According to Science" in *Theology Digest*, II (1954), 43–48; Cyril O. Vollert, S.J., "Evolution of the Human Body" in *The Church and Modern Science* (New York: America Press, 1953).

5. The existence of the Author of life can be proved from two other starting

points in the phenomena of life, namely (1) from the order, structure, and purposiveness of life which are explained only by an intelligent author; and (2) from the grades of life which participate in the highest form of life in a single ultimate author of all life who possesses perfect life.

6. Ernest C. Messenger, *Evolution and Theology: the Problem of Man's Origin* (New York: Macmillan, 1932), pp. 87–88 holds this view. Cf. also his chapter 16, "The Origin of Man in St. Thomas Aquinas." St. Thomas briefly speaks of successive souls in *Summa contra Gentiles*, III, chap. 22.

7. St. Thomas Aquinas, *Summa Theologiae*, I, q. 76 on the unity of the soul.

8. The fact of tubal pregnancies suggests that infusion of the soul does not wait until implantation of the fertilized ovum in the womb.

Chapter 7.   The Supreme Goal of Human Life, pages 79–93

1. Aristotle, *Nicomachaean Ethics*, I, chap. 1, 4–12; X, chap. 6–8. Aristotle is a guide in philosophical method, but he does not reach all the answers on man's purpose in life.

2. Thomistic passages on the best good and the best activity include *Summa Theologiae*, I–II, qq. 2–4; *Summa contra Gentiles*, III, chap. 25–40.

3. Aristotle, *Nicomachaean Ethics*, IX, chap. 9–10; X, chap. 7 for the philosophic happy life and the need of friends for this.

4. On natural desire for beatitude, *Summa Theologiae*, I, q. 12, a. 1; 62, a. 1; I–II, q. 5, a. 1; *Summa contra Gentiles*, III, chap. 25, 50, 57; *Compendium of Theology*, chap. 104. On natural inability to attain perfect (supernatural) happiness, *Summa Theologiae*, I, q. 12, aa. 4, 5, 11; 56, a. 3; 62, a. 1; I–II, q. 5, a. 5; 62, a. 1; *Summa contra Gentiles*, III, chap. 50, 52, 57; *Truth*, q. 8, a. 3; *Quodlibetum* X, q. 8.

5. *Nicomachaean Ethics*, X, chap. 7–8 on contemplative activity.

6. The following readings may help to appreciate the infinity of God and the intensity of the soul's experience in knowing and loving Him: St. Thomas Aquinas, *Summa Theologiae*, I, q. 4, a. 2; q. 7, a. 1; q. 26, a. 4; *Summa contra Gentiles*, III, chap. 63; St. Augustine, *Confessions*, translated by F. J. Sheed (New York: Sheed and Ward, 1942), I, chap. 1, 4; M. C. D'Arcy, S.J., *Death and Life* (London: Longmans, Green, fourth impression, 1948), p. ix; Charles P. Bruehl, Sheen, *God and Intelligence* (London: Longmans, Green, 1925), Part II, chap. 7.

Chapter 8.   The Purposes of Life on Earth, pages 94–105

1. Rebuttals to this charge may be read in M. C. D'Arcy, S.J., *Death and Life* (London: Longmans, Green, fourth impression, 1948), p. ix; Charles P. Bruehl, *This Way Happiness* (Milwaukee: Bruce, 1941), pp. 45–46; Alban Goodier, S.J., *The Meaning of Life and Other Essays* (St. Meinrad: St. Meinrad Press, American edition, 1946), pp. 11–14; Pope Pius XI, "The Christian Education of Youth" reprinted in Joseph Husslein, S.J., *Social Wellsprings*, II (Milwaukee: Bruce, 1943), pp. 120–121, nos. 99, 100, quoting Tertullian on the same problem; Richard M. Weaver, *Ideas Have Consequences* (Chicago: University of Chicago Press, 1948), pp. 117–118. See also the statements on incarnational humanism by the Holy

Fathers scattered in the symposium on Christian Humanism in *Social Order*, III (May–June, 1953).

2. St. Augustine, *City of God*, translated by Marcus Dods and others (New York: Hafner, 1948, 2 vols.), XXII, chap. 24.

3. Charles D. Boulogne, *My Friends, the Senses*, translated by Jane Howes (New York: Kenedy, 1953), has many humanistic and optimistic attitudes to the natural bodily life of man.

Chapter 9. The Dignity of Human Life, pages 106–118

1. St. Thomas Aquinas, *Summa Theologiae*, I, q. 29, a. 3.

2. St. Thomas Aquinas, *Summa contra Gentiles*, III, chap. 111. Cf. *Summa Theologiae*, I–II, Prologue; *Power of God*, q. 9, a. 1 ad 3.

3. *Summa Theologiae*, I, q. 18, articles 1, 3.

4. Psalm 8. Shakespearean praises of man are from *Hamlet*, Act II, scene 2. A more interesting Litany of Man is found in Laurent of Paris, O.F.M.Cap., *Palais de l'Amour divin*, cited and translated in part in Henri Brémond, *A Literary History of Religious Thought in France*, translated by K. L. Montgomery (New York: Macmillan, 1928), pp. 283–284.

5. The basis of this idea of man as image comes from Genesis 1:27. It is a favorite idea of the Greek Fathers, of St. Augustine, and of St. Bonaventure. Cf. technical discussion in St. Thomas Aquinas, *Summa Theologiae*, I, q. 93; q. 35; q. 91, a. 4; *Truth*, q. 10, a. 6; Edward P. Cronan, *The Dignity of the Human Person* (New York: Philosophical Library, 1955), chap. 4.

6. *Summa contra Gentiles*, III, chap. 112, fourth paragraph; III, chap. 25, 51, 57, 61–63. This supremacy of man's good must not be interpreted in a Kantian sense which seems to make man autonomous even from God.

7. Rudolf Allers, "Microcosmus from Anaximandros to Paracelsus," *Traditio* II (1944), 319–407 brilliantly discusses microcosm and gives many Thomistic texts.

8. *Summa contra Gentiles*, III, chap. 112–113; Pope Pius XII, *The Mystical Body of Christ* (New York: Paulist Press, 1943), nos. 65–66.

9. 2 Peter 1:4.

10. In *Summa contra Gentiles*, IV, chap. 44–45, St. Thomas writes of man's new awareness of his dignity because of Christ's Incarnation.

11. Citations from Pascal on this subject in Anton C. Pegis, *Wisdom of Catholicism* (New York: Random House, 1949), pp. 628–634.

12. The modern attitudes to indignity of man appear brutally in racial troubles, in the practices of concentration camps and slave political labor, in Communist trials and persecutions, in Freudian attitudes to the inferiority of women, in lingering contempt for manual and menial labor in some circles. For intellectual currents that have demeaned regard for man see Alfred Noyes, *The Unknown God* (New York: Sheed and Ward, 1934), chap. 17–18; Pitirim A. Sorokin, *The Crisis of Our Age* (New York: Dutton, 1941), 242–244.

13. United States Hierarchy, "The Dignity of Man" reprinted in *Catholic Mind*, Vol. 52 (January, 1954), pp. 123–128.

14. On the confused, exaggerated, and wrong bases for human dignity see John

H. Hallowell, *Main Currents in Modern Political Thought* (New York: Henry Holt, 1950), the long section on Liberalism, especially pp. 110–118; Russell Kirk, *Academic Freedom* (Chicago: Regnery, 1955), *passim;* Pope Leo XIII, *Human Liberty (Libertas Praestantissimum)*, reprinted in Etienne Gilson, ed., *The Church Speaks to the Modern World* (Garden City: Doubleday, Image books, 1954), pp. 57–85; F. J. Sheed, *Society and Sanity* (New York: Sheed and Ward, 1953), p. 34 on Shylock's wrong reasons for protesting against mistreatment.

Chapter 10. Growth in Living, pages 119–129

1. Pope Pius XI, *Christian Education of Youth*, translated from the Italian given in *Acta Apostolicae Sedis,* 1929 (Vol. 21), p. 723 ff.

2. Suggestions on growth will be found in Rudolf Allers, *Self Improvement* (New York: Benziger Brothers, 1939); Ernest R. Hull, S.J., *Formation of Character* (St. Louis: Herder, 1909); and Bakewell Morrison, S.J., *Character Formation in College* (Milwaukee: Bruce, 1938).

3. Charles Darwin, *Life and Letters* (New York: Appleton, 1891), I, pp. 81–82.

4. St. Thomas Aquinas, *Summa Theologiae*, I–II, questions 51–52, 65; II–II, q. 23, articles 7–8.

5. Henri Frédéric Amiel, *Journal*, translated by Mrs. Humphry Ward (London: Macmillan, 1885).

6. Cf. Mt. 4:4.

Chapter 11. The Intellectual Life, pages 130–141

1. A. D. Sertillanges, *The Intellectual Life: its Spirit, Conditions, Methods,* translated by Mary Ryan (Westminster, Md.: Newman, 1948); St. Thomas Aquinas, *How to Study*, translation and exposition by Victor White, O.P. (London: Blackfriars, 1953).

2. Etienne Gilson, *Wisdom and Love in St. Thomas Aquinas* (Milwaukee: Marquette University Press, 1951), notes 3 and 22 on the dependence of the intellectual virtues on the will.

3. Studiousness is discussed by Christian Pesch, S.J., *Praelectiones Dogmaticae* (Friburg, Brisgoviae: Herder, 1899), IX, pp. 93–96; Joseph Pieper, *Fortitude and Temperance*, translated by Daniel F. Coogan (New York: Pantheon, 1954), pp. 109–114; St. Thomas Aquinas, *Summa Theologiae*, II–II, questions 166–167.

4. Plato, *Republic*, V, 473; VII; *Phaedo*, near the end.

5. Aristotle, *Nicomachaean Ethics*, X, chap. 7, 8; *Metaphysics*, XII, chap. 7.

6. Lk. 10:38–42.

7. *Summa Theologiae*, II–II, q. 182, a. 1 lists eight reasons, but the first and eighth seem to be almost identical. In the discussion of the ways of life, St. Thomas several times shows his preference for the mixed life, in which contemplative life overflows into action for others, as in teaching; even here, however, the life should be primarily contemplative, secondarily active, if it is to qualify as the best life.

8. *Summa contra Gentiles*, I, chap. 2.

9. John Henry Cardinal Newman, *The Idea of a University, Defined and Illustrated* (New York: Longmans, Green, C. F. Harrold edition, 1947), especially

Part I. Cf. Fernal McGrath, S.J., *Newman's University: Idea and Reality* (New York: Longmans, Green, 1951).

10. Bertrand Russell, *In Praise of Idleness and Other Essays* (New York: Norton, 1935), "Useless Knowledge." Though very far from Newman in its witty, astringent, and somewhat tragic spirit, Russell agrees with Newman's idea of the liberal and humanistic notion of knowledge and pities Bacon's knowledge for power and use.

11. St. Augustine, *"Intellectum valde ama"* from *Epistolae* 120, 3, 13–14 (*Patrologia Latina*, 33, p. 459).

12. William H. Cornog, "Bread and Hyacinths," *School and Society*, Vol. 72 (July 8, 1950), p. 20.

13. Henri Brémond, *A Literary History of Religious Thought in France*, translated by K. L. Montgomery (New York: Macmillan, 1928), especially Vol. I.

14. Jacques Maritain, "Thomistic Views on Education," in Nelson B. Henry, ed., *Modern Philosophies and Education* (Chicago: University of Chicago Press, distributor for National Society for the Study of Education, 1955), pp. 57–90.

Chapter 12. *The Good Life*, pages 142–154

1. Aristotle, *Nicomachaean Ethics*, I, chap. 7, 1098a; X, chap. 7–8; *Politics*, IV, chap. 11; *Rhetoric*, I, chap. 5.

2. St. Thomas Aquinas, *Summa Theologiae*, I–II, q. 57, a. 3; 58, articles 3–4; and many other places.

3. *Summa Theologiae*, I–II, q. 57, a. 5.

4. Some scholastics hold to the Aristotelian statement that right reason is the norm and point to its use by St. Thomas. But reason is right when it is conformed to reality; reason's judgment of human goodness is right when it is measured by the objective reality of human nature. St. Thomas himself uses human nature as the test of reasonableness or goodness, e.g. in *Summa contra Gentiles*, III, chap. 129. The other proposed standards of right order or of direction to the true end of man are either included in or, if properly qualified, can be reduced to the view that man as such is the moral standard.

5. F. J. Sheed, *A Map of Life* (New York: Sheed and Ward, 1933 and 1938), pp. 95–97 uses this analogy in regard to auto manufacturers.

6. Plato, *Laws*, IV, 716; Aristotle, *Nicomachaean Ethics*, X, chap. 7. Besides these Greek ideas on following a divine standard, the same appears in many contexts in St. Thomas, e.g., in discussing man as image of God and God as exemplar, in discussing the eternal law and the Augustinian definition of sin as transgression of the eternal law, and in the discussion of assimilation to God.

7. This discussion of the four stages differs from the theory of the three ways of the spiritual life, purgative, illuminative, and unitive. Cf. Joseph de Guibert, S.J., *The Theology of the Spiritual Life*, translated by Paul Barrett (New York: Sheed and Ward, 1953).

8. Cited in *Summa Theologiae*, I–II, q. 19, a. 10, ultimately based on St. Augustine's *Commentary on the Thirty-second Psalm*. Cf. Col. 3:17; Etienne Gilson, *Spirit of Mediaeval Philosophy*, translated by A. H. C. Downes (New York: Sheed and Ward, 1950), chap. 17. In terms of the three moral determinants

of a definite act, this means that the agent's intention outweighs the act and its object and the intrinsic circumstances.

9. Aristotle, *Politics*, IV, chap. 11 on the special dangers of different social backgrounds of wealth and poverty.

10. The rule of the mean in Aristotle, *Nicomachaean Ethics*, II, chap. 6–7; *Summa Theologiae*, I–II, q. 64.

11. St. Paul's praises of charity's properties and effects in 1 Cor. 13. On the problem of the existence of a natural charity, see Etienne Gilson, *The Christian Philosophy of St. Thomas Aquinas*, translated by L. K. Shook, C.S.B., (New York: Random House, 1956), pp. 339–350.

Chapter 13. Man's Place in Nature, pages 155–166

1. St. Augustine, *Confessions*, translated by F. J. Sheed (New York: Sheed and Ward, 1942); Philip Hughes, *History of the Church* (London: Sheed and Ward, second edition, 1949), II, pp. 380–384 on the Albigensians.

2. Jean Mouroux, *The Meaning of Man*, translated by A. H. C. Downes (New York: Sheed and Ward, 1948), chap. 3; Fulton J. Sheen, *Three to Get Married* (New York: Appleton-Century-Crofts, 1951), chap. 8.

3. This is very different from Kant's view of our knowledge of nature. Because of his theory of knowing nature and his interpretation of Galileo's experimental method, the German philosopher regards man as the judge of nature, not its pupil; nature answers the judge's questions.

4. Pope Pius XII, "The Technological Concept of Life," reprinted in *Irish Ecclesiastical Record*, 83 (Apr., 1955), pp. 298 ff.

5. Wisd. 5:18–24 on nature as God's avenger.

6. St. Thomas Aquinas, *Summa Theologiae*, I, q. 22, a. 2 ad 3, 4; q. 103; I–II, q. 1, a. 2 on the subject of God's operations in nature. On nature's capacity to help man toward God and to protect him from religious errors, see *Summa contra Gentiles*, II, chap. 2–3.

7. Dan. 3:56–90.

Chapter 14. Living Under God and for God, pages 167–180

1. F. Sherwood Taylor, *Two Ways of Life: Christian and Materialist* (Westminster, Md.: Newman, 1949, second printing), p. 110.

2. John Henry Cardinal Newman, *The Idea of a University, Defined and Illustrated* (New York: Longmans, Green, Charles F. Harrold ed., 1947), Discourses II, III, IV; Walter Moberly, *The Crisis in the University* (London: S C M Press, 1949), pp. 71–93, 111.

3. F. Sherwood Taylor, *op. cit.*, 43 ff. The mystics show us the greatest intimacy with God and that full transformation that the spirit desires in its search for likeness to God. For some of the best insights on the phenomena of conscience see John Henry Cardinal Newman, *An Essay in Aid of a Grammar of Assent* (New York: Longmans, Green, Charles F. Harrold ed., 1947). On the need of understanding both the transcendence and immanence of God for a religious humanism, see Emmanuel Cardinal Suhard, "The Meaning of God" in *The Church Today* (Chicago: Fides, 1953).

4. United States Hierarchy, "Religion our Most Vital National Asset," reprinted in *Catholic Mind*, 51 (1953), 56–64; James Keller, M.M., *Government is Your Business* (Garden City: Doubleday, 1952), chap. 9; Keller, *All God's Children* (Garden City: Hanover House, 1953); President Eisenhower's statement in the daily press of February 6, 1956, for the American Legion's "For God and Country" observance.

5. St. Thomas Aquinas, *Summa Theologiae*, II–II, questions 81–91 on the virtue of religion.

6. *Codex Juris Canonici* (Rome: Vatican Press, 1917), canons 487–488.

Chapter 15. Life in Society, pages 181–192

1. On the sociality of man and woman see John L. Thomas, S.J., "The Social Web of Marriage," in *Social Order*, May, 1956, reprinted in *Catholic Mind*, Sept., 1956 (Vol. 54), 523–529; Carl C. Zimmerman and Lucius F. Cervantes, S.J., *Marriage and the Family* (Chicago: Regnery, 1956), Part II, chap. 15, "Complementarity."

2. Aristotle, *Politics*, III, chap. 4, 13; VII, chap. 14; N. S. Timasheff, *An Introduction to the Sociology of Law* (Cambridge: Harvard University Press, 1939), in Index of Subjects, s.v. "dominance-submission," "domination," "obedience," and "principle of domination."

3. John Donne, *Devotions Upon Emergent Occasions*, No. XVII. For context one may consult *The Complete Poetry and Selected Prose of John Donne and the Complete Poetry of William Blake* (Random House: New York, 1941). Caryll Houselander has remarks more beautiful and penetrating than Donne's, especially when she writes of suffering and sinful men and the mystical union of the redeemed in Christ.

4. Pope Pius XII, *Summi Pontificatus* (*On the Unity of the Human Race*), reprinted in Harry Koenig, ed., *Principles for Peace* (Washington: National Catholic Welfare Conference, 1943, distributed by Bruce), No. 1406.

5. One of the best treatments of friendship is in Aristotle's *Nicomachaean Ethics*, books VIII and IX.

Chapter 16. The Life of the Citizen, pages 193–207

1. Pope Pius XI, *Quadragesimo Anno* (*Restoring a Christian Social Order*), reprinted in Joseph Husslein, S.J., *Social Wellsprings* (Milwaukee: Bruce, 2nd printing, 1943), II, pp. 206–207, Nos. 79–80, the principle of subsidiarity. Extensive discussions of this principle appear in John F. Cronin, *Catholic Social Principles* (Milwaukee: Bruce, 2nd ed., 1955), and Johannes Messner, *Social Ethics*, translated by J. J. Doherty (St. Louis: Herder, 1949).

2. Walter Lippmann, *The Public Philosophy* (Boston: Little, Brown, 1955); Clinton Rossiter, *Seedtime of the Republic* (New York: Harcourt, Brace, 1953), 440–449.

3. Examples include President Eisenhower's statements on the public philosophy of his wing of the Republican Party made at Denver, September 10, 1955, and published the next day in the press, and much of the literature of Freedom Foundations which encourages intelligent discussion of the principles and loyalties of the American way of life. But partisan promotion of some slanted interpretation

of our way of life can be very bad, as is shown in the doctrine of secularism sponsored by Protestants and Others United for Separation of Church and State.

4. James Keller, M.M., *Government is Your Business* (Garden City: Doubleday, 1952) gives many practical suggestions for civic activity within every one's power.

Chapter 17. The Ideal Human Life, pages 208–222

1. Samples of this literature on the ideals of different times will be found in these works, arranged by periods: Ancient Greece and Rome — Plato, *Republic*, *passim*, especially V, 473, VI, and VII; *Laws*, *passim*; Aristotle, *Nichomachaean Ethics*, IV, chap. 3, 4, on the magnanimous man; IX, chap. 11; *Politics*, VII, chap. 1, 13; Epictetus, *Discourses*, *Manual*, and fragments from the *Encheiridion* (New York: Putnam, 1928); Werner W. Jaeger, *Paideia, the Ideals of Greek Culture*, translated by Gilbert Highet (New York: Oxford University Press, 3 vols., 1939–1945); Jaeger, *Humanism and Theology* (Milwaukee: Marquette University Press, 1943); Edward Gibbon, *The Decline and Fall of the Roman Empire* (New York: Random House, n.d.) I, chap. 23–24 on the self-righteous character of Julian the Apostate; Harry V. Jaffa, *Thomism and Aristotelianism: a Study of the Commentary by Thomas Aquinas on the Nicomachaean Ethics* (Chicago: University of Chicago Press, 1952), chap. 5–6, for biting comment on the magnanimous man as treated by St. Thomas. Biblical ideals — Prov. 31; Ecclus. 31, 51. Medieval period — Etienne Gilson, *The Spirit of Mediaeval Philosophy* (New York: Sheed and Ward, 1950), chap. 18–20; Régine Pernoud, *The Glory of the Medieval World*, translated by Joyce Emerson (New York: Roy, 1950); Johan Huizinga, *Herbst des Mittelalters* (Stuttgart, Kröner, 1952); Huizinga, *The Waning of the Middle Ages*, reprint (Garden City: Doubleday Anchor books, 1954); St. Thomas Aquinas, *Summa Theologiae*, II–II, qq. 23, 25, 27, 129, a. 3 ad 5; qq. 179–184; *Summa contra Gentiles*, II, chap. 2; III, chap. 69–70; *Sermo V in Dominica secunda Adventus* (in *Opera Omnia*); Gerald G. Walsh, S.J., *Medieval Humanism* (New York: Macmillan, 1942). Renaissance and later — Desiderius Erasmus, *The Education of a Christian Prince*, translated by Lester K. Born (New York: Columbia University Press, 1936); Jakob C. Burckhardt, *The Civilization of the Renaissance in Italy*, translated from the fifteenth ed. by S.G.C. Middlemore (London: Harrap, 1929); Henri Brémond, *A Literary History of Religious Thought in France*, translated by K. L. Montgomery (New York: Macmillan, 1928), especially I, chap. 1, 18; Alexander Pope, *An Essay on Man*, edited by Maynard Mack (New Haven: Yale University Press, 1951). Modern — Jacques Maritain, *True Humanism*, translated by Margot Adamson (New York: Scribner's, 1938); A. Messineo, S.J., "L'umanesimo integrale" in *La Civiltà Cattolica*, anno 107, Vol. III (Sept. 1, 1956), 449–463 which sharply criticizes Maritain's views as insufficiently Christian; Walter Moberly, *The Crisis in the University* (London: S C M Press, 1948); Pope Pius XI, *The Christian Education of Youth* (confer note 4).

2. John Henry Cardinal Newman, *The Idea of a University, Defined and Illustrated* (New York: Longmans, Green, Charles F. Harrold ed., 1947), Discourse VIII, passages on the gentleman and criticism. The ideal is largely drawn from Shaftesbury's *Characteristics of Men, Manners, Opinions, Views*. Comment on Newman by Ernest R. Hull, S.J., *Formation of Character* (St. Louis: Herder, 1909), chap. 2–5, especially chap. 3.

3. See the six superb papers in the symposium, "Christian Humanism," *Social Order*, III (May–June, 1953). The difficult point of eschatological humanism is commented on at times: pp. 194, 203–206, 238–242, 262–263, 271, 280, 284–285.

4. Pope Pius XI, *The Christian Education of Youth* (*Rappresentanti in Terra*, 1929) reprinted in Joseph Husslein, S.J., ed., *Social Wellsprings* (Milwaukee: Bruce, second printing, 1943), II, pp. 107, 118–120, Nos. 59, 96–99.

5. St. Thomas Aquinas, *Summa Theologiae*, I, q. 1, a. 8; q. 60; q. 62; II–II, q. 10, a. 10.

6. Comments on Christ the model will be found in many works studying the Gospels and the life of Christ. Cf. Alban Goodier, S.J., *Jesus Christ, the Model of Manhood*, reprinted in George D. Smith, ed., *The Teaching of the Catholic Church* (New York: Macmillan, 1949), I, No. 12; Goodier, *The Public Life of Our Lord Jesus Christ; an Interpretation* (London: Burns, Oates, Washbourne, 1930); Columban Marmion, *Christ, the Life of the Soul* (London: Sands, sixth ed., n.d.), Part I, chap. 2; Pope Pius XI, *op. cit.*, No. 101.

7. Romano Guardini, *The Church and the Catholic*, translated by Ada Lane (New York: Sheed and Ward, new edition, 1953), chap. 2–3; Frederick Wilhelmsen in F. J. Sheed, ed., *Born Catholics* (New York: Sheed and Ward, 1954), p. 67 on the man made by the Church.

8. St. Thomas Aquinas, end of the hymn "Panis Angelicus," the divine office of Corpus Christi.

Chapter 18. The Place of Suffering, pages 223–237

1. Eccles. 1–4 laments man's follies, worries, and wretchedness. Cf. St. Augustine, *City of God*, translated by Marcus Dods and others (New York: Hafner, 1948, 2 vols.), XIX, chap. 4–8.

2. Camus is cited by Albert Dondeyne, "The Existence of God and Contemporary Materialism" in Jacques de Bivort de la Saudée, ed., *God, Man, and the Universe*, translated (New York: Kenedy, 1953), p. 11.

3. M. C. D'Arcy, S.J., *Death and Life* (London: Longmans, Green, fourth impression, 1948), chap. 8–9 treats the sufferings of hell and purgatory.

4. Boethius, *Consolation of Philosophy*. English translations include that by W. V. Cooper (London: Dent, 1940), and that by I. V. and H. F. Stewart in the Loeb classical series (New York: Putnam, 1918).

5. The maxim "Always consider the whole" has a long philosophical and theological tradition. Cf. Plato in *Laws*, 903, Marcus Aurelius and other Stoics, Plotinus, St. Irenaeus, and Boethius. It often occurs in St. Thomas Aquinas' works, e.g. in *Summa Theologiae*, I, q. 22, a. 2; *In II Sent.*, d. 32, q. 1, a. 1; *Summa contra Gentiles*, III, chap. 71; *Power of God*, q. 3, a. 6 ad 4. On the individuality of God's providence over men and their actions see the splendid chapters of *Summa contra Gentiles*, III, chap. 111–113.

Chapter 19. Christ's Contribution to a Theory of Life, pages 238–247

1. Etienne Gilson, *The Spirit of Mediaeval Philosophy*, translated by A. H. C. Downes (New York: Sheed and Ward, 1950) gives a brilliant historical demonstration of this superiority of Christian thought.

2. Frederick Copleston, S.J., *A History of Philosophy* (Westminster, Md.: Newman, 1950), II, 408–411 compares Aristotle and St. Thomas on the virtue of religion.

3. Edward Leen, C.S.Sp., *Why the Cross?* (New York: Sheed and Ward, 1938), pp. 178–181.

4. Jn. 6:45 (the Rheims Version).

5. Jn. 6:69–70.

6. Gal. 2:20.

7. Mt. 25:40.

8. Jn. 15:12–17.

9. For the influence of Christ on the interior life see Alban Goodier, *The Inner Life of a Catholic* (London: Longmans, Green, 1933); His influence on man's knowledge of his dignity, St. Thomas Aquinas, *Summa contra Gentiles*, IV, chap. 54; His influence on literature and art, Alfred Noyes, *The Unknown God* (New York: Sheed and Ward, 1934), chap. 22.

Chapter 20.   The Life of Peace, pages 248–261

1. The notable literature on peace should include these passages: in the Bible, Isa. 9:6; 32:17; 45:6–7; Ps. 84:9–11; 118:165; Job 9:4; Lk. 2 (Christmas); 24:36; Jn. 14:27; 17:33; 20:21–23; Rom. 15:33; 16:30; 1 Cor. 14:33; 2 Cor. 5:18; Eph. 2:13–14; Phil. 4:9; 1 Thess. 5:23; 2 Thess. 3:16; Hebr. 13:20; James 4:1; St. Augustine, *The City of God*, translated by Marcus Dods and others (New York: Hafner, 1948, 2 vols.), Bk. XIX, chap. 12–27; (Pseudo)-Dionysius the Areopagite, *The Divine Names*, translated by C. E. Rolt (New York: Macmillan, 1951 reprint), C. 11; St. Thomas Aquinas, *Summa Theologiae*, II–II, q. 29; for peace writings of the popes see the collection by Harry C. Koenig, ed., *Principles for Peace: Selections from Papal Documents, Leo XIII to Pius XII* (Washington: National Catholic Welfare Conference, 1943; distributed by Bruce); statements by Pius XII subsequent to 1943 and especially his Christmas peace statements will be found in February issues of *The Catholic Mind* (New York: America Press).

2. St. Augustine, *op. cit.*, XIX, chap. 13.

3. On order, see papal expositions in Koenig, *op. cit.*, Nos. 1327, 1470, 1497, 1756 ff., 1815, 1829, 1834–1838, 1853–1854. On tranquillity, *ibid.*, Nos. 23, 47, 768, 863, 1140, 1615, 1828–1829, 1838–1839, 1853.

4. The principal treatment of the peace of Christ is in Pope Pius XI, *Ubi Arcano Dei* (*The Peace of Christ in the Kingdom of Christ*), reprinted in Koenig, *op. cit.*, Nos. 758–823, especially 786–787, 790–793, 800–801. Cf. in the same collection Nos. 23, 283, 559, 863–864, 914–917, 1117, 1500.

5. Mt. 5:9.

6. Bernard W. Maturin, *Laws of the Spiritual Life* (London: Longmans, Green, 1908), chap. 8; St. Augustine, *De Sermone Domini in Monte*, I, chap. 2, used in the third nocturn of the feast of St. Boniface, June 5.

7. St. Augustine, *The City of God*, XIX, chap. 14.

8. *The Roman Missal*, "Missa pro pace." Cf. the widely circulated prayer of St. Francis of Assisi, "Lord, make me an instrument of your peace, etc."

Index

Adam, 13, 19

Aristotle, on contemplative life, 135; on definition of soul, 34 f; on immanent action, 25, 29; on method of knowing man, 39; on proof of intellect, 45 f; on temporal happiness, 142

Augustine, St., on happiness in truth, 89; on the intellect, 138; on peace, 249 ff; rules for peace, 258; on temporal happiness, 100

Authority, limited, 204 f; need for, 186 f; scope of, in the state, 199; *see also* Subsidiarity

Beatitude, *see* Happiness

Blessed Trinity, 242

Body of man, dignity of, 62, 108, 115, 157; origin and evolution, 72 ff; origin of first human body, 73

Boethius, on suffering and providence, 225 ff

Book of Wisdom, 3 f

Causes, kinds of, 6 f

Censorship, as instrument of totalitarian state, 206; reasonable, 141

Character and religion, 171 ff

Charity, 243; and Christian humanism, 102; highest virtue, 221; integrates all virtues, 152 f; and life of peace, 259 f

Choice, freedom of, 50 ff, 110

Christ, 17, 19, 20; on contemplative life, 134; contributions to a theory of life, 238 ff; the ideal, 220 ff; as model, 128, 219; model of peace, 256 f; Prince of Peace, 255 ff; union with, 243

Church of Christ, 16, 222, 244, 247

Conscience, 172; controls moral judgment, 121; and inner peace, 254; nature of, 137

Constitution of the United States, preamble to, 196

Culture, 138 ff; Christian, 246 f

Cultus, 176; *see* Worship

Death, happy, 93, 96; and a philosophy of life, 18 f; role of, 237

Defense of life, 77

Detachment, need for, 166

Dignity of man, *see* Man, dignity of

Docility and intellectual life, 132

Donne, John, on human unity, 184 f

Education, and intellectual life, 136, 140 f; and life of peace, 251; must consider "whole" man, 64; parents' role in, 189 f, 192; primarily looks to man's spirit, 69; and religion, 169; state's role in, 192

End, *see* Purpose

Equality of men, 185, 241 f

Evidence, as criterion for philosophy of life, 21 ff

Evil, nature of, 227 f; prevention and cure of, 229, 237; problem of, 223 ff

Family, as school of virtue, 187, 190; basis for, 78; life in, 187; a natural society, 188 ff; nobility of, 63; priority of, 190 ff

Friendship, nature of, 186

Future, the, 231 f, 235; *see* Immortality of the soul

Gentleman, nature of, 213, 218

God, Author of human life, 72 ff; Author of life, 71; Author of nature, 158, 160 f; cares for human life, 75 f; Creator of human soul, 73 ff; in ethical systems, 170; the Father, 242; glory of, 76, 81; goodness of, as measure of moral goodness, 146 f; goodness of, as object of beatitude, 83, 85; government of, 233 ff; and happiness, 85 ff; His place in life, 168 ff; justice of, 225, 232; knowledge of, 167 ff; knowledge of all, 226 f; and man, 15; mercy of, 234 f; and peace, 260; perfections and operations of, 170 f; perfect life in, 31; permission of evil, 227 ff; and philosophy of life, 242; providence of, 153; sovereign over man, 76; will of, 148, 254; *see also* Law

Goodness, in human life, 142 ff; moral, 142 ff; standard of, 16 f

Government, as danger to liberty and welfare, 202 ff; *see also* Authority, Leadership, State

275